SOCIAL SCIENCE RESOURCES IN THE ELECTRONIC AGE

SOCIAL SCIENCE RESOURCES IN THE ELECTRONIC AGE

Volume V
Geography

**Elizabeth H. Oakes and
Jeffrey A. Gritzner**

GREENWOOD PRESS
Westport, Connecticut • London

Library of Congress Cataloging-in-Publication Data

Oakes, Elizabeth H., 1964–
   Social science resources in the electronic age.
     p. cm.
   Includes bibliographical references and indexes.
     Contents: v. I. World history / Elizabeth H. Oakes and Mehrdad Kia — v. II. U.S. history /
Elizabeth H. Oakes and Michael S. Mayer — v. III. Government and civics / Elizabeth H.
Oakes and Jeffrey D. Greene — v. IV. Economics / Elizabeth H. Oakes and Michael H.
Kupilik — v. V. Geography / Elizabeth H. Oakes and Jeffrey A. Gritzner.
     ISBN 1–57356–589–X (set : alk. paper) — ISBN 1–57356–474–5 (v. I : alk. paper) —
ISBN 1–57356–473–7 (v. II : alk. paper) — ISBN 1–57356–476–1 (v. III : alk. paper) —
ISBN 1–57356–477–X (v. IV : alk. paper) — ISBN 1–57356–475–3 (v. V : alk. paper)
     1. Social sciences—Computer network resources. 2. Humanities—Computer network
resources. I. Title.

H61.95.O25   2004
025.06′3—dc22   2003060400

British Library Cataloguing in Publication Data is available.

Library of Congress Catalog Card Number: 2003060400
ISBN: 1–57356–589–X (set)
     1–57356–474–5 (vol. I)
     1–57356–473–7 (vol. II)
     1–57356–476–1 (vol. III)
     1–57356–477–X (vol. IV)
     1–57356–475–3 (vol. V)

First published in 2004

Greenwood Press, 88 Post Road West, Westport, CT 06881
An imprint of Greenwood Publishing Group, Inc.
www.greenwood.com

Printed in the United States of America

The paper used in this book complies with the
Permanent Paper Standard issued by the National
Information Standards Organization (Z39.48–1984).

10 9 8 7 6 5 4 3 2 1

Contents

Introduction

Social Science Resources in the Electronic Age: Geography is designed as a one-stop resource for cutting through the chaos of the Internet to find authoritative, age-appropriate information. The book is divided into five chapters. In the first chapter, "Resources in Geography," you'll also see how specific kinds of electronic services and print media can be mined for your research projects. We also point you to the Web's top-notch sites offering general information about geography.

The heart of the book, "Researching Individual Geography Topics on the Internet," provides you with a treasure map to quality information on the Web, which will save you hours of your own research time. We have searched for and found the crème de la crème of Web sites providing specific information on key topics in geography. These topics were chosen based on a review of national curriculum standards and were screened by an expert in the field.

For each topic, you'll find reviews of several Web sites, giving you all of the goodies you need to know: the name, URL, appropriate grade range, and a thorough discussion of how to use the site for research. When you log on to the Web to find a tidbit about the greenhouse effect or to gain a fuller understanding of Hinduism, you'll now have three or four handpicked sites, as opposed to the thousands that might turn up with a keyword search. In case you choose to conduct your own online search for a key topic, we let you know which search engine and keywords provide the best hits.

The following chapter, "Materials and Resources for Geography Teachers," reviews a number of excellent Web sites that offer materials and resources for geography educators, such as free maps, government document reprints, lesson plans, quizzes, and downloadable geography software.

"Museums and Summer Programs for Geography Students" surveys Web sites offering unique online museum exhibits, interpretive centers, summer programs, and other interactive opportunities for students of geography.

The final chapter of the book, "Careers," turns its attention to Web sites that provide students with career information in the field of geography. Here we've reviewed sites for professional associations, academic groups, conferences, workshops, programs, clubs, and other outlets for students interested in working or doing an internship in the subject.

HOW TO USE THIS BOOK

There are two ways you can find information in *Social Science Resources in the Electronic Age: Geography*. First you can look at the detailed table of contents. If you are researching a particular topic in geography, you can immediately go to the alphabetical listing of topics in Chapter 2. You can also use the index, which expands our coverage significantly. Because we had to limit the number of topics in Chapter 2, we added as much detail as possible to our site reviews. These include names of people and countries, events, and other topics covered in the Web site but not included in our topic list. All of these have been indexed. Also, don't forget to refer to "The Basics" section in Volume I of this set for general information.

1

⸻꩜⸻

Resources in Geography

FORMATS OF RESOURCES

Library Electronic Services

Specialized Databases

A number of topic-specific databases are popular among geography students and researchers. The following represents just a handful of those that you might find at your library. Check with the library staff about which databases would be useful for your project.

World Geography. ABC-Clio's subscription-only Web site of geography resources for schools.

Energy Research Abstracts. Indexes U.S. Department of Energy reports from energy centers and labs. Also includes articles, books, and theses.

Environment Abstracts Annual/Enviroline. Covers environmental research.

GeoRef. The American Geological Institute's comprehensive index to periodicals in the geosciences.

Ethnic Newswatch. Full-text newspapers, magazines, and journals from the ethnic, minority, and native press. Covers the years 1994 through the present.

Stat-USA. International and domestic data and statistics from federal agencies. It includes National Trade Data Bank, Country Commercial Guides, Economic Bulletin Board (Commerce Business Daily, etc.). Current.

CD-ROMs

Unlike print reference tools, CD-ROMs can cross-reference and link information together. Small Blue Planet's *The Real Picture World Atlas* presents a good example. It features a world relief map in accurate to-pographical detail. Using a looking glass tool, you can zoom in on sat-ellite images of many parts of the world. Click on a country to hear a human chorus that speaks 12 phrases in over one hundred languages. A linked almanac provides ecological, historical, political, and cultural background for each country. This CD-ROM also has tools for anno-tating images with your own notes. To gather a collection of information like this, you would have to rely on a variety of print reference books.

There are a number of other affordable CD-ROMs that might be of interest to geography students and teachers. Microsoft's *Encarta Virtual Globe* offers a CD-ROM version of a world atlas that includes 1.2 million place names, home pages of almost two hundred countries, seven thou-sand geographical articles, 3-D virtual flights over countries, detailed moon maps, panoramic views, street maps, global statistics, and a ge-ography glossary. Mindscape's *National Geographic Maps 2.0* is an eight-CD-ROM set of every foldout map that *National Geographic* magazine has ever published. It features cartographic facts, map tours and thematic tours, including Space, the Environment, and Peoples of the Past. The printable black-and-white or color maps are handy for reports or proj-ects. For more in-depth information, check your library for *The Complete National Geographic*, a 30-CD-ROM multimedia archive of every issue of the magazine.

E-Mail

Ask-an-Earth-Scientist (http://www.soest.hawaii.edu/GG/ASK/askanerd. html) is an excellent ask-an-expert service. Faculty at the University of Hawaii's Department of Geology and Geophysics will answer your ques-tions on volcanoes, geochemistry, geophysics, earthquakes, minerals and gems, sediments and sedimentary rocks, hydrology, and natural hazards.

Ask a Hurricane Hunter (http://www.hurricanehunters.com/askus.htm) puts you in direct communication with the 53rd Weather Reconnais-sance Squadron, the folks who fly airplanes into the eyes of hurricanes.

Scientific American: Ask the Experts about the Environment (http://www.sciam.com/askexpert/environment/index.html) offers answers to questions as diverse as "Why do clouds float when they have tons of water in them?" to "Does burying garbage reduce the amount of carbon in the air?"

You could also check out *AllExperts.com* (http://www.allexperts.com/). Follow the links from "Homework Help" to "Sciences" to "Geography." You can choose among several scholars with different areas of expertise.

Mailing Lists

Here are some examples of geography-related mailing lists:

MAPHIST

Map History Discussion List

To subscribe, send mail to LISTSERV@HARVARDA.HARVARD. EDU with the command: subscribe MAPHIST

CULTURALGEOG

Cultural Geography Discussion List

To subscribe, send mail to LISTSERV@LISTSERV.OKSTATE.EDU with the command: subscribe CULTURALGEOG

WRG12

World Geography Discussion List

To subscribe, send mail to LISTSERV@LISTSERV.UAFORTSMITH. EDU with the command: subscribe WRG12

CLIO3@LISTS.UNEP.FR

Climate and Ozone Discussion Forum

To subscribe, send mail to LISTSERV@LISTS.UNEP.FR with the command: subscribe CLIO3

GEOGRAPHY_240

Cities: An Introduction to Urban Geography

To subscribe, send mail to LISTSERV@EMAIL.RUTGERS.EDU with the command: subscribe GEOGRAPHY_240

To find other mailing lists of interest, check these Web sites:

CataList: The Official Catalog of Listserv Lists http://www.lsoft.com/lists/listref.html

Liszt: The Mailing List Directory http://www.liszt.com/

Topica: The Email You Want http://www.topica.com/

Usenet Newsgroups

If you are studying a particular country, you're sure to find a newsgroup dedicated to discussing its culture and geography (i.e., soc.culture.

Austria). Other newsgroups of interest to geographers include the following:

soc.culture.europe Discussion about European culture.

soc.culture.baltic Discussion about Baltic culture.

sci.geo.eos Discussion about the Earth Observation System.

sci.geo.earthquakes Discussion about earthquakes.

sci.geo.satellite-nav Discussion on satellite navigation.

sci.anthropology.paleo Discussion on anthropology topics.

To find and subscribe to newsgroups that interest you, check out these two Web sites:

Deja News http://www.deja.com/usenet/

CyberFiber Newsgroups http://www.cyberfiber.com/index.html

E-Journals

A few e-journals of interest to researchers in geography include the following:

The Electronic Green Journal
http://egj.lib.uidaho.edu/index.html

Provides peer-reviewed articles, book reviews, news, and information on current printed and electronic sources concerning international environmental topics.

Focus on Africa Magazine
http://www.bbc.co.uk/worldservice/africa/features/focus_magazine/index.
    shtml

Find news reports, feature articles, and color pictures covering the latest political, social, cultural, and sporting developments in Africa.

Digital Libraries

One good digital library resource for those interested in geography is *American Memory* (http://memory.loc.gov/ammem/ammemhome.html). This was created to digitally capture the distinctive, historical Americana holdings at the Library of Congress. These extensive digital collections include "Mapping the National Parks," documenting the history, cultural aspects, and geological formations of areas that eventually became national parks.

Two other digitized collections that provide images which may be of interest to geography students and teachers are the following:

Aerial Photography http://sunsite.berkeley.edu/AerialPhotos/

Jan T. Kozak Collection/Images of Historical Earthquakes http://www.eerc.berkeley.edu/kozak/

Reference Books

You will find a great deal of both background information and specific topical material in general dictionaries and encyclopedias. These include *Dictionary of Human Geography, Longman Dictionary of Geography: Human and Physical, Modern Dictionary of Geography, Geography and Cartography: A Reference Handbook, Encyclopedia of the First World, Encyclopedia of the Third World, Larousse Encyclopedia of World Geography,* and *Encyclopedia of Human Geography.*

If you're looking for biographical information on important people in geography, two are particularly helpful: *Biographical Dictionary of American Geography in the Twentieth Century* and *Biographical Dictionary of Geography.*

TYPES OF WORLD WIDE WEB RESOURCES

Reference Sites

Glossary of Population Terms
http://www.prb.org/template.cfm?Section = Glossary

Here's a basic online glossary from the Population Reference Bureau that covers key terms in population studies and demographics. It's easy to use and quite comprehensive. Type in the word you want to find or use the A to Z feature to browse topics.

Geography Glossary
http://geography.about.com/library/misc/blgg.htm?once = true&

Here's the *About.com* geography glossary. It's a general glossary of very basic geography terms that's weighted heavily toward physical and environmental geography.

StudyWeb
http://www.studyweb.com/

StudyWeb is a subject guide designed for student researchers who need to find information as easily as possible. With over 141,000 quality Web links reviewed and categorized into numerous subject areas, you can narrow in on a topic for a report, find background material for a project, begin research for a paper, or just increase your knowledge of a particular topic.

The home page for *StudyWeb* is clutter-free and easy to navigate. For starters, click on the "People and Places" topic link, which is then further broken into the categories of "Biographies," "Geography," "U.S. Geography," and "Sources of Current Events." When you enter the "Geography" section, you can narrow your search to "Africa," "Asia/Pacific," "Canada," "Central America/Caribbean/Mexico," "China," "Europe," "Middle East," "South America," "USSR (Former)," "World," or "Interactive Maps." Within each of these listings, there are "General Resources" Web links, as well as a handful of links to sites about the specific countries. *StudyWeb* helps you decide if the link is appropriate for your research by giving the site a score for visual interest, describing its contents, and indicating which age group the material is geared toward.

InfoPlease
http://www.infoplease.com/

InfoPlease is the online spin-off of a company that's produced almanac publications and reference databases for more than 60 years. This colorful site lets you tap into a massive collection of almanacs on almost every imaginable topic—chock-full of millions of authoritative factoids. For instance, you can quickly find the latitude and longitude for hundreds of international cities, find out where the world's 14 highest mountain peaks are, and discover the strongest Atlantic hurricanes on record.

Click on the subject area "World" and you'll find "Atlas," "Geography," "Countries," "World Statistics," "International Relations," "Current Events," "Disasters," and more. Within "U.S.," there's "Cities," "States," "Statistics," and "Geography." Inside "Weather Climate," you can learn about "Deadliest Hurricanes," "Climate of Selected Cities," "Weather Extremes," and so forth. Online maps in *InfoPlease*'s atlas are easy on the eye and provide text links to related info elsewhere in the site, such as country profiles, flags, geography facts, and statistics.

You can search for keywords within *Infoplease*'s almanac database and come up with an impressive amount of information—more than some general search engines provide. For example, the keywords "human geography" resulted in over 30 relevant hits in *InfoPlease*'s world almanac, science almanac, and encyclopedias, as well as brief biographies of important historical figures in the field of human geography. If you know the kind of information you need, you can use a pulldown menu to restrict your search to *InfoPlease*'s dictionary, biographies, or encyclopedia.

Commercial Sites

National Geographic
http://www.nationalgeographic.com/

The National Geographic Society, founded in 1888, has certainly done its part to keep up with the times. This lively site uses Web technology to pursue the society's mission—"the increase and diffusion of geographic knowledge"—with interactive gusto. It's a great site to visit when you want to trigger ideas for research *or* to seek out specific information.

The home page gives you a sense of the enormous amount of information here. The site, which is composed of more than 10,000 pages, breaks down into these main areas: "Interactive Features," "Travel," "Adventure and Exploration," "Maps and Geography," "Photography," "News," "Kids," "Education," "Forums," "Live Events," and "Exhibitions." To search the site, simply use the search box located on every page. You'll find information on a host of geography research topics, from acid rain to Buddhism to Zaire.

The section on "Maps and Geography," called "MapMachine," contains great resources, including dynamic maps, atlas maps, flags and facts, and additional, frequently updated information. Read, for instance, a feature called "Round Earth, Flat Maps" that explores the mapmaker's dilemma and the reasons why every map is distorted. You can also click on "View from Above" to get an astronaut's view of Earth through satellite images.

And of course, you're given plenty of opportunities on the site to support the National Geographic Society with a membership or the purchase of books, CD-ROMs, and magazines.

The Weather Channel
http://www.weather.com/

Your parents probably remember waiting for the nightly news to get their lone chance to find out about tomorrow's weather. Now, we all can get our weather fix 24 hours a day, seven days a week, on television, thanks to the ubiquitous Weather Channel. The enterprise is also thriving online with current conditions and forecasts for over 1,700 cities worldwide, along with weather-related news, a weather glossary, a storm encyclopedia, and seasonal features.

While it might not surprise you that this is a site to go for breaking weather news, it's also a top-notch source for satellite maps, in-depth special reports on physical geography topics, and other educational material. You can use the internal search feature to find specific terms or topics of interest, or click on "Learn More" to enter a section designed for students and educators. Here, you can access information about careers in weather, a weather glossary with 800 terms, and a storm encyclopedia, which explains topics from severe weather to historic events.

One of the best finds in this whole site, however, is almost buried. The Weather Channel has produced a number of superb special reports on weather topics. For instance, "Hot Planet" discusses global warming and provides expert interviews, an online discussion center, and links to related Web sites. Another report called "Eye of the Storm" brings you interactive information about hurricanes. To check the archive of these special reports, go directly to http://www.weather.com/weather_ center/special_report/index.html.

MapQuest
http://www.mapquest.com/

This commercial site aims to provide maps and map information for the average Joe or Jill. Its strength is in its simplicity. After all, if you're looking for driving directions, the last thing you want to do is get confused at a map Web site.

While there are more powerful and sophisticated mapping tools available online, this site is straightforward and easy to use. For a research project, you could use *MapQuest*'s world atlas, where you'll find maps for continents and countries, as well as ocean floor maps and polar region maps. Each country, province, and state map also provides quick facts. You'll also find interactive U.S. Geological Survey topographic maps for the entire United States, searchable by place name or latitude/longitude. Another section devoted to the national parks provides detailed park maps, photos, descriptions, and contact information.

A clickable map legend explains what the symbols and colors indicate on each map. For further information, you can also click on topics such as "What Is a Topographic Map?" and "How to Read a Topographic Map." Other features like online driving directions, travel deals, city guides, and yellow and white pages might not help you much with your current research project, but who knows? They just might be useful on your next road trip.

Government Sites

Central Intelligence Agency (CIA)
http://www.odci.gov/

As you probably know, the Central Intelligence Agency's (CIA) mission is to collect foreign intelligence to assist the U.S. president and other policymakers in making decisions relating to national security. At this site, you can tap into some of their intensive research.

If you need up-to-date information on a turbulent geographic region, or want to gain a fuller understanding of a country's dynamics, the CIA's *World Factbook* is a sound place to begin your investigations. Its full text is available on the Web site and can also be downloaded for use offline. In the *Factbook*, you'll find a detailed listing for every country in the world, providing background information and data on the country's geography, people, government, economy, communications, transportation, military, and transnational issues, along with reference maps.

Also of interest here are links to related sites, including sites with declassified satellite imagery from the U.S. Geological Survey and records from the National Archives and Records Administration.

Environmental Protection Agency
http://www.epa.gov/

The Environmental Protection Agency's (EPA) Web site exemplifies a government site that's striving for an open dialogue with concerned citizens. For certain topics in geography, you will find a wealth of well-organized information here, running the gamut from functional to fun.

To get an overview of what the agency handles, click on "Browse EPA Topics," then choose from such areas as "Air," "Ecosystems," "Emergencies," "Pollution Prevention," "Water," and more. Each of these broad topics is further broken down. Under "Ecosystems" for example, you'll find "Wetlands," "Watersheds," "Endangered Species," and so forth. Or you could click on "Information Sources" to locate environmental data via EPA libraries and information centers, hotlines, technical report clearinghouses, publications, newsletters, listservs, and online and downloadable software tools. Want to find out something about your own neighborhood? Try the "Community" section, where you can enter your zip code and then choose which database to search for information about your community: Envirofacts, Enviromapper, Surf Your Watershed, or UV Index.

There's also a thorough "Student Center" that posts students reports and ongoing projects, offering ways for students to become involved in many EPA initiatives. Here, you can read what other students have written about ozone depletion, global warming, watersheds, biomes, and more; read a guide to environmental laws; or access a glossary of terms. Information about the EPA's internships, fellowships, and student programs is also listed here.

The Library of Congress: Country Studies
http://lcweb2.loc.gov/frd/cs/

This link takes you directly to the home page for the *Country Studies* published by the Federal Research Division of the Library of Congress. Most resources at the Library pertain to American history, but the *Country Studies* handbooks present a description and analysis of the social, economic, political, and national security systems and institutions of countries throughout the world. They also examine the interrelationships of those systems and the ways they are shaped by cultural factors. At the time of this book's publication, 101 countries and regions are covered in the handbooks. Notable omissions include Canada, France, the United Kingdom, and other Western nations, as well as a number of African nations. The date on which information for each country was posted appears on the title page for each country and at the end of each section of text.

National Oceanic and Atmospheric Administration
http://www.noaa.gov/

The home page for the National Oceanic and Atmospheric Administration (NOAA) resembles the front page of *USA Today*, with its clean design and vivid photos. For general, up-to-date information on weather, environmental, and oceanic activity, you can read daily news coverage here. For more targeted research, you'll want to tap into the major sections: "Weather," "Ocean," "Satellites," "Fisheries," "Climate," "Research," "Coasts," and "Charting and Navigation." Considering how much quality information is contained, each of these sections could constitute a Web site unto itself. Under "Satellites," for example, you can see real-time imagery from environmental, geostationary, and polar satellites. The "Climate" section contains material about El Niño and La Niña, global warming, drought, climate prediction, paleoclimatology, and more.

NOAA also maintains an extensive online photo library, with more than 12,000 public domain photos of reefs, coastal scenes, and more. Also be sure to visit NOAA's visualization lab, which uses 3-D technology to create graphics of severe weather events, such as tropical storms, fires, solar radiation storms, and hurricanes.

Click on a link to the "GLOBE Program" (Global Learning and Observations to Benefit the Environment) to learn about NOAA's well-respected, international interactive project for students. In GLOBE, students are responsible for daily observations of local weather in an effort to help scientists unveil information about long-term climate patterns.

U.S. Census Bureau
http://www.census.gov/

For housing such a wealth of data, the U.S. Census Bureau's Web site is reassuringly straightforward and easy to navigate. Use the A–Z index if you have a specific topic in mind. Otherwise, you can search by keyword or subject, or delve into the general sections, which include "People," "Business," "Geography," "News," and "Special Topics." If you're looking for data about the population and socioeconomics of the United States, this is the preeminent source.

The Census Bureau is also a good source for maps, courtesy of the TIGER map server, which produces high-quality, detailed maps using public geographical data. You can generate maps of anywhere in the United States, right down to your street, using the TIGER database. These maps have simple GIS capabilities such as point display and statistical choropleth mapping.

Other good research tools at this site include the American Fact-Finder, an interactive database that can provide you with data from the 1997 Economic Census, the American Community Survey, the 1990 Census, the Census 2000 Dress Rehearsal, and Census 2000. To get information at the national, state, and county level, you could click on another tool called QuickFacts. Also be sure to check out the population clocks for the United States and the world that reveal, minute-by-minute, just how rapidly our populations are increasing. The site also provides excellent links to other government sites with useful social, demographic, and economic information.

Organization Sites

United Nations Children's Fund
http://www.un.org/partners/civil_society/m-child.htm
high school and up

This is the home page of the United Nations Children's Fund (UNICEF) and a good bet for finding information on many issues concerning children around the world, including some useful statistics. If you're interested in child health and development, there's a link to the World Health Organization's *Child and Adolescent Health and Development* Web site, which has an entire section devoted to data and statistics.

United Nations Educational, Scientific, and Cultural Organization
http://www.unesco.org/

This is home base for the United Nations Educational, Scientific, and Cultural Organization (UNESCO), whose mission is "to contribute to

peace and security in the world by promoting collaboration among nations through education, science, culture, and communication in order
to further universal respect for justice, for the rule of law, and for the
human rights and fundamental freedoms which are affirmed for the peoples of the world, without distinction of race, sex, language or religion,
by the Charter of the United Nations." Whew. As you can tell, this
organization has its hands in a little bit of everything, and you can find
out about all of it at this stellar Web site.

There is a section devoted to UNESCO documents, one devoted to
publications and audiovisual material, and one devoted to statistics.
These are the three you will likely find most useful in your research.
The site is also easy to search, so try the search feature if you have a
specific topic in mind.

World Bank
http://www.worldbank.org/

The World Bank collects and publishes social and economic data on
most countries around the world. Click on "Data and Statistics" in the
home page menu. You will be given the following choices: "Country
Data," "Data by Topic," "Data Query," and "Working with Data."

"Country Data" contains national statistics for countries and regions,
including country-at-a-glance tables and data profiles. "Data by Topic"
will put you in touch with indicator tables, sector data, and links to
other data sites. You should also browse the box of special features.
When we visited, it contained links to "Latest Stats on Gender" and
"Health, Nutrition, and Population Stats," among other topics.

World Health Organization
http://www.who.int/home-page/
high school and up

As the major organization concerned with world health, the World
Health Organization (WHO) has created a Web site that's a great starting point for research on disease. Use the "Information" section to find
a multitude of WHO publications, such as the *Weekly Epidemiological
Report* and the annual *World Health Report*. The "Press Media" section
also provides many useful resources, such as press releases, fact sheets,
and multimedia clips.

Look in the "Disease Outbreaks" section to find information on current outbreaks or older ones in historical archives arranged by year (1996
to 2000) and disease. The "News" section is another best-bet for finding
information about topical issues on disease.

Just click on "Data and Statistics" in the menu at the left side of the home page for an analysis, complete with numerous charts and graphs, of the worldwide estimates for morbidity and mortality among children.

Or if you want statistics on human rights for children, child refugees, or child labor, you'll find sections here that contain documents and data of all types on these topics too.

Academic and Educational Sites

Center for Improved Engineering and Science Education
http://njnie.dl.stevens-tech.edu/

The Center for Improved Engineering and Science Education's (CIESE) Web site provides information about a wide array of collaborative projects, real-time data projects, and partner programs between colleges and K–12 schools that you and your class can become involved with. These programs are designed to enhance or reinforce science and math curriculum with the use of technology.

Click on "Collaborative Projects" to learn about participating in such projects as the Global Water Sampling project, in which students compare the water quality of their local rivers, streams, lakes, or ponds with other freshwater sources around the world. In another project, called the Noon-Day project, students from across the globe collaborated by measuring the length of a shadow cast with a meter stick, sharing the data electronically, making comparisons with scale drawings and a spreadsheet, and finally using this information to estimate the circumference of the earth.

Under "Real-Time Data Projects" you'll discover several that hit the mark for high-school geography students. In the Musical Plates project, students use earthquake data to explore the relationship between earthquakes and plate tectonics, and in the Gulf Stream Voyage project, they use real-time data to investigate the mysteries of the Gulf Stream.

You can also click on links to "Partner Projects," such as the Rainforest Connection, in which a university research team traveling through Panama's rainforests communicates with students via e-mail and the Web.

Geography World
http://members.aol.com/bowermanb/101.html

This index of geography sites is truly oriented toward the student researcher. The home page offers you several dozen categories to choose from that range across the many subdisciplines in geography. You'll find "Africa," "Agriculture/Farming," "Earth's Land," "Earth's Water,"

"Environment/Conservation," "Europe," "Flags," "Latin America," "Tectonics," "World Culture," and much more.

Each category takes you to a page of links that are alphabetically arranged and very briefly but helpfully annotated with keywords. Little smiley faces indicate exceptionally good sites and the word "new" is highlighted beside new entries to the list. For each category, you can count on at least 25 sites that have been created especially for secondary school student researchers. And the bottom of the list always contains sites for games, puzzles, and quizzes.

GeoSource
http://www.library.uu.nl/geosource/index.html

This site is a matter-of-fact presentation of a collection of links to Web sites with information on the subjects of cartography, human geography, physical geography, environmental science and policy studies, and planning science. It aims to provide academic communities in the fields of geography, planning, geoscience, and environmental science with a comprehensive, categorized subject gateway to relevant sites, filling the gap between search engines and nonacademic subject directories.

GeoSource does not rate every Web site listed, but a small selection of sites receive the designation "topsource," on the value of its content. New links are added four days a week. *GeoSource* has been well received in the science community: it has been selected by the *Scout Report for Science and Engineering* and by *SciCentral,* and has also received a seal of approval from *Argus Clearinghouse.*

University of Michigan Inter-university Consortium for Political and Social Research
http://www.icpsr.umich.edu/

For polls and surveys on a wide range of political and social topics, try this well-organized academic site. Just go straight to the section called "Access and Analyze Data." A dozen or more subtopics will let you narrow your initial search. Read the instructions on using the search feature before you use it. You're more likely to have success that way.

Interactive/Practical Sites

GeoGlobe
http://library.thinkquest.org/10157/

This site, a winner of the ThinkQuest Internet Challenge, is the product of three students from geographically diverse regions: British Columbia, Canada; Springfield, Illinois, United States; and Warsaw, Poland.

The students created six interactive geography games that you can play online. In *Geo-Find*, select one of three skill levels and try to find the locations of countries, cities, rivers, lakes, and mountains. *Geo-Quest* is a 10-question version of the 20-questions game in which you try to uncover mystery animals from around the world. In *Geo-Tour*, you are given clues leading you to interesting landmarks—a "reversing river," ancient cities, the world's deepest lake, and so on. In *Geo-Seas*, follow a maze through the ocean, answering questions along the way. *Geo-Adapt* explores how plants have adapted to various international habitats. *Geo-Layers* allows you to investigate what's above and below the Earth's surface.

The games here are innovative and well designed. It's truly interactive, in that you can shape the evolution of the site by making your own contributions to the games. The one big question mark about this site is whether it is maintained or updated on any regular basis.

How Far Is It?
http://www.indo.com/distance/

Here's a simple, interactive site that provides *fast* answers to a single question: How far is it? Using data from the U.S. Census and a supplementary list of cities around the world, this site quickly calculates the distance between them (as the crow flies). It also provides a map showing the two places, using the Xerox PARC Map Server.

We found out in mere seconds, for example, that the distance between Lincoln, Nebraska, United States, and Ho Chi Minh City, Vietnam, is 8,584 miles, 13,814 km, or 7,459 nautical miles. You'll also get nutshell information on the cities' population and latitude and longitude.

How to Use a Compass
http://www.uio.no/~kjetikj/compass/

Kjetil Kjernsmo may just be a 20-something dude in Norway with a love of orienteering, but his illustrated guide on how to use a compass is a standout personal site. If you're looking for someone to hold your (virtual) hand while you learn to use a compass, you could do worse than Kjetil. His step-by-step tutorial site is informative and downright entertaining.

The lessons included in his tutorial are on the compass alone, compass and map interaction, magnetic declination and uncertainty, navigating under difficult conditions, finding directions without a compass, buying a compass, and suggested exercises. You'll also find a handful of links to related sites here.

Where in the World? Online Geography Games and Quizzes
http://www.geography-games.com/index.html

If you're into geography trivia, you'll appreciate the scope of games provided at this site. Click on a region ("World," "Canada," "USA," "Australia," "Europe," "Asia," "South America," or "Africa") and then choose to play either a find game, word game, or quiz game about that region.

The rest of this site is somewhat of a geography potpourri, probably representative of the passions of its author. You can access geography clip art, learn about endangered animals and biodiversity, and check your seismic hazard risk.

Map Collections

Historical Atlas of the Twentieth Century
http://users.erols.com/mwhite28/20centry.htm

If you want a good general atlas of the twentieth century, turn to this site. It has hundreds of maps, charts, and graphs dealing with historical topics worldwide. The number of American maps is small, but we have included the site because it links to a superb collection of other sites that are very useful for American history. To find the sites, click on "Links" under "Broad Outline" on the left side of the home page. Then scroll down to "America" under "Human History Organized by Place rather than Time" and click on "United States."

Images of American Political History
http://teachpol.tcnj.edu/amer_pol_hist/_browse_maps.htm

Images of American Political History concentrates on maps illustrating border changes or showing the results of presidential elections. While the territorial change maps are inclusive, running from 1768 to 1920, the election maps span only 1796 to 1968. The collection also contains a few demographic maps, but this is not the site for demographic information. It is, however, a good site for political geographers interested in maps of American growth, population, and election figures.

Geography and Map Division, Library of Congress
http://memory.loc.gov/ammem/gmdhtml/gnrlhome.html

This is an extensive—as in more than 4.5 million items—searchable collection of historical and contemporary maps covering such diverse categories as "Cities and Towns"; "Conservation and Environment"; "Discovery and Exploration"; "Cultural Landscapes"; "Military Battles and Campaigns"; and "Transportation and Railroads." Each collection contains an overview as well as a history of mapping the topic.

You can search map collections by keyword, geographic location, subject, map creator, and title.

See *MapQuest* in this chapter. Also see description in "The Basics" section in Volume 1 of this set.

Perry-Castañeda Library Map Collection
http://www.lib.utexas.edu/maps/map_sites/hist_sites.html#general

The Perry-Castañeda Library Map Collection at the University of Texas at Austin is the most extensive online map collection on the Internet. From the home page, just choose a part of the world to search the site's collection or browse the extensive list of links to other historical map sites. This is no small feat. There are hundreds of map sites, but chances are very good that you'll find what you're looking for without ever venturing beyond the borders of this site.

United States Military Academy (West Point) Map Library
http://www.dean.usma.edu/history/dhistorymaps/MapsHome.htm

This site contains nearly 1,000 maps that were created over many years for a course entitled the "History of Military Art." Some of the maps you'll find here are titled "Ancient Warfare"; "Dawn of Modern Warfare"; "Colonial Wars"; "Napoleonic Wars"; "War of 1812"; "Mexican War"; "Spanish-American War"; "Chinese Civil War"; "World War One"; "World War Two—Europe Theater"; "World War Two—Asia Theater"; "Korean War"; "Arab-Israeli Wars"; "Vietnam War"; "Wars and Conflicts since 1958."

Be forewarned that the files for these maps are quite large and thus slow to load. If you want to do some research here, use the fastest machine you can find, and leave yourself plenty of time.

Primary Sources

Ahlul Bayt Digital Islamic Library Project
http://www.al-islam.org/organizations/dilp/

The Digital Islamic Library Project is an effort to digitize important Islamic resources and make them available to the masses through the Internet. Its ultimate goal is the creation of an Islamic Study Database. You'll find an extensive section of full-length texts and journal articles, as well as a section of links to multimedia sites, including such ones as "Translations Corner," where you'll find information on planned translations of Islamic texts and "Online Islamic Courses," in case you're looking to sign up for a class.

African-American Mosaic
http://www.loc.gov/exhibits/african/intro.html

Part of the Library of Congress's *Exhibitions* site, *African-American Mosaic* is a great resource for primary material in four areas of African American studies: abolition and slavery; the controversy over colonization of free blacks in Africa; the migration of African Americans to the West following the Civil War; and the Great Migration to the North during the early twentieth century. It also contains a large amount of material from WPA (Works Projects Administration) programs in the 1930s including ex-slave narratives. Although the focus is on primary documents, the text accompanying the exhibit gives you an excellent overview of the topics.

Center for World Indigenous Studies
http://www.cwis.org/

This site aims, in its own words, "to present the online community with the greatest possible access to Fourth World documents and resources." The *Fourth World Documentation Project* is an online library of texts that record and preserve the struggles of Fourth World people to regain their rightful place in the international community. These texts include "Tribal and Inter-Tribal Resolutions and Papers"; "African Documents"; "UN Documents"; "Treaties"; and documents from each region throughout the world.

The site is searchable from the home page and is available in French, Spanish, Portuguese, Dutch, Italian, and Norwegian, as well as English.

Internet History Sourcebooks
http://www.fordham.edu/halsall/

Paul Halsall of Fordham University has collected primary source material and secondary texts in a number of different subject areas into what are called sourcebooks. These sourcebooks include some of the largest collections of subject-specific online textual sources, and they are presented in an easy-to-follow chronological outline for educational use. There's no advertising or fancy graphics to get in your way, just a rich array of primary source material, with annotated links so that you can efficiently pick and choose your resources.

His sourcebooks include the Internet *Ancient History Sourcebook, Internet Medieval Sourcebook, Internet Modern History Sourcebook,* and nine subsidiary sourcebooks in the following subject areas: African, east Asian, Indian, global, Jewish, Islamic, lesbian/gay, science, and women's studies.

The Islamic Texts and Resources Metapage
http://wings.buffalo.edu/student-life/sa/muslim/isl/isl.html

Located at the University of Buffalo, this site includes a section of introductory texts, followed by sections dedicated to scriptures and prophetic traditions, Islamic thought, and Islamic language and art resources. It is, in its own words, "an attempt to provide a 'springboard' for exploring texts and resources on Islam and Islamic thought, ideas, and related issues."

The introductory section may be especially useful if you're looking to get acquainted with the ideas and practices of Islam. These texts are written for those with little exposure to Islam, so they cover the basics very well.

Among the other resources found here is a FAQs section, which covers questions on women, marriage laws, and human rights, among other topics.

Slave Movement during the Eighteenth and Nineteenth Centuries
http://dpls.dacc.wisc.edu/slavedata/index.html

This site from the Data and Program Library Service at the University of Wisconsin provides access to the raw data and documentation that contains information on the following slave trade topics from the eighteenth and nineteenth centuries: records of slave ship movement between Africa and the Americas; slave ships of eighteenth-century France; slave trade to Rio de Janeiro; Virginia slave trade in the eighteenth century; English slave trade (House of Lords Survey); Angola slave trade in the eighteenth century; internal slave trade to Rio de Janeiro; slave trade to Havana, Cuba; Nantes slave trade in the eighteenth century; and slave trade to Jamaica.

A handy-dandy link at the top of the page takes you to a section called "What the Slave Movement Site Can and Cannot Do for You." There's also helpful instructions on how to cite the resources found at this site and links to other related Web sites.

READY TO RESEARCH

Evaluating Web Material

For excellent subject guides specific to the fields of geography and other geosciences, check out *GeoGuide* (http://www.geo-guide.de/index.html), *Odden's Bookmarks* (http://oddens.geog.uu.nl/index.html), *GeoSource* (http://www.library.uu.nl/geosource/index.html), and *Geography World* (http://members.aol.com/bowermanb/101.html).

2

---∽∽∽---

Researching Individual Geography Topics on the Internet

Researching a specific geography topic on the Internet can be overwhelming. Type a topic such as "apartheid" into a search engine, and you'll pull up hundreds—if not thousands—of Web pages, some of which are only remotely connected to your subject.

This chapter is designed to help you over this major hurdle to online geography research. In it, you'll find a list of about 200 topics in geography, such as "Animism," the "Green Revolution," and "Women." For each of these topics, you'll see several key terms listed that will make searching the Internet a little easier. For instance, under "Animism," you'll learn that it might be helpful to search by keywords like "nature worship" and "ancestor worship." The best search engine to use will also be listed.

Below these recommendations on how to search, you'll see the names and descriptions of Web sites that best cover the topic. Some of the Web sites give basic overviews, some are multimedia extravaganzas, and some make primary source material available to you. Because each main topic is so broad, some of these Web sites will only look at a particular facet of the topic. Use these tried-and-true sites as a jumping-off point, and then follow the links until your heart's content . . . and your paper topic has come into crystal-clear focus.

ACCULTURATION

Best Search Engine:	http://www.sprinks.com/
Key Search Terms:	Acculturation
	Cultural anthropology

Diffusion and Acculturation: A Guide Prepared for Students by Students
http://www.as.ua.edu/ant/Faculty/murphy/diffusion.htm
high school and up

You'll find this site to be one of your best bets for acculturation info on the Web. The graduate students in the anthropology department at the University of Alabama who created the site covered all the bases. It's just too bad that nobody spruced up the look and design of the site—it's crying out for a face-lift: new font, some visual eye-candy, and better use of current Web technology.

From an academic and historical standpoint, this site provides great information and provides you with some essential background and historical perspective on acculturation and diffusion, as well as directing you to books with more information. It's arranged much as a book would be, with short chapters covering basic premises, points of reaction, leading figures, key works, principal concepts, methodologies, accomplishments, criticisms, sources and bibliography, and, sadly, an empty section called "Related Web Sites." Despite flaws, the site has been lauded by both *StudyWeb* and the *Scout Report for Social Sciences*.

Acculturation Depot
http://www.ocf.berkeley.edu/~psych/depot.html
high school and up

Designed for researchers who already understand *what* acculturation is, this site provides methods for measuring acculturation. The site was created in 1998 by a Ph.D. student who hoped to create a depot to house measures and scales of psychological acculturation.

These measures and scales include the Benet-Martinez Acculturation Scale, which measures acculturation through language/media exposure, cultural identity, and types of biculturalism; the Flannery Listing Index of Preferences, which measures culture and gender preferences in a subtle, indirect fashion; the General Ethnicity Questionnaire, which measures acculturation of Chinese Americans and European Americans; the Cultural Beliefs and Behaviors Adaptation Profile, which is designed to access an individual's cultural beliefs and behaviors based on the theoretical concepts of independence. To see the full text for each of these scales, just click on the name. With permission from the authors, most of these scales can easily be adapted for your own research.

Acculturation (Anthropology)
http://www.orst.edu/instruct/anth210/accult.html
high school and up

This site was originally created for students enrolled in an anthropology course at Oregon State University. Essentially, it's a fact sheet on the topic of acculturation, providing a definition, a list and definitions of related terminology, and brief descriptions of three acculturation processes: directed, nondirected, and other.

To get the most out of this site, scroll down to the globe-shaped symbols at the bottom of the page. Click on the symbol with letters to access class notes on specific cultures and key concepts. Here—for you masochists who don't have enough homework of your own—you'll also find sample quiz questions. Click on the lightning bolt globe to find links to sites relevant to the instructor's course material (which will, naturally, be useful for those of you planning to take the quiz).

ACID RAIN

Best Search Engine: http://www.looksmart.com/

Key Search Terms: Acid rain

Acid rain + education

Clean Air Market Programs: Acid Rain (United States Environmental Protection Agency)
http://www.epa.gov/airmarkets/acidrain/
middle school and up

This Environmental Protection Agency (EPA) site will answer your basic questions about what acid rain is, what causes it, and how it is measured. In particular, the effects of acid rain are covered in great detail, with links to comprehensive pages describing how acid rain affects surface waters, forests, car paint, visibility, and human health. The EPA clearly developed this site with students in mind, offering excellent science experiments, learning activities, and a lengthy glossary of terms related to clean air.

If you're interested in helping tackle the problem of acid rain on a local level, you'll find specific guidelines. You'll also find a progress report on the EPA's efforts to reduce emissions of sulfur dioxide (SO_2) and nitrogen oxides (NO_x), the primary causes of acid rain.

Acid Rain Data and Reports (U.S. Geological Survey)
http://bqs.usgs.gov/acidrain/index.htm
high school and up

As the leading federal agency for the monitoring of wet atmospheric deposition, the U.S. Geological Survey (USGS) has created an excellent site for locating current scientific data on acid rain. You can access a number of scientific reports, including a primer on acid rain written by USGS scientists, a report on the effects of Clean Air Act amendments, and an interesting report on acid deposition's devastating effect on historical buildings in Washington, D.C.

You can also download maps of atmospheric deposition and read about scientific research and assessments to evaluate the effects of atmospheric deposition on aquatic and terrestrial ecosystems.

AGRIBUSINESS

Best Search Engine: http://www.google.com/
Key Search Term: Agribusiness

Global Agribusiness Information Network (GAIN)
http://www.fintrac.com/gain/
college level

This is a great site for any research project that calls for accurate and up-to-date facts and figures from the agribusiness industry. Click on "Postharvest and Production Guides" for information on producing and maintaining postharvest quality in crops ranging from arugula to zucchini. The section entitled "Wholesale Prices" will give you daily updates on wholesale prices from North American, South American, European, and Japanese markets. Under "Trade Statistics," look for historical, annual, and monthly trade statistics for a variety of agricultural commodities. In the section called "Trade Regulations," you'll find import regulations and industry standards for a wide range of agricultural products and most major markets.

There are lots of other goodies here, including an events calendar with listings of the most important worldwide agricultural industry events, and a photo library with dozens of downloadable pictures of fruits, vegetables, and other agricultural products. And while you're at the site, be sure to check out "GAIN Select," a handful of agricultural Web sites that the Global Agribusiness Information Network (GAIN) recommends.

AgriBiz
http://www.agribiz.com/
high school and up

AgriBiz is another commendable site for info on agribusiness. (*Argus Clearinghouse*, *LookSmart*, and the *Scout Report* have all given their nods of approval.) *AgriBiz* has set its site on organizing a vast amount of Web information and resources specific to the global agricultural trading community.

The site is divided into three main sections: "Articles and Trade News," "Markets and Analysis," and "Search and Research." In the "Article and Trade News" section, you'll find links to numerous sources of agricultural news. In the "Markets and Analysis" section, look for links to price quotes and research reports on agricultural commodities. Under "Search and Research," there are research tools from various federal, state, and commercial agricultural agencies. Here you can also learn about weekly crop conditions and weather reports from around the country and the world.

AGRICULTURE

Best Search Engine: http://www.google.com/

Key Search Terms: Agriculture + geography

Agriculture Network Information Center
http://www.agnic.org/
high school and up

You'll appreciate the streamlined feel of the *Agriculture Network Information Center's* (*AgNIC*) Web site, which houses an incredible selection of quality agricultural information on the Internet, as selected by the National Agricultural Library, land-grant universities, and other institutions.

From the home page, you can dive right into the browsable subject categories. These categories include "Animal and Veterinary Sciences"; "Aquaculture and Fisheries"; "Consumer and Family Studies"; "Earth and Environmental Sciences"; "Economics, Business, and Industry"; "Extension and Education"; "Farming and Farming Systems"; "Food and Human Nutrition"; "Forestry"; "Geographical Locations"; "Government, Law, and Regulations"; "Medical and Biological Sciences"; "People, Organizations, and History"; "Plant Sciences"; and "Science and Technology." You can also access specific keyword information using the site's advanced and simple search engines.

Be sure to check out *AgNIC's* excellent "Ask a Question" tool, where you will find links to designated centers of excellence for reference and question and answer services on topics as diverse as the American cranberry, plant genetics, swine, and water quality.

Food and Agriculture Organization of the United Nations
http://www.fao.org/
high school and up

This site is an excellent place to conduct your research on topics in sustainable agriculture. The Food and Agriculture Organization (FAO) works to raise levels of nutrition and standards of living, to improve agricultural productivity, and to better the condition of rural populations.

You may need to spend some time browsing FAO's crowded home page, which gives space to everything, including "Subject Categories," a FactFile archive, "News and Highlights," "Press Releases," "In-Depth Features," "Global Watches," "Conferences," "Summits," and more.

Some of the best research resources at the FAO site are the reports on global conditions and trends, such as *The State of Food Insecurity in the World; The State of Food and Agriculture;* and *The World Food Survey.* Tucked into the upper right corner of the home page, you'll also find a link to WAICENT (World Agricultural Information Centre), which provides quick access to FAO's extensive data and analyses on agricultural subjects such as biodiversity, biotechnology, desertification, ethics, gender, organic agriculture, rural youth, small islands, and trade.

ANIMISM

Best Search Engine:	http://www.northernlight.com/
Key Search Terms:	Animism
	Nature worship
	Ancestor worship

Animism in Vietnam
http://mcel.pacificu.edu/as/students/vb/Animism.HTM
middle school and up

This page—part of a comprehensive site examining the evolution of Buddhism in Vietnam—offers a brief look at animism and ancestor worship as practiced at one time in Vietnam.

Created as part of an Asian Studies Web collection at Pacific University, this page will give you a glimpse into how animism was practiced, who its believers were, and how it eventually blended with Buddhism in the peasant regions of Vietnam. Although its scope is limited to Vietnam, this site could be useful for general cultural research on animism.

Practical Animism
http://hpwsys.com/dave/
high school and up

If you're curious about how animism might be practiced in the modern age, check out this site. It presents the argument that practical animism is alive and well in the United States. Regardless of how you feel about animism's supposed revival, this site presents an interesting description of current animism practices and beliefs. The creator of this site, Dave Huckleberry, works as a modern-day shaman, creating power objects to help people.

Since this site obviously falls into the category of personal sites, you'll want to use and cite any material gleaned here accordingly.

"Animism," Microsoft Encarta Online Encyclopedia 2000
http://encarta.msn.com/index/conciseindex/5F/05FAA000.htm
high school and up

If you're seeking a straightforward definition of animism, look no further. In this encyclopedia entry, you'll learn that the word animism was coined in the eighteenth century to describe a chemist's theories on organic development. In the following century, however, a British anthropologist borrowed the term to describe the inception of religion and primitive beliefs. In turn, this anthropologist's theories on animism were attacked by another anthropologist, who described his own theories on animism and preanimism. For further reading, click on a link to the *Encarta* page that describes ancestor worship.

ANTARCTICA (SEE ALSO GLACIATION, GLACIER)

Best Search Engine: http://www.yahoo.com/
Key Search Terms: Antarctica
    Antarctica + education
    Antarctica + geography

Secrets of the Ice (Boston Museum of Science)
http://www.secretsoftheice.org/
middle school and up

While there are a number of other excellent Web sites about Antarctica, this one might just take the cake. It's easy to navigate, and it offers professional and comprehensive tools and data for understanding Antarctica.

The introductory section, entitled "Explore Antarctica," takes a broad look at the continent's wilderness, climate, past history, and its human discovery. "Ice Core Research" offers an introduction to the ice core time machine and how scientists use ice core data to interpret global environmental changes. In "Scientific Expedition," you can follow a team of scientists as they travel to the South Pole over four field seasons, collecting ice core samples to evaluate how humans have impacted climate changes. You can click on "Projects" to read research summaries of projects involving meteorology, remote sensing, geophysics, ice coring, and surface glaciology.

In "Expedition Headquarters," click on "Visitor Q&A" or "FAQs" to find out what daily life is like for the scientists. You can listen to archived broadcasts or access recent media coverage of events in Antarctica. If you favor a hands-on approach to learning, click on "Learning Resources" for a list of student activities and tools.

Glacier
http://www.glacier.rice.edu/
middle school and up

This vast Web site focuses on Antarctica and the role Antarctica plays in the global system of weather, climate, oceans, and geology.

For the full tour, start in the "Introduction" section. Click on "Where?" to learn precisely where Antarctica is and see simple maps of the region. "Who?" provides a description of Antarctica's native population, both on land and below water. You'll learn about the flora and fauna unique to the ecosystem. Other pages within the introduction cover topics such as "Ice," "Ice Size," and "Poles Apart."

An "Expedition" section captures what it's like to live and work in Antarctica, with detailed essays and photos about traveling there, training camp life, station life, remote camping, and ship life. As with all of the site's main sections, you'll find an expedition-specific glossary, bibliography, and a list of other resources. The three other main sections—"Weather," "Ice," and "Ocean"—all do a good job of delving thoroughly into the topic at hand.

PBS: Nature: Antarctica: The End of the Earth
http://www.pbs.org/wnet/nature/antarctica/
middle school and up

This site is well researched and well written, as you'd expect from PBS's Nature series. While you probably wouldn't want to use this site as a primary research tool, you'll find plenty of interesting facts here to flesh out your research on Antarctica.

The site is divided into sections, each featuring great photos and visuals that capture the extremes of life in Antarctica. The sections include "Of Time Machines and Icebergs," where you'll explore the secrets that ice holds about the past; "Unequaled Extremes," which presents Antarctica's records as the earth's coldest, driest, and windiest place; and "Life in the Icebox," which highlights the unusual strategies that Antarctica's animals use to survive.

APARTHEID

Best Search Engine: http://www.askjeeves.com/

Best Search Question: What is apartheid?

Apartheid
http://www.encyclopedia.com/articles/00616.html
high school and up

The *Columbia Electronic Library* offers this straightforward resource on apartheid. You'll find a general definition of what apartheid is, as well as sections with in-depth information on apartheid history, the separate development policy, the Bantustans, and opposition, and repeal.

In addition, you'll find a short bibliography of print resources on apartheid and access (for a price) to *Electric Library's* document library of photos, newspaper and magazine articles, and maps.

Historical Documents Archive: African National Congress
http://www.anc.org.za/ancdocs/history/
college level

This incredible site represents an enormous effort by the African National Congress (ANC) to preserve and catalog documents pertaining to South Africa's political and social history. It contains scores of documents either produced by the ANC about the role of the ANC and its allies, or directly concerned with the ANC.

Click on "World against Apartheid" to find speeches, press statements, reports, and letters written by organizations and individuals in support of the liberation struggle. You'll find items documenting the major campaigns and struggles against apartheid—in some instances, entire books have been archived chapter by chapter. You'll also find personal letters, articles, and lectures written by influential political and cultural leaders, such as Martin Luther King, Mahatma Gandhi, Jean-Paul Sartre, and W. E. B. DuBois.

The History of Apartheid in South Africa
http://www-cs-students.stanford.edu/~cale/cs201/apartheid.hist.html
high school and up

This Stanford University student site opens with a page on the history of apartheid and continues with a page that explores the ethical question posed to the international community and another page that lists the tallies of votes, broken down by state, in the 1994 democratic elections. Charts and photographs throughout the site graphically illustrate the brutality of apartheid.

You'll also find current information at this site on the criminal justice system, policing and security, crime and crime prevention, and the Truth and Reconciliation Commission, among other topics.

Crime, Justice, and Race in South Africa
http://www.uaa.alaska.edu/just/just490/
middle school and up

Click on "History" midway down the page to explore South Africa's history of apartheid policies under the Nationalist government from 1948 to 1993. You'll find links to recent history topics first, followed by older historical topics and a section on Nelson Mandela. At the bottom of the page you'll find "Other Resources," which includes a link on "Computers and Apartheid" that explores the enabling technology of computers and how they were used to support the oppression. Two other links take you to award-winning photographs of South Africa's first democratic elections in 1994.

AQUACULTURE

Best Search Engine: http://www.ixquick.com/
Key Search Term: Aquaculture

Aquanic
http://aquanic.org/
high school and up

Here's an amazing site for anyone with an interest in aquaculture. The site can be accessed in a variety of ways. On the home page, you'll see a "For Beginners" menu, where you can choose either the species (baitfish, yellow perch shellfish, shrimp, etc.) or the system (cage, farm pond, levee pond, etc.) to access an array of publications, Web sites, discussion groups, videos, photographs, and experts relevant to the particular subject.

Use the toolbar at the top of the home page to access useful calculators and dictionaries, such as a fish name translator (in case you'd like to translate "tuna" into 20 other languages), a pond plumbing calculator, and a bead filter size calculator. The site also has sections where you can quickly access aquaculture publications (federal, regional, and state), newsletters, Web sites and listservs, multimedia resources (photos, slide sets, software, video), news briefs, and educator information.

Getting Started in Freshwater Aquaculture
http://ag.ansc.purdue.edu/courses/aq448/index.htm
high school and up

This site provides an excellent college-level course in freshwater aquaculture. The course, sponsored by the National Sea Grant College Program, Purdue University, the University of Illinois, and the Illinois-Indiana Sea Grant College Program, ties a ton of information and resources into a neat, user-friendly package. Surprisingly, the course is described as still being in development, so one can only imagine how good it's going to become.

The "Introduction" section gives you an overview of the course, answers frequently asked questions, and provides an hour-by-hour look at life on an aquaculture farm (revealing how shockingly few hours a fish farmer actually spends sleeping). You can move on next to the body of the course, which is broken into 10 complete sections: "Water Resources," "Species," "Production Methods," "Marketing," "Business Planning," "Diseases," "Reproduction," "Nutrition," "Transportation," and "Assessment." Within each section, you'll find truly interactive offerings—some PowerPoint and video presentations, a list of pertinent online publications, and a full glossary of terms.

The World Aquaculture Society
http://www.was.org/
high school and up

The World Aquaculture Society (WAS) is an international nonprofit society with members in 94 countries. Founded in 1970, its primary focus is communication and information exchange within the aquaculture community.

The site, quite honestly, doesn't compare to *Aquanic* (http://aquanic. org/) in terms of education or outreach. It's intended primarily for paid members, who can access portions of the site that are off-limits to the rest of us. Nonetheless, you'll want to visit the site, if only to tap into its exhaustive list of links to aquaculture associations and societies, aquaculture suppliers, and other aquaculture-related Web sites. The database is searchable, which comes in handy for research pertaining to a specific topic. For example, our keyword search for "internship" turned up a number of links within the database, as did a search for "striped bass."

AQUIFER (SEE ALSO HYDROLOGIC CYCLE)

Best Search Engine: http://www.google.com/
Key Search Terms: Aquifer

Aquifer + geography

Groundwater + geography

EPA's Office of Water: Ground Water and Drinking Water
http://www.epa.gov/safewater/
high school and up

Here's a site that really delivers on any topic related to groundwater and drinking water. The site's "Frequently Asked Questions" section is a smart place to begin your research. Here, you'll find information on water quality, drinking water standards, testing, specific contaminants, drinking water sources, and more—all with hyperlinked text to further information.

For information specific to aquifers, go to the site's "Source Water" section. Here, you can tap into subsections, such as "Source Water Basics," "Source Water Assessment," "Source Water Protection," "Contamination Prevention Strategy," and more. For other information, use the topic index or the site search engine, both provided on the home page.

The Groundwater Foundation
http://groundwater.org/
middle school and up

The Groundwater Foundation is an aptly named nonprofit organization dedicated to informing the public about—you guessed it!—groundwater. To begin your research, just click on the section called "Groundwater Basics." Here, you'll find information and statistics on groundwater protection, contamination sources, the hydrologic cycle, wells, and conservation. Be sure to check out "Groundwater ABCs," a glossary of terminology. You can also access the foundation's *Source Water Assessment and Protection (SWAP) Workshop Guide and Training Materials*, which were designed to educate and motivate community members on groundwater issues.

The Hydrologic Cycle (Online Meteorology Guide)
http://ww2010.atmos.uiuc.edu/(Gh)/guides/mtr/hyd/grnd.rxml
high school and up

The University of Illinois's excellent series of online instructional modules pulls it off again. As a section within the *Meteorology Guide*, the "Hydrologic Cycle" module is organized into the following topics: "Earth's Water Budget," "Evaporation," "Condensation," "Transport," "Precipitation," "Groundwater," "Transpiration," "Runoff," and "Summary and Examples." The URL provided here takes you directly to the "Groundwater" page, where you can watch a colorful animation of water penetrating the earth's surface and then read about the zone of aeration and the zone of saturation, the two layers of soil where groundwater is stored.

This site is well designed, with excellent diagrams and animations interspersed throughout the text. Thanks to a toolbar on the left side of the home page, the site is also easy to navigate. Highlighted text link to a glossary of terms and relevant case studies. On the "Groundwater" page, you can link to a case study on the upper midwest spring floods of 1997 and to a separate page on runoff. And unlike other online courses that cater to students with lightening-fast computers, this site is available in both graphics and text-only versions.

ARCTIC

Best Search Engine: http://www.webscout.com/
Key Search Term: Arctic

Arctic Studies Center
http://www.mnh.si.edu/arctic/
high school and up

This powerful Smithsonian Institution site uses multimedia technology to its fullest advantage to bring the impact of a museum right to your computer. The site features 10 exhibits, each loaded with information, images, and sounds of the arctic landscape, people, and wildlife. An exhibit on the Viking age, for example, explores the origin and impact of the rise of Scandinavian kingdoms during the Viking age to the demise of the Greenland colonies. While visiting the exhibit, you can view a Viking ship in vivid 3-D or watch a movie of Viking ships at sea.

Another exhibit presents the impressive collaboration of native Alaskan people, researchers, and museum professionals, using photographs, video, and sound to bring traditional Yup'ik masks to life within their native context. Other exhibits focus on arctic wildlife, northern clans, the Yamal people, and repatriation. Each exhibit offers a list of relevant Web and print resources, and for more general resources on the arctic, simply click on "Web, Publications, and Research" on the site's home page.

Arctic Theme Page: National Oceanic and Atmospheric Administration (NOAA)
http://www.arctic.noaa.gov/
high school and up

A visit to this site is a must for anyone researching the arctic. Recognized for excellence by *USA Today*, *Scientific American*, the *Scout Report for Social Sciences*, and *Science* magazine, its purpose is to provide arctic data and information to scientists, students, teachers, and the general public.

Information is organized into "Scientific," "General Interest," "Photo Gallery," "Essays," and "FAQ" sections. If you're searching for data, maps, climate indexes, and links to other arctic research programs, check out the "Scientific" section. The "General Interest" section holds a variety of resources on education, arctic exploration, the Bering Sea, the North Pacific Ocean, the northern lights, archaeology and native people, ships, animals, and the environment. The "Essays" and "FAQ" sections offer excellent expert responses to questions about the arctic.

ATMOSPHERE (SEE ALSO BAROMETER, CLIMATE, WEATHER)

Best Subject Directory: http://www.scout.cs.wisc.edu/index.html
Key Search Term: Atmosphere

Encyclopedia of the Atmospheric Environment
http://www.doc.mmu.ac.uk/aric/eae/english.html
middle school and up

Produced by the U.K. Atmosphere, Climate, and Environment Information Programme, this site is a handy resource for information on atmospheric issues.

From the topic tree on the left side of the home page, select "Atmosphere." Here, you'll find an introduction to the atmosphere, plus easy-to-digest encyclopedia entries on atmospheric topics such as aerosols, air, atmospheric gases, atmospheric layers, aurora, blue sky, clouds, coriolis force, cosmic rays, energy, exosphere, ionosphere, jet stream, magnetosphere, mesosphere, meteors, moisture, nitrogen, oxygen, ozone hole, ozone layer, pollution, pressure, stratosphere, temperature, thermosphere, trace gases, troposphere, weather, and wind. Many entries include a list of Web links and recommended reading.

Forces and Winds: Online Meteorology Guide
http://ww2010.atmos.uiuc.edu/(Gh)/guides/mtr/fw/home.rxml
high school and up

The University of Illinois's excellent series of online instructional modules strikes gold again. As a section within the *Meteorology Guide*, this "Forces and Winds" module is organized into the following topics: "Pressure," "Pressure Gradient Force," "Coriolis Force," "Geostrophic Wind," "Gradient Wind," "Friction," "Boundary Layer Wind," "Sea Breezes," and "Land Breezes."

You'll see that the first two topics provide a broad introduction to the subject of atmospheric pressure, while the remaining topics focus on specific aspects. The site is well designed, with good use of graphics and QuickTime movies. Thanks to a toolbar on the left side of the page, the site is easy to navigate. And unlike other online courses that cater to students with lightening-fast computers, it's available in both graphics and text-only versions.

BALANCE OF TRADE

Best Search Engines:	http://www.scout.cs.wisc.edu/index.html and http://www.lii.org/
Key Search Term:	Balance of trade

Foreign Trade Statistics
http://www.census.gov/foreign-trade/www/index.html
college level

This site's a winner for statistical information relating to the balance of trade. Look in the "Statistics" section to find current and historical information on imports, exports, and balance for just about every country in the world. You can also use this section to find out what categories of products were traded in any given year and month. In other words, if you need to know what U.S. trade with Belgium was like during February of 1999, look no further.

Tracking Major Economic Indicators on the World Wide Web
http://www.methodist.edu/business/tracking.htm
high school and up

Created by the Reeves School of Business at Methodist College, this site provides excellent resources on the major economic indicators.

The section dedicated to "Balance of Trade" does a nice job of defining what balance of trade is and why it matters, as well as pointing you in the direction of other useful Web sites. Back at the home page, you'll also find sections with information on the consumer price index, Federal Reserve data, foreign exchange rates, gross domestic product, leading indicators, and more.

BAROMETER (SEE ALSO ATMOSPHERE)

Best Search Engine: http://www.ixquick.com/

Key Search Terms: Barometric pressure

Barometer

Atmospheric pressure

Understanding Air Pressure
http://www.usatoday.com/weather/wbarocx.htm
middle school and up

Produced by *USA Today*, this site devotes itself to answering the questions of you weather hounds. This particular section sets out to explain how air pressure impacts the weather. You'll find explanations of how air pressure is measured, its relation to air density, how a barometer works, and how wind-barometer readings are used for forecasting. You'll also be supplied with the mathematical formulas used to describe air's decreasing pressure with altitude.

Simply click on highlighted words to link with related topics, such as atmosphere tables, a weather calculations index, the *Federal Meteorological Handbook*, and a storms and fronts index.

Atmospheric Pressure/Introduction to Physical Geography
http://www.geog.ouc.bc.ca/conted/onlinecourses/geog_111/5d.html
high school and up

Though designed for students in a college geography course, this site is quite accommodating to Web interlopers. This page on atmospheric pressure is part of the "Climatology" section of the course. There are short descriptions of Torricelli's barometers and aneroid barometers and how each measures air pressure. You'll find a good explanation of how gravity influences atmospheric processes and graphics illustrating how pressure systems develop at different times of the year.

By clicking on any highlighted text, you'll go to a glossary of terms. To explore other aspects of physical geography offered in this course, simply click on the "Course Outline" button at the bottom of the page.

BARRIER ISLAND

Best Search Engine: http://www.google.com/

Key Search Terms: Barrier island + reference

How Barrier Islands Work
http://www.howstuffworks.com/barrier-island.htm
middle school and up

This info-packed site will clue you in on barrier islands. A lot of basic information is covered in the section entitled "What Are Barrier Islands?" Here, you'll learn not only what they are, but where they are found, theories about how they form, a U.S. Geological Survey diagram of the various zones of a barrier island, and more—and that's just in the first section!

Other sections provide text, photos, and graphs on barrier island ecology, shifting island conditions, and island development problems. Finally, you'll appreciate the section offering book and journal recommendations and links to other relevant sites.

Coasts in Crisis (U.S. Geological Survey)
http://pubs.usgs.gov/circular/c1075/
high school and up

This online document, written by U.S. Geological Survey (USGS) scientists, provides an excellent overview of the United States' varied coastal environments and the natural and human processes that are constantly altering them.

The site introduces you to types of coasts—such as rocky shores, sandy shores, coastal wetlands, and coral reefs—and to changes affecting those coastlines. In the text that's about coastal change, you'll find information specific to barrier islands. The section on coastal conflict also focuses on the problems of urbanization and natural erosion on barrier islands.

BIODIVERSITY (SEE ALSO BIOGEOGRAPHY, BIOSPHERE)

Best Search Engine: http://www.lii.org/

Key Search Term: Biodiversity

Biodiversity: Measuring the Variety of Nature
http://www.nhm.ac.uk/science/projects/worldmap/
college and up

Created by researchers at the Natural History Museum, this no-nonsense site provides a worthy introduction to biodiversity and conservation.

You'll find four main sections: "Measuring Biodiversity Value," "Measuring Rarity and Endemism," "Assessing Conservation Priority and Gap Analysis," and "Developments in Biogeography." Each section contains text and graphics to illustrate the various approaches, methods, theories, and examples pertaining to biodiversity and conservation. The site's "Key References," "Publications," and "Related Links" sections also enhance its usefulness as a research tool.

BIOGEOGRAPHY (SEE ALSO BIODIVERSITY, BIOSPHERE)

Best Search Engine: http://www.yahoo.com/
Key Search Term: Biogeography

Biogeography.com
http://www.biogeography.com/
high school and up

This site is manna from heaven for students who are researching topics in biogeography. It's designed to encompass three broad areas: concepts, topics, and tools in biogeography.

Within the "Concepts" section, you can simply click on a concept of interest—such as island biogeography, invasive species, or evolution—to find links to dozens of Web sites on that subject. While it's not made entirely clear what the difference between a concept and a topic is, you'll want to tap into "Topics" to find links to sites with information on biomaps, ocean life, forests, fauna, general biology, protected areas, and more. Inside "Tools," you'll find an excellent glossary of biogeography terms, along with some great links to Web forums, journals, organizations, and university departments.

Biogeography Lab at University of California, Santa Barbara
http://www.biogeog.ucsb.edu/
high school and up

The Biogeography Lab within the Department of Geography at the University of California, Santa Barbara is one of the few university biogeography programs with a strong Web presence. The lab's research work focuses on the ecology, distribution, and conservation status of species and ecosystems, utilizing tools such as geographic information systems and remote sensing.

At this frequently updated site, you'll find extensive information on the lab's research projects, its funding partners, and the status of projects. Projects are loosely divided into two major areas: "Conservation Planning and Spatial Decision Support Systems" and "Ecological Inventory, Monitoring, and Assessment." Recent research has included regional scale mapping and modeling of vegetation cover types, wildlife distributions, and long-term vegetation change. Other recent work described here involves the design of networked nature reserves to help protect biodiversity.

Another valuable research tool is the "Publications" section, where you'll find full-text journal articles, book chapters, conference proceedings, technical reports, and dissertations.

Introduction to Biogeography
http://www.valdosta.edu/~grissino/geog4900/geog4900no.htm
high school and up

Hats off to Dr. Henri Grissino-Mayer of Valdosta State University for creating this excellent Web resource on biogeography. While not created as an online course per se, this professor's lecture notes are comprehensive enough that, with some tweaking, he could easily call this a virtual classroom.

The course examines the patterns of distribution of living organisms across the earth's surface, and why these patterns arise. The notes are broken into these major topics: "Introduction to Biogeography"; "Biodiversity"; "Patterns of Distribution"; "Communities, Ecosystems and Climate"; "Biomes"; "Island Biogeography"; "Causes of Glaciations"; "Evidence from Glacial, Ocean, and Pollen Records"; "Biogeography during the Holocene"; and "Disturbance History." Within each section, you'll find lengthy and meticulously outlined lecture notes. And just think, you don't have to take the exams!

BIOMASS

Best Search Engine: http://www.dogpile.com/
Key Search Terms: Biomass + education
                        Bioenergy

American Bioenergy Association
http://www.biomass.org/
middle school and up

The American Bioenergy Association (ABA) aims to be the leading voice in the United States for the bioenergy industry. Click on "Get the

Facts" to view an excellent fact sheet on bioenergy technologies. It describes what biomass is, how it is used, and what its economic, energy, and environmental benefits are.

You'll also find information here about specific legislative efforts and clean energy caucuses in Congress. Under "Helpful Links," there's a variety of good links to sources of information about biomass and other renewable energy technologies, many compiled by the U.S. Department of Energy.

The Education Site: Future Sources of Electricity
http://www.the-education-site.com/bio.html
middle school and up

This British site was designed for students and teachers interested in understanding possible future energy sources. The sources covered include biomass, nuclear fusion, solar power, oceans, nuclear fission, fuel cells, fossil fuels, and wind. The biomass page contains a lengthy description of how various materials are used to create biomass energy, including trees, plants, animal waste, straw, and rubbish (best known to Americans as garbage). There's gobs of useful information and statistics here. However, it would be *more* useful if original sources for the facts were also cited.

BIOMES (SEE ALSO BIODIVERSITY, ECOLOGY, ECOSYSTEM)

Best Subject Directory: http://www.ixquick.com/
Key Search Term: Biomes

WorldBiomes
http://www.worldbiomes.com/
middle school and up

WorldBiomes is an educational site that presents excellent information on five major biomes—aquatic, desert, forest, grasslands, and tundra. From the site's main page, simply click on your selected biome to find a brief description of the biome, color photos, suggested links, and a reading list. You'll read about various subdivisions within each biome and see examples that can help you distinguish one from another.

Major Biomes of the World
http://www.runet.edu/~swoodwar/CLASSES/GEOG235/biomes/main.
   html
high school and up

As part of the Virtual Geography Department Project at Radford University, this site offers a learning module on the world's major biomes. You'll want to start with the introductory section, "Introduction to the Biome Concept," then peruse the comprehensive list of biomes.

For each of the eight biomes—tundra, boreal forest, temperate broadleaf deciduous forest, tropical broadleaf evergreen forest, tropical savanna, desert scrub, temperate grasslands, and Mediterranean scrub—you'll find a discussion of climate, soil, subclimaxes, vegetation, structure and growth forms, fauna, and distribution. Each page contains graphics, photos, and a map representing the geographic range of the particular biome.

BIOSPHERE

Best Search Engine: http://www.dogpile.com/

Key Search Terms: Biosphere

Biosphere + geography

Hands-On: Living in the Biosphere
http://www.colorado.edu/geography/virtdept/module/biosphere/toc.html
high school and up

This virtual geography course is an incredible resource for students and teachers alike. It is broken into four distinct and comprehensive learning units. If you have the time, it's worthwhile to work your way through the entire site. However, if time's short or you have a particular topic in mind, just use the toolbar on the left side of the screen.

Unit 1 is entitled "Introduction to Biogeography and the Human Dimensions of Global Change." It provides an overview of biospheres, biogeography, global change research, and basic concepts of ecology. As is the case for all of the units, you'll not only find excellent text and graphical material, but interesting student worksheets with ideas for activities and an instructor's guide to the material. Unit 2 is focused on production, the food web, and human interactions with the food web. Unit 3 looks at abundance and spatial patterns of distribution, along with how disturbances affect patterns. Unit 4 takes biodiversity as its key subject.

To view definitions of highlighted terminology used throughout the units, simply click on the text. You can also click to access a collection of supporting materials and suggested readings.

World Network of Biosphere Reserves
http://www.unesco.org/mab/wnbr.htm
high school and up

This site houses vital information about the biosphere reserves that
have been established across the globe. The site's "Biosphere Reserve
Directory" can provide information on any biosphere reserve or any
region. Simply select from an alphabetical country list or use the excellent interactive map. With the map, just click on a region to find out
about its biosphere reserves. For instance, click on "North America,"
then "United States," and then choose one of the reserves. Each reserve
is accorded a page with key information such as major ecosystem type,
location, current research and monitoring activities, Web site address,
and other contact information.

Be sure to check out the site's curiously hard-to-find section called
"Biosphere Reserves in a Nutshell" (http://www.unesco.org/mab/nut
shell.htm), which answers questions about the definition and origin of
biosphere reserves, how they are selected and organized, the benefits of
reserves, and the purpose of a world network.

BIRTHRATE (SEE ALSO DEMOGRAPHY,
POPULATION, VITAL STATISTICS)

Best Search Engine: http://www.askjeeves.com/
Key Search Term: Death rate

Countries of the World
http://www.countryreports.org/
middle school and up

This terrific site, selected as one of the best sites on the Web for
teachers, is also one of the best sites for students. Basic demographic
research on people from all over the world is easy and quick. Go to the
home page and click on "World Countries" for a comprehensive database of the world's countries with extensive demographic information
on each one. Once you choose a country, you'll be given a menu of the
following: "Economy," "Defense," "Geography," "Government," "People," "National Anthem Lyrics," and "Related Links." Pick "People."

Among many other statistics, you'll find information about birthrate.
Other really helpful information here includes overall fertility rate, age
structure, infant mortality rate, population growth, religious affiliations,
languages spoken, literacy, and more.

You won't get detailed information about the birthrate here. You'll have to continue your search for that elsewhere. But you will get accurate information to start you on your way.

BOUNDARY AND BOUNDARY CONFLICTS

Best Search Engine: http://www.google.com/

Key Search Terms: Boundary conflicts + geography

Limits and Boundaries
http://www.unifr.ch/geoscience/geographie/Research/HUMAN/WL/
     bound.html
middle school and up

This simple but very useful site from a geography professor in Switzerland covers "Boundaries," "Marginality and Marginal Regions," and "Impact of Immigration." You will probably come to this topic thinking about political boundaries or geographic boundaries, but what you'll learn from this site is that there are numerous other kinds of boundaries and boundary conflicts at work in our world. These other types of boundaries are discussed in the "Marginality and Marginal Regions" section of the site. Professor Leimgruber writes that "marginality is the (temporary) state of having been put aside, of living in relative isolation, at the edge of a system (cultural, social, political, or economic). Included in this definition is the marginality in the mind, when one excludes certain domains or phenomena from one's thinking because they do not correspond to the 'mainstream' philosophy." He goes on to discuss how nature has been marginalized in our thinking.

Whether you're interested in the boundaries established by different cultural practices, such as religious practices, the physical boundaries between one mountain range and the next, the political boundaries between countries, or the boundaries between Third World, marginalized peoples and people of the developed world, you'll find something of interest here.

Specific boundary conflicts explored on the site—most of them are theses or studies done by graduate students—include "The Integration of Highly Qualified Immigrants," "Mental Maps and the Integration of Immigrants," "Identity between Tradition and Modernity—The Case of the Sikhs," and "The Partition of British India."

The International Boundaries and Research Unit
http://www-ibru.dur.ac.uk/pubs/bsb.html
high school and up

Once you understand the scope of what can be included under the terms "boundaries" and "boundary conflicts," it's time to branch out and explore some of the specific boundary issues around the world. There isn't a much better place at which to do this than at the Web site for the International Boundaries and Research Unit (IBRU) at the University of Durham in England.

This Web site is divided into four main sections: "Events and Training," "Publications," "Services and Resources," and "General." The "International Boundary News Database" will probably hold the most interest for you if you're researching specific boundary issues. It's located under "Services and Resources." Just click on the link for the database and you'll be taken to its home page, where you can read instructions on the best way to search. It's really pretty simple, though, to locate information. If you're interested in the Indian-Pakistan border dispute, just type in "India Pakistan," and you'll be given a chronological list of events that have occurred in that ongoing conflict. The India-Pakistan list dates back to 1991 and probably includes several hundred entries.

You'll also want to check out the links page, also found under "Services and Resources." The collection of links is broken into the following four categories: "Specific Boundaries and Territorial Issues," "Organizations with Boundary Related Interests," "Reference Material," and "Miscellaneous." The "Miscellaneous" section contains a wonderfully eclectic group of links. Browse for fun.

BUDDHISM

Best Search Engine: http://www.webscout.com/
Key Search Term: Buddhism

BuddhaNet: Buddhist Studies
http://www.buddhanet.net/e-learning/index.htm
high school and up

Regardless of whether your research on Buddhism is general or in-depth, you'll be impressed with *BuddhaNet's Buddhist Studies* Web site. It contains educational material on all aspects of Buddhism, including a basic Buddhism guide, information on Buddhist scriptures and basic teaching, an online study guide, information on Buddhist history and culture, and an encyclopedic look at the Buddhist world.

There are simply too many research goodies to adequately describe in this review. But we'll try. In the online study guide alone, you'll find several biographies of the Buddha; overviews of the teachings; time lines and historical info; overviews of the scriptures; and meditation, Theravada, and Mahayana texts. Buried in the "Basic Teachings" section of the site, you'll also find the "Good Questions, Good Answers" Web page, which answers your questions about basic concepts, monks and nuns, rebirth, meditation, vegetarianism, the five precepts, and becoming a Buddhist.

Religion Religions Religious: Information and Links for Study and Interpretation
http://www.clas.ufl.edu/users/gthursby/rel/
high school and up

If your research on Buddhism is broadening into a larger analysis of world religions, this site is a great stop. The creation of an associate professor at the University of Florida, this site is broken into the following sections: "Religious Traditions"; "Religion: Modernity and Beyond"; "Research and Teaching Resources"; "Other Reference Sources"; and "Religious Experience."

Each section offers several subtopics, each with numerous Web links. For instance, go to "Religious Traditions" and choose "Traditions from South and East Asia." Click on "Buddhist" to view an extensive annotated list of relevant Web links.

Journal of Buddhist Ethics
http://jbe.gold.ac.uk/
college level

The *Journal of Buddhist Ethics* site will no doubt exceed your expectations of an obscure online journal. And not just *your* expectations—it's been given awards by *Magellan*, *USA Today*, and *WebScout* as a great resource for information on Buddhism.

You can read current and archived issues to cull interesting opinions and informed voices on Buddhism. The articles focus on a variety of issues, such as Buddhist contributions to social welfare, Buddhism and the morality of abortion, and Buddhist case law on theft. For other intriguing articles, click on "Online Conferences," where you'll discover conference papers useful to your general research with titles such as "A New Buddhism," "The Free Tibet Movement," and "Widening the Circle: Black Communities and Western Buddhist Convert Sanghas."

Other research jackpots at this site are the sections entitled "Global Resources for Buddhist Studies" and "Scholarly Resources." Both sections offer excellent links for more information on Buddhism.

CARBON CYCLE

Best Search Engine: http://www.google.com/

Key Search Terms: Carbon cycle + geography

Exploring Environment: Earth on Fire
http://www.cotf.edu/ete/modules/carbon/efcarbon.html
middle school and up

This carbon cycle page is part of a larger site called *Exploring Environment*, where you can look into, among other subjects, the Florida Everglades, the Yellowstone National Park fires of 2000, and global climate change. The site is designed for students and teachers, so you'll find lots of curriculum-specific goodies here. The site includes a glossary, a related links page, a references page, teacher pages, and more.

But on the topic at hand, you'll find an excellent overall explanation of the carbon cycle, which you'll learn is one of the biogeochemical cycles at work. The term "carbon cycle" refers to the movement of carbon between the biosphere, atmosphere, oceans, and geosphere, and you'll see this process illustrated in several graphs on this page. Don't expect the site to go into much detail, but do expect an excellent introduction that will help you get on your way to understanding the basics of the carbon cycle. To go more in depth on the topic, check out the *Chemical Carousel* site below.

Chemical Carousel: A Trip around the Carbon Cycle
http://www.thinkquest.org/library/lib/site_sum_outside.
    html?tname=11226&url=11226/
middle school and up

This *Thinkquest* site was created by several North Carolina high-school students to illustrate the carbon cycle. It's much more in-depth than the *Exploring Environment* entry above, so if you want to delve deeper into the carbon cycle, this site is where you'll want to begin. It takes a little persistence to actually get into the site. There are lots of explanations on the home page about how the *Thinkquest* sites are created. But persevere by clicking where it says "Click Here to Enter the Site" and you'll arrive at the introduction.

The introduction is helpful to read because it explains the thoughts of the students who created *Chemical Carousel*—why they chose this topic and their objectives in developing the site. Click the arrow at the bottom of the page to continue. The lesson truly begins here with the page called, appropriately, "What Is the Carbon Cycle?" Continue to click the "Click Here" buttons at the bottom of the pages to proceed through the lesson.

After learning what the carbon cycle is, you'll go to a page on how to use the site. At the bottom of this page are two links—one for "The Protein Cycle" and one for "The Carbohydrate/Fuel Cycle." Here you'll meet Captain Carbon and begin to explore the carbon cycle for real. Just pick where you want to enter the cycle—as a protein or carbohydrate/fuel—and follow the links on the left side of the page to learn about different aspects of these cycles. A diagram accompanies each page so that you can visualize what's happening as well.

CARTOGRAPHY

Best Search Engine: http://www.mamma.com/

Key Search Term: Cartography

Odden's Bookmarks: The Fascinating World of Maps and Mapping
http://oddens.geog.uu.nl/index.html
high school and up

If you're searching for cartographic information on the Web, you can't help but stumble across this site. Its collection of over 13,000 Web links is considered by many professional geographers to be *the* premier Web resource on cartography. Links are updated and added regularly; in fact, it's not unusual for *Odden's Bookmarks* to add 1,000 new sites each month.

To find the cartography information that you need, simply use the search engine or browse the broad topic categories. These categories include "Maps and Atlases," "Map Collections," "Cartographic and Geographic Societies," "Carto- and GeoServers," "Government Cartography," "Departments of Cartography," "Libraries," "Literature," "Gazetteers," and "Sellers of Cartographic Material."

The Fundamentals of Cartography
http://atlas.gc.ca/english/carto/index.html
high school and up

This site, created by the National Atlas of Canada, provides students and teachers with interactive educational units on the fundamentals of cartography. While the self-contained units are arranged in sequential order, you can easily skip around to find the info you need. Each unit includes suggestions for further reading, as well as a brief quiz.

The unit entitled "Maps: What Are They?" contains basic information about maps and how they are used. In "Map Projections," you'll find a detailed examination of the properties and classifications of various map projections. "Map Content and Design for the Web" explores the specific arena of designing maps for online usage; it covers the topics of color design, symbology, and typography. Another useful section is the extensive glossary of cartographic terms.

CASTE SYSTEM

Best Search Engine: http://www.google.com/
Key Search Terms: Caste system + geography

Mr. Dowling's Electronic Passport: Caste System
http://www.mrdowling.com/612-caste.html
middle school and up

For the briefest introduction to India's caste system, try *Mr. Dowling's Electronic Passport.* You won't get much more than a definition and a tiny bit of historical context, but for some reason the Web is unusually sparse when it comes to caste system resources. Nothing goes into much depth on this complex and entrenched Indian social structure.

One good thing about Mr. Dowling's caste system page is that it's part of a larger group of pages on the Indian subcontinent. Use the menu at the top (and bottom) of the page to access other related topics, such as "Subcontinent," "The Himalayas," "Monsoon," "Mohenjo-Daro and Harappa," "The Untouchables" (very relevant to the caste system topic), "Hinduism," "Siddhartha Gautama," "Buddhism," "Indian History," "The Moguls," "The British in India," "Gandhi," "Partition," "India since Independence," "One Billion People," "Pakistan and Bangladesh," and "Sri Lanka, Nepal, and Bhutan."

Invest in India: India's Social Customs and Systems: The Caste System
http://www.investindia.com/newsite/social/castes.htm
high school and up

This is a more comprehensive resource on the Indian caste system than what you'll find at *Mr. Dowling's Electronic Passport.* It's also written from an Indian perspective, so keep that in mind while reading. It actually advocates maintaining the caste system until it can be replaced by another system that would maintain social order. This article argues that the caste system has been quite effective at not only maintaining social order but also maintaining social morality.

The article is divided into three sections. There's a brief introduction, and that is followed by a general section on the caste system, and then a section titled "The Depressed Classes." While most resources on the caste system will tell you that there are four castes in India—the Brahmin (priests, teachers, and judges), the Kshatriya (warriors), the Vaisya (farmers and merchants), and the Sudras (craft workers and laborers)—this article suggests that there are more than 2,000 castes that are arranged in a complex system of social differentiation. Wow.

The article goes into quite a bit of detail on a sampling of these different social groups and how they operate within the same culture. The final section on the depressed classes discusses those who fall in the lower castes.

CHILDREN—LIFE

Best Search Engine   http://www.google.com/
Key Search Terms   Children + geography

The Children's Rights Council
http://www.gocrc.com/
high school and up

This is the Web site of an advocacy group for children that is particularly concerned with the issue of shared parenting for children of divorce. The council provides research and other resources to support children and parents in their efforts to maintain children's relationships with both parents and with their extended families regardless of the parents' marital status.

This site is useful to look at if you are interested in children's issues, especially with divorce, and want to see how one organization makes use of census data. Its report on "The Best States to Raise Children" makes use of various statistics to determine its ranking of states.

Voices of Youth
http://www.unicef.org/voy/
middle school and up

This is a fairly new site that was developed in celebration of the United Nations Children's Fund's (UNICEF) 50th anniversary. The site was created to give children a place to communicate with others around the world. It houses three forums—"The Meeting Place," "The Learning Place," and "The Teacher's Place."

"The Meeting Place" is where users can read ideas on current global issues that affect children and share their thoughts on these ideas. A quick visit one day revealed sections on "Children and Work," "Children's Rights," "Children and War," "The Girl Child," and "Cities and

Children." Click on any of these sections, and you'll be presented with links in three categories—"Explore," "Discuss," and "Take Action." At "The Girl Child," for example, you can explore images and stories, take the girl child quiz, or add information to *Voices of Youth* on a project or organization related to the topic.

"The Learning Place" has a number of interactive learning projects implemented by volunteers—quizzes on various topics and ideas to implement in your school. The goal of the site is to have schools and groups from around the world work together on the projects, but when we visited there were no ongoing projects. Perhaps this is something that has yet to be developed. In any case, it will be a nice addition to the site if it ever happens, but it's not necessary to make the site worth your time. There are many other stellar resources here.

"The Teacher's Place" allows educators and workers in development agencies to exchange ideas and discuss the use of interactive activities and technology. This is an excellent place for teachers to create Internet-based lesson plans for social studies, political science, current events, and cultural studies classes. It is also a great place for students to check out on their own, or for education technology directors.

CHILDREN—STATISTICS ON (SEE ALSO VITAL STATISTICS)

Best Search Engine: http://www.google.com

Key Search Terms: Children + statistics

Children + health + statistics

Children + labor + statistics

UNICEF Statistics
http://www.unicef.org/statis/
high school and up

This United Nations Children's Fund (UNICEF) Web site gets right to the point. It's UNICEF's special place for statistical data, and it's easy to access what you need here because the site is not trying to do anything other than give you access to these statistics.

Scroll to the bottom of the page and browse the list of six categories, which includes "Child Survival and Health," "Child Nutrition," "Maternal Health," "Water and Sanitation," "Education," and "Additional Child Rights." If these topics are too broad, use the drop-down menu located just below these category links. It provides you with the indicators that fall under these broader six categories, things like birth weight, breastfeeding, child labor, and family planning.

Each indicator has its own page with detailed analyses and graphs, all in an accessible format. Click on "Malnutrition," for example, and you'll read about the challenge of addressing this problem, the indicators used to assess the problem, which include underweight, stunting, and wasting, and progress to date in addressing the malnutrition problem, as well as a brief section that addresses some disparities in the data.

United Nations Children's Fund
http://www.un.org/partners/civil_society/m-child.htm
high school and up

This is the home page of the United Nations Children's Fund (UNICEF) and a good bet for finding information on many issues concerning children around the world, including some useful statistics. If you're interested in child health and development, there's a link to the World Health Organization's *Child and Adolescent Health and Development* Web site, which has an entire section devoted to data and statistics.

Just click on "Data and Statistics" in the menu at the left side of the home page for an analysis, complete with numerous charts and graphs, of the worldwide estimates for morbidity and mortality among children.

Or if you want statistics on human rights for children, child refugees, or child labor, you'll find sections here that contain documents and data of all types on these topics too.

CHLOROFLUOROCARBONS (CFCS)

Best Search Engine: http://www.google.com
Key Search Terms: Chlorofluorocarbons + definition
                        CFCs + global warming

Global Warming: What's It All About?
http://www.nfu.ca/warming.htm
high school and up

Although this site gets quite detailed and in-depth at times, it's still fairly accessible to the high school student with little background in the subject. This is because the author, Carla Roeppel, puts everything in context. She starts out with a section explaining the importance of carbon and the various processes that either release carbon into the environment or remove it from circulation.

She provides several handy tables—one on the distribution of carbon on earth and the other on greenhouse gases. The table on greenhouse gases will show you the various chlorofluorocarbons (CFCs), hydrofluorocarbons (HFCs), and perfuorocarbons (PFCs) that are harmful to the environment, provide you with information on where they come from and how they are used, and explain exactly what harm they do to the atmosphere and what their lifespan is.

The article goes on to discuss how carbon affects climate and what the implications are for agriculture. Although you'll definitely have to put on your thinking cap to make use of this site, the effort is well worth it. You'll come away with a thorough understanding of CFCs as well as an excellent overview of the global warming issue.

Chlorofluorocarbons (CFCs)
http://www.bhs.berkeley.k12.ca.us/departments/science/APWEB/
    MECHAGODZILLA/html/cfcs.html
high school and up

This nifty little site was created by several California high school students to explore the issue of ozone depletion. The CFCs page is actually just one page of the overall site. If you're looking for a definition of CFCs, this site is your ticket. It defines the two main types—those used in aerosols and those used in air conditioning systems.

The neatest part about the site, however, is not the boring definitions but the colorful graphic that portrays, visually and with accompanying explanatory text, how these CFCs work their misery on the ozone. The diagram takes you from step one, when ultraviolet radiation strikes a CFC molecule, through the disintegration of the CFC molecule, to the final step when a chlorine atom is released to destroy more ozone.

After you're done here, you may want to continue your research by reading the sections on "How Ozone Is Destroyed Naturally," "Source of Destroyers," and "Ozone Chemistry."

CHRISTIANITY

Best Search Engine: http://www.scout.cs.wisc.edu/index.html

Key Search Term: Christianity

Yale University Library Research Guide for Christianity
http://www.library.yale.edu/div/xtiangde.htm
college level

Yale University Library Research Guide for Christianity goes above and beyond the average click-and-find subject directory on the Web. It provides substantive advice and direction on how to research particular areas or topics in Christian studies.

Resources are organized by format, which include "Library Catalogs"; "Indexes and Abstracts"; "Reference Tools and Bibliographies"; "Selected Electronic and Print Journals"; "Selected Internet Sites"; "Primary Sources"; "Organizations and Institutions"; and "Electronic Discussion Lists." Or, you can conduct your research by subject area. Areas offered are "The Bible"; "Church/Denominational/Ecumenical Resources"; "Church History"; "Ethics and Social Issues"; "Missions and World Christianity"; "Systematics/Doctrinal Theology"; "Practical Theology"; and "Religion and the Arts."

Christianity Chronology
http://campus.northpark.edu/history/WebChron/Christianity/Christianity.
    html
college level

Developed by the history department at North Park University, the *Web Chronology Project* offers a series of linked chronologies that depict world, regional, and cross-cultural history. The *Christianity Chronology* is part of the cross-cultural collection, which also includes chronologies of Islam, Buddhism, Western civilization, and technology.

Designed for use in survey history courses, this chronology is hardly an exhaustive account of Christianity. However, it's useful for gaining a broad overview and for fact checking. You'll find time line information on the apostolic era, the early church, the church in Germanic Europe, the church in eastern Europe, the church outside the Roman Empire, and Christian missions. There are also links to related chronologies, in-depth articles, and related Web sites.

CITIES

Best Search Engine: http://www.google.com/

Key Search Terms: Cities + geography

Demographia: World's Twenty Largest Urban Areas Population and Density: 1991
http://www.demographia.com/db-wldurb91.htm
middle school and up

Although this site is from 1991 statistics, over a decade old, it's still a fascinating look at the world's cities. The table was compiled by the U.S. Census Bureau and shows the rank, name, population, number of residents per square mile (and kilometer), and number of people per square mile (and kilometer).

Tokyo is the largest city on the table, followed by Mexico City, São Paulo, Seoul, and New York in the top five. Cities on the list that may surprise you? Teheran. Take a look for yourself. There isn't much in the way of interpretation at this simple site page, but click on "Demographic Briefs" at the bottom of the page, and you'll be taken to a table of contents for demographic information of all sorts on all parts of the world.

In the "International Index" alone, you can find a section called "International Urban Areas: Transport and the Environment" with links to topics such as "Traffic Intensity by International Urban Area—1990," "International Journey to Work Times Less Where Sprawl Greater," and "Air Pollution Intensity Variation by Geography." There are statistics here on more urban geography issues than you could imagine. There's even data on religion, taxation, and parks.

U.S. Cities A–Z
http://members.aol.com/bowermanb/citiesaz.html
middle school and up

This site lists links to the home pages for nearly 100 cities in the United States. You'll find all kinds of information at these sites, everything from sightseeing maps and sections on local government to lists of annual festivals and descriptions of schools. You may be interested in the demographic information found at many of these sites, or the crime reports, or the neighborhood news sections. Each site is different from the next, but you're sure to find interesting geographic information at each one. Many sites list detailed information on the projects and plans underway in the city. At the Burlington, Vermont site you can read key documents like the "Open Space Protection Plan" and then visit the page for the department responsible for the document, in this case the Department of Planning and Zoning.

The New Urbanist Lexicon
http://www.mnapa.com/urbanlex.html
high school and up

This page from the *Planning Minnesota Online* site is a great introduction to the topic of new urbanism, which is a movement devoted to human-scaled cities. There are seven articles here on topics of primary importance to the movement, and for the most part these articles are concerned with defining a lexicon for the movement, hence the name of the site. Topics covered in this lexicon include "complete neighborhood," "walking distance," "pedestrian continuity," "community," "countryside," "corridor," "neighborhood," "district," "hamlet," "village," "town," and other commonly used terms that are being reevaluated by the new urbanists.

If your interest in cities lies in the realm of planning, you're sure to find much food for thought at this site. It's a wonderful and in-depth introduction to new urbanism. And the site is simple to use. Just scroll from top to bottom to read the articles. There's a link at the end of each article that will take you back to the top of the page if you want. Otherwise there's not much to distract you from the topic at hand . . . unless you happen to be interested in Minnesota in particular, in which case you can head back to the home page of the site and find many more interesting resources related to cities and planning in that state.

CITY-STATE

Best Search Engine: http://www.google.com/

Key Search Terms: City-state + geography

City-States—Social Structure—Government
http://www.crystalinks.com/greeksocial.html
middle school and up

This *Crystalinks* page covers what are probably the most famous city-states in all of history, those of the ancient Greeks. While you won't get an overall view, you will get a decent description of what these Greek city-states were like and how they functioned both together and individually.

Part of the "Ancient and Lost Civilizations Index," this page is part of the "Ancient Greece" section and thus also contains information about Greek government, which might be helpful to read if your research revolves around the Greek city-states.

Why Did Greece Develop City-States?
http://www.pbs.org/empires/thegreeks/background/9b_p1.html
middle school and up

This page is part of a larger PBS site on the Greek empire. It's a simple page but very worthwhile if you're researching the Greek city-states. It explains, from a geographical point of view, why the Greeks developed city-states instead of larger centers of power. As you might guess, the mountainous terrain, the Mediterranean Sea, and the aristocracy all played a hand in this unique organization of the ancient Greek population.

Read this site with the one above if you're looking for simple, straight-forward information on the Greek city-states. Together they cover the basics fairly well.

Cities in History
http://www.owlnet.rice.edu/~arch343/
high school and up

From the table of contents, choose "Athens: The City and Politics" to read a fascinating, if somewhat academic, article on what is arguably the greatest city-state of all time. Taken from a group of 10 lectures for a "Cities in History" course taught by Dr. Richard Ingersoll of Rice University's School of Architecture, this lecture provides historical background about the history of Athens as well as much insight into the function of the city-state.

You'll find more detail here than at any other site on how city-states were formed and governed and how they compared to other great cities of the time, such as Memphis and Babylon. The physical geography of the Aegean is discussed in considerable detail, as are the topics of Athenian citizenship and architecture. In addition, there are sections on Sparta and Athenian democracy.

CLIMATE

Best Search Engine:	http://www.dogpile.com/
Key Search Terms:	Climate + geography

Climate Prediction Center
http://www.cpc.ncep.noaa.gov/
high school and up

The Climate Prediction Center was established in the 1980s by the National Oceanic and Atmospheric Administration to assess and forecast the impact of short-term climate variability. Look under "Outreach" to find educational materials, such as FAQs and fact sheets that explain the role of the climate system in peoples' lives and how to use climate forecasts. You'll also find excellent weekly, monthly, annual, and special publications about climate within this section.

For a suite of up-to-date climate forecasts, go to "Outlooks" or "Climate Highlights." Here you'll find both maps and text for several time spans (i.e., 0–48 hours, 8–14 days), as well as an analysis of current U.S.

threats, the winter outlook, a drought assessment, and more. In "Monitoring and Data," you'll find information on how the raw data used for forecasts and threat assessments is collected.

Institute for Climate Research
http://www.geo.umnw.ethz.ch/
college and up

If you want to know about climate, who better to turn to than the Institute for Climate Research? The institute supports two main research groups, one focusing on global climate and the other on climate and water cycle.

While the site is not set up as an educational venue, you'll be able to uncover some valuable project data, names of experts, and lists of relevant publications here. Click on the tab called "Research" to learn what projects are underway. Within each research area (i.e., alpine dynamics, climate of polar regions, hydrological modeling), you can read about specific topics under investigation. For instance, the team studying the climate of polar regions provides data here about the mass balance of Greenland, the energy exchange at the atmosphere/ice interface, and the sensitivity of the polar ice caps to anthropogenic climate changes.

WorldClimate
http://www.worldclimate.com/climate/index.htm
middle school and up

If you're looking for general historical weather patterns around the world—as opposed to current weather reports—this site is the ticket. *WorldClimate* has gathered a worldwide range of climate data. These historical weather averages show what the weather is typically like each month, averaged over a range of years.

Just type in the name of a city—say, Athens—and up pops a selection, from Athens County, Ohio, to Athens, Greece. Click on your intended city—in this case, Athens, Greece, to see average climate data such as temperature, rainfall, and sea-level pressure. If you have any questions or concerns about the data, just go to the original Web sources, which are provided here as well.

To date, around 85,000 climate records are online for tens of thousands of places around the world. The site's plans for 2002 included a better collection of non-U.S. data, as well as some snow, sunshine, humidity, and wind data.

CLIMATE ZONES

Best Search Engine: http://www.google.com/

Key Search Terms: Climate zones + geography

Examples of Earth's Climate Zones
http://www.fsl.noaa.gov/~osborn/CG_Figure_14a.gif.html and http://
    www.fsl.noaa.gov/~osborn/CG_Figure_14b.gif.html
middle school and up

Each of these links shows color images of seven of the earth's climate zones. The first link shows you tropical and dry climate zones; the second link shows you rainy and cold climate zones.

In all, you'll see pictures of 14 different world climates. There isn't anything in the way of interpretive text, but sometimes pictures speak louder than words, and in this case that's definitely true. You can see in vivid contrast the differences between the polar climate—alpine tundra and the cool snow—forest climate, for example. Or the difference between the polar climate—alpine glacier and the polar climate—high Arctic, which is definitely a more subtle difference.

These pages are part of *Climgraph*, a site devoted to providing educational documents and graphics on global climate change and the greenhouse effect, so you may want to backtrack to the home page, which is easily accessible through a link at the bottom of each of these pages, to find other resources on world climate.

Climate Zones
http://www.yourgreenthumb.com/climate.html
middle school and up

Climate zones are often discussed on regional or even local terms. For example, the Department of Agriculture in the United States recognizes 11 climate zones, but then each of these areas has numerous regional climate zones. And within one of those regional climate zones, there may be many different local climate zones. Even a single residential backyard may have several different climate zones.

To understand how this works, just check out this gardening site. There's a nice map of the United States with the hardiness zones for growing plants marked. A separate link for each of the 11 climate zones in the United States will take you to in-depth information on that zone.

Then, if you'd like to explore world climate zones further, go to the bottom of the page and use the links to access sites on Australian, African, Canadian, and European climate zones. The information is all geared toward gardening, but you'll get a basic understanding of climate zones by looking at the colorful maps and reading the accompanying text. Who knows, you may even pick up a few gardening tips, too!

World Climate Regions
http://www.geocities.com/slauson6th/worldclimateregions.htm
middle school and up

This *Geocities* site provides an excellent overview of the 12 main climate regions of the world—tropical rain forest, tropical savannah, marine west coast, Mediterranean, humid continental, humid subtropical, subarctic, tundra, ice cap, highland, desert, and steppe. These are climate regions, not climate zones, but the two are closely related, and you'll learn a lot about climate zones at this site.

Click on "Tropical Rainforest," for example, and you'll find a list of features that define rain forests, a list of places around the world where rain forests occur, like the Amazon River Basin and the east coast of Madagascar and Central America, and really nice color photographs of rain forests.

World Climates
http://www.uwsp.edu/geo/faculty/ritter/geog101/lectures/climates_toc.html
high school and up

For in-depth information on the world's climates, try this site, which is easy to use and neatly organized. The table of contents on the home page offers you links to various climate regions that have been organized into the following categories: "Low Latitude Climates," "Midlatitude and Subtropical Climates," and "High Latitude Climates."

The climates are broken down into smaller, more specific regions than you'll find at the *World Climate Regions* site above, which allows for more detailed information. At this site you'll be able to research humid subtropical and dry summer subtropical climates, for example. Click on "Humid Subtropical," for example, and you'll find information on the geographic distribution of these climates, controlling factors, and characteristics, as well as an image that illustrates the climate.

CLOUDS

Best Search Engine: http://www.google.com
Key Search Terms: Clouds + definition

PSC Meteorology Program Cloud Boutique
http://vortex.plymouth.edu/clouds.html
middle school and up

The Plymouth State College (PSC) Meteorology Program has developed this server to provide explanations of and access to detailed pictures of some basic cloud forms. In addition to the wonderful cloud pictures, there's an explanation of cloud classification, with a little chart on altitude distinctions for clouds, and then the main section, which is on cloud descriptions and pictures. This is not an all-inclusive list, so don't expect to find every cloud imaginable here. The page is intended to be a general cloud reference. Some clouds you can expect to find here are cirrus, altostratus, nimbostratus, fog, mammatus, and more.

You'll find descriptions of high clouds, middle clouds, low clouds, and multilayer clouds, as well as orographic clouds. Each description is embedded with links to pictures that illustrate the particular features discussed. The cloud images are relatively large (640 × 480) in order to show detailed structure and features, so be patient when the site is loading images and use the fastest machine you have.

Clouds from Space
http://www.hawastsoc.org/solar/eng/cloud1.htm
middle school and up

This site contains a wonderful selection of space shuttle images of clouds with informative text. Start by reading the introduction, which gives a good introduction to the study of clouds as related to understanding the greenhouse effect.

The section called "Images of Clouds from Space" provides thumbnail images of clouds with a paragraph or two of explanation about each one. You'll find jet stream cirrus, Florida squall line, cloud margin, Bering Sea, unique cloud lanes, Oman, anticyclonic clouds, typhoon Odessa, and many more fascinating images of clouds taken from space. Just click on a thumbnail image if you wish to download the picture.

Martian Clouds
http://www.windows.ucar.edu/tour/link = /mars/atmosphere/
    martian_clouds.html
middle school and up

Part of a Martian atmosphere site, this is not your basic clouds site. If you want to branch out a bit, try looking at some of the clouds found on Mars. You'll learn that clouds on Mars are found only around the equatorial region of the planet, for example, and you can see images of some of these clouds and read explanatory text.

The text has embedded hyperlinks that take you to separate pages on such topics as the Mariner Mission to Mars, precipitation, the Mars Pathfinder, and temperatures.

COLONIALISM

Best Search Engine: http://www.metacrawler.com/
Key Search Term: Colonialism

"Colonialism and Colonies" Microsoft Encarta Online Encyclopedia 2000
http://encarta.msn.com/index/conciseindex/61/0610E000.
　htm?z = 1&pg = 2&br = 1
high school and up

This is far, far more than just an encyclopedia article. Weighing in at more than five screens, it's currently the only comprehensive analysis of colonialism on the Web.

If you're searching for material about a specific aspect of colonialism, use the pull-down menu outline at the top of the first page. If it's a broad overview you're looking for, simply read from start to finish. After an introductory paragraph that distinguishes colonialism from imperialism, the article breaks down into five major sections. "Types of Colonies" explores the differences between colonies of settlement, colonies of exploitation, contested settlement colonies, and other types. "Motives for Colonization" looks at economic, strategic, and religious factors that played a role. "Colonial Economies" looks at export and subsistence sectors.

The lengthy section entitled "History of Colonialism" encompasses the periods known as the "Age of Exploration (1450–1700)," "European Merchant Empires (1700–1815)," "Imperialism of Free Trade (1815–1870)," and "New Imperialism (1870–1914)." There's also a strong section devoted to "Resistance to Colonialism." As you've come to expect from online encyclopedias, simply click on hyperlinked text that's scattered throughout to go to another *Encarta* page with more information.

Political Discourse: Theories of Colonialism and Postcolonialism
http://landow.stg.brown.edu/post/poldiscourse/discourseov.html
college and up

Although this site might be of greater interest to literature students than geography majors, it's worth noting. The site explores the aftermath of colonialism, as it is reflected in a culture's literature.

The section most pertinent for geography students is labeled "Themes and Issues in Theories of Colonialism and Post-Colonialism." Click here and you'll find a collection of academic essays and book chapters arranged in categories such as "What Is Post-Colonial?", "Nation(s) and Nationalism," "Women and Colonialism," and more. Under "Historical Context," there are also some good links for research projects that touch on contemporary issues affecting postcolonial regions like Australia, New Zealand, the Indian subcontinent, and much of Africa.

CONSERVATION (SEE ALSO BIODIVERSITY)

Best Search Engine: http://www.yahoo.com/
Best Subject Directory: Science > Geography > Conservation

Conservation International
http://www.conservation.org/
high school and up

The mission statement of this conservation biggie is "to conserve the Earth's living natural heritage, our global biodiversity, and to demonstrate that human societies are able to live harmoniously with nature." The home page will give you a general overview of the kind of work Conservation International (CI) does. If you're interested in CI's efforts in a particular region, click on "Where We Work" to see an index of locations where the group is conducting scientific programs, local campaigns, and economic initiatives. To better understand what's involved with CI's conservation efforts, click on "What We Do." You can also navigate the site using its search engine, an alphabetical site index, or a table of contents.

The "Library" section is a good resource as well, providing article reprints, CI fact sheets, field guides, policy papers, videos, and a great bunch of related links.

Student Conservation Association
http://www.sca-inc.org/
high school and up

If you'd like your research on conservation to come firsthand, check out the Student Conservation Association's (SCA) Web site. It's the largest and oldest provider of national and community conservation service opportunities and career training for youth in the United States. SCA volunteers and interns annually perform more than one million hours of conservation service in national parks, forests, refuges, and urban areas in all 50 states.

There are paid opportunities for college students, as well as many volunteer spots for high school students. SCA also organizes alternate spring breaks, where college students opt for a week of conservation service in places like Ocala National Forest in Florida, Cumberland Island National Seashore in Georgia, and the Grand Canyon National Park.

For miscellaneous information on conservation topics, the site offers "Ecobytes," a link to cutting-edge headline news from the *Environmental News Network* (http://www.enn.com/news/).

SpeakOut
http://www.speakout.com/Issues/
high school and up

This section of the *SpeakOut* Web site is designed to help you—the latent activist—find information on topics ranging from international affairs to food and farming to the environment. Although the site has an activist bias, you'll find that the information provided here on the environment is evenhanded and legitimate as a research source.

Click on the "Environment" button to see a selection of topics, including climate change; endangered species; oceans, lakes, and rivers; forests, deserts, and wilderness; and recycling and waste. Within each topic, there are neatly organized issues and subtopics. For instance, look inside "Oceans, Lakes, and Rivers" and click on "Should Old Dams Be Torn Down?" As with every subtopic, you'll get background information, history, and facts, as well as lucid on the one hand and on the other hand summaries. In this instance, the impressively diverse sources for information includes American Rivers, Trout Unlimited, and the National Hydropower Association. You'll also find good links to relevant organizations, as well as links to editorials and feature articles from other news sources.

CONTINENTAL DRIFT (SEE ALSO PLATE TECTONICS)

Best Search Engine: http://www.ixquick.com/

Key Search Term: Continental drift

Mountain Maker, Earth Shaker
http://www.pbs.org/wgbh/aso/tryit/tectonics/
middle school and up

This site gives you low-tech and high-tech ideas for exploring the theories behind continental drift. Using a cracked hard-boiled egg as a tiny model of the earth and its continents, you can see the process for yourself. Or use the site's Shockwave program to push and pull on tectonic plates and watch what happens to the earth.

In the text sections of the site, you'll be able to learn the distinctions between divergent, convergent, collisional, and transform boundaries.

There's also a touch of information about Alfred Wegener, who first came up with the theory of continental drift, and the scientists in the 1960s—Harry Hess, Robert Dietz, Fred Vine, and Drummond Matthews—who resurrected the theory, which gained acceptance as plate tectonics.

Alfred Wegener
http://pangaea.org/wegener.htm
high school and up

This site—as part of a larger site about continents—was selected by the National Science Teachers Association as a worthy one. Although it's limited to text only, you'll find plenty of good material about the German climatologist and geophysicist, Alfred Wegener, who developed the original theory of continental drift, amidst skepticism by other scientists.

There's info about his professional training, the fossil and geological evidence he used to support his theory, and quotes from former colleagues. The site also provides a nice list of recommended reading, if you're still looking for more on old Alfred.

CORAL REEFS

Best Search Engine: http://www.askjeeves.com/
Key Search Term: Coral reefs

The Coral Reef Ecology Home Page
http://www.uvi.edu/coral.reefer/index.html
high school and up

This site is a great starting point for research on coral reefs. You'll find a general introduction to coral reefs, plus sections with information on coral anatomy, types of coral reefs, zooxanthellae, coral feeding, coral reproduction, coral diseases, coral bleaching, human threats to coral reefs, common Caribbean corals, and animals associated with coral reefs.

In addition, look under "Literature Cited" to find an excellent bibliography of print reference books about coral reefs.

NOAA's Coral Reef Online
http://www.coralreef.noaa.gov/
high school and up

You can always count on a Web site by the National Oceanic and Atmospheric Administration (NOAA) to be user friendly and packed with solid factual information. Its site on coral reefs is no exception—

it's a virtual labyrinth of fact sheets, conservation proposals, photographs, scientific data, and more.

For general research, you could begin by clicking on the NOAA article entitled "What Are Coral Reefs and Why Are They in Peril?" For more in-depth research into coral reefs, use the home page to link to sections with information on coral reef bleaching, coral health and monitoring, biodiversity and fisheries, and more.

CROP ROTATION (SEE ALSO AGRICULTURE)

Best Search Engine: http://www.copernic.com

Best Search Question: What is crop rotation?

Core 4: Conservation for Agriculture's Future: Crop Rotation
http://www.ctic.purdue.edu/Core4/CT/Choices/Choice6.html
high school and up

This site provides a simple explanation of crop rotation and its benefits in terms of pesticide usage, water quality, and pest management. You'll also find some technical notes that explain how to design a crop rotation plan.

Core 4's larger focus is on improving farm profitability while addressing environmental concerns. You'll find information on how sustainable soils increase productivity, how agriculture can actually protect water quality, and how the latest technologies can bring about greater cropland productivity. You can also view fact sheets on related subjects like conservation tillage, crop nutrient management, weed and pest management, and conservation buffers.

New Crops Resource Online Program (NewCROP)
http://www.hort.purdue.edu/newcrop/default.html
college level

If you're looking for the big picture on crops and crop rotation, check out *NewCROP*, an information-rich site related to crop plants. Here, you can utilize CropSEARCH, a search engine that accesses crop information or use CropINDEX for information on a huge number of crops. There's a reference section with lists of books and manuals about crops, a discussion group, and links to related Web sites, databases, and libraries.

The site is a project of the Purdue University Center for New Crops and Plant Products and is associated with the New Crop Diversification Project and the Jefferson Institute.

CROPS (SEE AGRICULTURE, CROP ROTATION)

CULTURAL ADAPTATION

Best Search Engine:　　http://www.google.com

Key Search Terms:　　Cultural + adaptation

India Cultural Tips
http://www.stylusinc.com/business/india/cultural_tips.htm
high school and up

Cultural adaptation is defined as the complex strategies human groups employ to live successfully as part of a natural system. This site is designed to assist people traveling, working, or volunteering in India as they attempt to adapt to the culture. You'll learn abut cultural adaptation here by exploring what it's like to be a foreigner in India. Much of what you learn is applicable in any locale around the world.

This wonderful site is both entertaining and very useful, and it's full of tips on adjusting to Indian culture. You'll find the following articles: "Regional Differences in India," "Communicating Cross-Culturally," "Doing Business in India," "There's No WalMart in India," "Americans Are Too Independent," and more.

Read the introduction first to get an overview of the purpose and goals of the site. Then pick the articles that seem most interesting to you and let your imagination take over. Even if you've never been to India, or even out of the country, you've probably been a foreigner or an outsider in some situation, and you may remember what it was like to try to adapt to that new environment.

CULTURAL ECOLOGY

Best Search Engine:　　http://www.google.com/

Key Search Term:　　Cultural ecology

Notes on the Development of Cultural Ecology
http://www.indiana.edu/~wanthro/eco.htm
high school and up

This site provides a brief academic overview of the field of cultural ecology. You'll learn about the history of this field of study, the important themes, and useful journals and Web sites. You'll also find a chart of traditional and current lines of research in cultural ecology and other charts showing various definitions of "adaptation," "adaptive strategy," and "niche" that have been used by experts in the field.

Cultural Ecology Specialty Group (CESG)
http://www.u.arizona.edu/~batterbu/cesg/cesg.html
high school and up

The Cultural Ecology Specialty Group (CESG), a specialty group of the Association of American Geographers, created this site to distribute info on scholarly activities on cultural ecological topics. You can make marginal use of the *Cultural Ecology Newsletters* to find book reviews, meeting notes, student papers, and more. But the real highlight for cultural ecology zealots would be the CESG listserv, which you can sign up to access here. The listserv is for general exchange of information, news, views, debates, questions, and answers by the members of the specialty group.

CULTURAL GEOGRAPHY

Best Search Engine: http://www.yahoo.com/

Key Search Term: Cultural geography

The Human Mosaic
http://www.whfreeman.com/jordan/
high school and up

This site was created for use in conjunction with the textbook *The Human Mosaic*, but it stands on its own feet too. More than just a marketing vehicle, the site provides you with summaries, Web activities, Web links, and flash cards for each chapter.

To access these resources, select from the following chapters: "The Nature of Cultural Geography," "People on the Land," "The Agricultural World," "Political Patterns," "The Mosaic of Languages," "Religious Realms," "Folk Geography," "Popular Culture," "Ethnic Geography," "The City in Time and Space," "The Urban Mosaic," and "Industrial Geography." You'll find the Web activity suggestions especially helpful for developing your own research project ideas.

Cultural Profiles Project
http://cwr.utoronto.ca/cultural/
high school and up

This is a wonderful resource for your research into a particular country's cultural geography. Designed to aid in cultural awareness of new immigrants to Canada, the *Cultural Profiles Project* is a stellar source of information on countries around the world.

For over 70 countries, you'll find a detailed cultural profile providing an overview of life and customs, as well as information about landscape and climate, history, family life, work life, sports and recreation, health-care, education, food, communication, spirituality, holidays, and arts and literature. Many of the profiles also include photographs.

CYCLONES

Best Search Engine: http://www.ixquick.com/

Key Search Terms: Cyclone + tropical

FAQs: Hurricanes, Typhoons, and Tropical Cyclones
http://www.aoml.noaa.gov/hrd/tcfaq/tcfaqHED.html
high school and up

Although this site purports to be *just* answers to frequently asked questions, it offers an amazingly comprehensive factual resource on tropical cyclones. For instance, simply click on the question "Why Are Tropical Cyclones Named?" and you'll get historical and current information on why cyclones are named, who names them, what the upcoming names will be in the northern and southern hemispheres, and why some names are retired. And that's the answer to one question!

You'll also find information here about frequency, forecasting, and the likelihood of tropical cyclones for various regions. There's also information directing you to useful journals, nontechnical and technical books, and articles on tropical cyclones.

Midatlantic Cyclones
http://ww2010.atmos.uiuc.edu/(Gh)/guides/mtr/cyc/home.rxml
high school and up

The University of Illinois's excellent WW2010 series of online instructional modules hits pay dirt again. As a section within the "Meteorology Guide," this "Midatlantic Cyclones" module is organized into the following topics: "Definition," "Winds," "Air Masses," "Satellite Images," and "Upper Air Features."

These topics offer information on the general structure and distinct characteristics of a cyclone, the associated air masses and fronts, wind barbs, troughs, amplification, and jet streaks. The site is well designed, with good use of graphics and QuickTime movies. Thanks to a toolbar on the left side of the page, the site is easy to navigate. And unlike

other online courses that cater to students with lightening-fast computers, it's available in both graphics and text-only versions.

DEATH RATE (SEE ALSO DEMOGRAPHY, POPULATION, VITAL STATISTICS)

Best Search Engine: http://www.askjeeves.com/

Key Search Term: Death rate

Countries of the World
http://www.countryreports.org/
middle school and up

This terrific site, selected as one of the best sites on the Web for
teachers, is also one of the best sites for students. Basic demographic
research on people from all over the world is easy and quick. Go to the
home page and click on "World Countries" for a comprehensive database of the world's countries with extensive demographic information
on each one. Once you choose a country, you'll be given a menu of the
following: "Economy," "Defense," "Geography," "Government," "People," "National Anthem Lyrics," and "Related Links." Pick "People."

Among many other statistics, you'll find information on death rate.
Other really helpful information here includes overall fertility rate, age
structure, infant mortality rate, birthrate, population growth, religious
affiliations, languages spoken, literacy, and more.

You won't get detailed information about the death rate here. You'll
have to continue your search for that elsewhere. But you will get accurate information to start you on your way.

DECIDUOUS (SEE ALSO BIOMES, FORESTS)

Best Search Engine: http://www.askjeeves.com/

Key Search Term: Deciduous forest

Temperate Broadleaf Deciduous Forest
http://www.runet.edu/~swoodwar/CLASSES/GEOG235/biomes/tbdf/tbdf.
    html
high school and up

As part of the *Major Biomes of the World* Web site, this page focuses
in detail on the deciduous forest biome. You'll find information here
that succinctly describes a deciduous forest's climate, growing season,
and precipitation; specific genera and species; the five layers of growth

forms; soils and utisols; characteristic fauna; and parts of the world where you can find deciduous forests.

You can click to find information about the other major biomes. However, this site could be strengthened with the addition of links to other Web sites related to deciduous forests.

Deciduous and Coniferous Trees
http://www.alienexplorer.com/ecology/e71.html
middle school and up

Want a description of the difference between deciduous and coniferous trees? Look no further. This five-paragraph Web site is essentially an encyclopedia entry explaining the two major categories of trees and how to distinguish one from the other.

DEFORESTATION

Best Search Engine:	http://www.google.com/
Key Search Terms:	Deforestation
	Rain forest + Amazon + deforestation

Forest Conservation Portal
http://forests.org/
high school and up

The *Forest Conservation Portal* is maintained by *Forests.org*, which "works to end deforestation, preserve old-growth forests, conserve and manage other forests for sustainability, maintain climatic systems, and commence the age of ecological restoration." At the *Portal*, users will find a large series of news articles and resources on forests, forest regions, forest ecology, forest destruction and protection, and related information. In addition the site contains current news with international coverage.

Although the site is intended for activists and activism—action alerts are one of the first things you'll notice when you enter the home page— student researchers will find much of value here as well. There's an archive of forest news articles, organized chronologically, a list of forest conservation news links, and a list of general forest links that organizes Web sites in the following categories: "Forest Types," "Forest Regions," "Forest Ecology," "Forest Information," "Forest Destruction," "Forest Protection," "Forest Campaigns," and "What You Can Do."

Click on "Forest Destruction" and you'll be offered, among other subtopics, a section called "Deforestation." Voila! Nine annotated links are listed here, and these are the crème de la crème when it comes to deforestation sites. This is where you'll want to spend your time . . . checking out sites like the *World Rainforest Report* and the *Landsat NASA Pathfinder Humid Tropical Deforestation Project*, which maps global deforestation in the humid tropics, focusing on the Amazon basin, central Africa, and Southeast Asia.

Human Impact: Deforestation and Desertification
http://www.nationalgeographic.com/eye/deforestation/deforestation.html
middle school and up

This is an international page from National Geographic that includes photos, causes, and the results of deforestation and desertification. The overall site, *Eye in the Sky*, is broken down into four sections, one of which is "Human Impact." "Human Impact" addresses floods and dams, ozone and pollution, and overpopulation in addition to its page on deforestation and desertification.

Divided into four sections, this page opens with a brief introduction. From there click on "The Effect" to read about forest holocaust. There's a gallery of images and two videos—one that shows forest destruction in Costa Rica due to fire and logging, and another that shows Amazon forest destruction in Bolivia. You can download Real Media or Windows Media Player right on this page if you don't already have them on your computer.

The next section, "The Phenomena," talks about creeping sand, or desertification. You'll get a good definition and overview of desertification issues, as well as access to a video of winds sweeping across a desert wasteland.

The final section, "The Science," has a section called "Toward a Greener Earth" that discusses the importance of trees and the complex reasons why deforestation continues despite our desire to stop it.

World Rainforest Movement: What Are Underlying Causes of Deforestation?
http://www.wrm.org.uy/deforestation/indirect.html
middle school and up

Part of the *World Rainforest Movement* Web site, this page on the causes of deforestation discusses the forces behind unsustainable agriculture, the consequences of globalization, land tenure policies and inequalities, consumption and production patterns, the many actors involved in the issue, the role of the military, and how we can move forward in our efforts to preserve the forests.

It's an excellent overview of deforestation issues, complete with links to other relevant sites and other *World Rainforest Movement* articles.

Food and Agriculture Organization of the United Nations
http://www.fao.org/NEWS/1999/990301-e.htm
high school and up

This United Nations report from 1999 summarizes the deforestation occurring around the world and discusses the steps being taken, both internationally and nationally to curb the rate of deforestation. A graph on the site illustrates the change in forests around the world from 1980 to 1995. This is really a brief overview of deforestation on an international level. To get a more in-depth view of deforestation in specific parts of the world, try locating national forestry departments for specific countries.

For more international information, links are provided at the bottom of this page for accessing the Food and Agriculture Organization of the United Nations (FAO) Forestry Department, the minutes of a meeting on sustainability issues in forestry, "National and International Challenges," and a "News and Highlights Archive," which contains articles on all issues of concern to the FAO, including deforestation.

DELTA

Best Search Engine: http://www.metacrawler.com/
Key Search Terms: Delta + wetlands
                                   Wetlands + education

Rivers: From Source to Sea
http://geography.about.com/library/weekly/aa031897.htm?terms=delta
middle school and up

This concise article about rivers traces the course of a river from its origin to its final destination, the sea. Along the way, the river encounters its delta just before merging with a larger body of water, or at least most rivers do, and this is where the article gives you the lowdown on what a delta is and the chief factors that affect the formation of deltas. It also mixes in a link to an article on the Nile River, which contains information on the Nile Delta in case you'd like to continue reading on the subject.

DEMOGRAPHY (SEE ALSO POPULATION)

Best Search Engine: http://www.metacrawler.com/
Key Search Term: Demography

The White House: Social Statistics Briefing Room
http://www.whitehouse.gov/fsbr/demography.html
middle school and up

The White House calls this site its *Social Statistics Briefing Room on Demographics*—but don't be intimidated by the officious name. It's designed for easy use and puts tons of current data on demographics at your fingertips. For instance, click on the "U.S. PopClock" and you'll see the Census Bureau's population estimate, based on what's called component settings (i.e., one birth every 8 seconds, one death every 13 seconds).

You will find information here on world population, median household income, poverty rate, household wealth, homeownership, earnings and field of degree, and more. Each area is supported with charts, graphs, source references, and links to other government sites with related information.

Internet Guide to Demography and Population Studies
http://demography.anu.edu.au/VirtualLibrary/
high school and up

Since demography is such a huge topic, this site is an excellent (if not mandatory) place to begin your research. It's a collection of international Web links, culled by researchers in the Demography Program at Australian National University.

The site is handily divided into the following sections: virtual libraries, census and data servers, electronic journals, historical demography resources, demography and population conferences, electronic mailing lists, and other links of interest. If you won't take our word that this is a great site, perhaps you'll be impressed that it received four stars from *Magellan*, as well as the *Argus* seal of approval.

World Wide Web of Demography
http://www.nidi.nl/links/nidi6000.html
high school and up

Here's another dandy for demographics research. This site aims at providing a comprehensive overview of demographic resources on the Web. There are over 500 links categorized and presented here, including a section with research institutions grouped by world region and further by country. This section could come in handy for collecting research on a particular country or continent.

You'll also find a section crammed with links to domestic and international Web sites with census, survey, and other statistical information. Another section presents numerous links to literature resources on demography and population studies, such as journals, newsletters, and abstracts. Additionally, there are sections with links to population-related conferences, mailing lists, and miscellaneous resources. The site is maintained by the Netherlands Interdisciplinary Demographics Institute.

DESERTIFICATION (SEE ALSO DESERTS)

Best Search Engine: http://www.google.com/

Key Search Term: Desertification

Desertification
http://www.fao.org/desertification/default.asp?lang = en
college level

This site, created by the Food and Agriculture Organization of the United Nations (FAO), is an incredibly rich resource for information on desertification. However, the site is most useful to those who've already narrowed their research focus. In the "Documents" section, for instance, you can locate FAO documents about desertification by selecting a region (Africa, Asia, Europe, Latin America, Near East, North America, or Pacific); theme (crop production; forest and rangelands management; land and water management; knowledge, information and communication; environmental conventions and cross-sector issues; and sustainable development); document category (maps and statistics, photos, text, and videos); and/or document type (field manual, success story, scientific/technical paper, etc.).

For more general information, click on "Institutions" to find links to international organizations carrying out desertification-related activities and other groups working in the field. The "Activities" section offers reports, strategy outlines, and other news about FAO's program to combat desertification.

Basic Fact Sheet about Desertification
http://www.unccd.int/publicinfo/factsheets/menu.php
high school and up

This excellent fact sheet, produced by the United Nations Convention to Combat Desertification, presents introductory information about the causes and consequences of desertification, its relation to climate change and sustainable development, and specific efforts to combat desertification in Africa, Asia, Latin America and the Caribbean, and the north Mediterranean.

DESERTS (SEE ALSO DESERTIFICATION)

Best Search Engine: http://www.google.com/

Key Search Terms: Desert + geography + biome

Arid Lands Newsletter
http://ag.arizona.edu/OALS/ALN/ALNHome.html
high school and up

Created by the Office of Arid Lands Studies at the University of Arizona's College of Agriculture, this Web site contains a browsable archive of current and past issues of the semiannual newsletter.

You'll find a variety of interesting and thought-provoking topics covered here, including desertification, ecotourism, biodiversity, climate change, cartography, desert architecture, and deserts in literature. These articles often provide further Web resources for your research into a particular topic pertaining to deserts.

Desert Biome
http://www.runet.edu/~swoodwar/CLASSES/GEOG235/biomes/desert/
    desert.html
high school and up

As part of the Virtual Geography Department Project at Radford University, this site offers a learning module on the world's major biomes, including deserts. You'll find a discussion of the desert scrub biome's climate, soil, sub-climaxes, vegetation, structure and growth forms, fauna, and distribution. Graphics, photos, and a map representing the geographic range of the desert scrub biome help supplement the text.

The World's Biomes: Deserts
http://www.ucmp.berkeley.edu/glossary/gloss5/biome/deserts.html
high school and up

The World's Biomes is an educational site that presents excellent information on five major biomes—aquatic, desert, forest, grasslands, and tundra. The section on desert biomes goes into detail about four major types of desert: hot and dry, semiarid, coastal, and cold. For these types of desert biome, you'll find information on geographic distribution, climate and rainfall, soil type, and representative plant and animal life.

DEVELOPING NATIONS

Best Search Engine: http://www.lii.org/

Key Search Term: Developing nations

World Factbook 2001
http://www.cia.gov/cia/publications/factbook/
high school and up

If you need up-to-date information on a developing nation, the CIA's *World Factbook* is a sound place to begin your investigations. Its full text is available on the Web site and can also be downloaded for use offline. In the *Factbook*, you'll find a detailed listing for every country in the world, providing background information and data on the country's geography, people, government, economy, communications, transportation, military, and transnational issues, along with reference maps. The section on each country's economy offers a detailed overview, gross domestic product, unemployment rate, percentage of country's population below the poverty line, and economic aid status.

Countries and Regions
http://www.worldbank.org/html/extdr/regions.htm
high school and up

This excellent site by the World Bank provides easy access to economic data, documents and reports, and initiatives and projects for over 100 developing nations and six regions of the world. Use the Country-at-a-Glance tables to find key indicators of social and economic development over the last three decades for each country. You can also tap into the GenderStats database, which offers summary gender indicators, basic demographic data, population dynamics, labor force structure, and education and health statistics, or utilize HNPStats (Health, Nutrition, and Population Statistics) to find summary indicators for health status, health determinants, and health finance.

DIASTROPHISM (SEE ALSO GEOMORPHOLOGY, LANDFORMS)

Best Search Engine: http://www.ixquick.com/

Key Search Term: Diastrophism

Diastrophism: Folded, Faulted, and Tilted Strata and Landforms Related to Structures
http://www.courses.unt.edu/hwilliams/GEOG_3350/examreviews/ diastrophism1.htm and
http://www.courses.unt.edu/hwilliams/GEOG_3350/examreviews/ diastrophism2.htm
college level

These two Web pages are part of the same site, providing an exam review for an upper-level geomorphology course. Although these are simply bullet-point reviews, they provide a surprising amount of key information on diastrophism.

You'll find information on three types of deformation that result from subjecting rock to stress (folds, faults, and joints); behavior of rock under stress; classification of folds and faults, including illustrations of each type; landforms developed on folded/tilted and faulted strata; outcrop patterns and landforms on geologic maps; and the influence of geologic structure on drainage patterns.

Lithosphere: Diastrophism
http://www.citytel.net/PRSS/depts/geog12/litho/diastro.htm
high school and up

This page on diastrophism is part of a larger Web site about the structure, composition, formation, and dynamics of the earth's lithosphere.

What you'll find here is a straightforward description of the folding and faulting processes that uplift, rift, dome, and tilt parts of the earth's crust, resulting in landforms. Click on the highlighted words "Folding" and "Faulting" to learn more about each diastrophic process and to see diagrams illustrating the processes.

DISEASES (SEE ALSO MEDICAL GEOGRAPHY)

Best Search Engine: http://www.msn.com/
Key Search Terms: Disease + geography

Centers for Disease Control and Prevention
http://www.cdc.gov/
high school and up

The Centers for Disease Control and Prevention (CDC) has created a Web site that's useful to professional and lay people alike. For your research into a particular disease, click on "Health Topics A–Z," where you'll find fact sheets, professional information, and mortality reports on all diseases in the CDC database. The fact sheets, for instance, on alveolar hydatid disease or Guinea worm disease offer an overview of the disease, geographic distribution, treatment, how infection occurs, likelihood of infection, symptoms, and preventative measures.

For research into international diseases, you can use the site's travel health "Outbreaks" and "Destinations" sections. Or take a look at the CDC's online *Emerging Infectious Diseases Journal,* which tracks trends and analyzes new and reemerging infectious disease issues around the world.

World Health Organization (WHO)
http://www.who.int/home-page/
high school and up

As the major organization concerned with world health, the World Health Organization (WHO) has created a Web site that's a great starting point for research on disease. Use the "Information" section to find a multitude of WHO publications, such as the *Weekly Epidemiological Report* and the annual *World Health Report*. The "Press Media" section also provides many useful resources, such as press releases, fact sheets, and multimedia clips.

Look in the "Disease Outbreaks" section to find information on current outbreaks or older ones in historical archives arranged by year (1996 to 2000) and disease. The "News" section is another best-bet for finding information about topical issues on disease.

DOMINO THEORY

Best Search Engine: http://www.altavista.com/
Key Search Terms: Domino theory

                       Domino theory + communism

Cold War International History Project
http://cwihp.si.edu/default.htm
college level

This is a phenomenal site and a must-visit for anyone researching the domino theory in the larger perspective of the Cold War. Established at the Woodrow Wilson International Center for Scholars, the Cold War International History Project (CWIHP) disseminates new information and perspectives on the history of the Cold War, especially new findings from previously inaccessible sources in the former Communist world.

You'll want to look at the *CWIHP Bulletin*, which publishes recently released and translated documents found in archives of former Communist countries. These documents are accompanied by brief introductions by leading Cold War historians and archivists. You can click on "Virtual Archive" to search for documents by keyword or browse the subject headings, which include "Rise and Fall of Détente," "Arms Race," "Cold War Leaders," "Le Duc Tho," and dozens of others.

American Government: Domino Theory
http://college.hmco.com/polisci/gitelson/am_gov/6e/students/mythboxes/
    domino.html
high school and up

This site establishes how the myth of the domino theory was born and its profound effect on political decisions during the 1950s and 1960s. The site also explores how the domino theory has lived on in the policies of recent administrations.

DROUGHT

Best Search Engine: http://www.google.com/
Key Search Term: Drought

National Drought Mitigation Center
http://enso.unl.edu/ndmc/
middle school and up

This is drought central for the United States, where you can find just about anything you need to know about droughts. And in this time of extended drought throughout much of the country, there is a lot you probably want to know. The center, in its own words, "helps people and institutions develop and implement measures to reduce societal vulnerability to drought." Based at the University of Nebraska, Lincoln, it stresses preparation and risk management rather than crisis management. And although this site is geared toward practical action, it also provides many educational resources.

The site is divided into 12 sections. You'll find "Drought Watch," "Drought Science," "Climatology," and "Impacts" among the most helpful, but you may also want to check out "Drought Links," "Mitigation," and "Methodologies," particularly if you're looking at the subject of drought prevention.

At "Drought Watch" you can get current on drought conditions throughout the United States, view maps, look at indices for drought, moisture, and vegetation conditions, study forecasts, read about current drought-related humanitarian issues, or follow a link for global climate and drought monitoring.

"Drought Science" is where you'll want to go to study what creates drought conditions. This section brings you definitions, articles on understanding drought, and resources on El Niño, for example. "Impacts" will inform you about "Drought Impacts and History," "U.S. Drought," "International Drought Impacts," "Current Drought Impacts," and more.

Other cool resources here include the "Network" section, where you can access drought planners nationwide and "What's New," where you can read the latest in drought news. There's so much good information at this site that you may not need to look beyond its pages, but just in case you want more international information than you find here, try the site listed below.

ReliefWeb
http://www.reliefweb.int/w/rwb.nsf
high school and up

Here's a more international resource on current droughts and other natural disasters affecting the world. It's designed to serve the information needs of the humanitarian relief community, so it provides updates on natural disasters and emergencies of all kinds around the globe. You can search the site by country, by "Complex Emergencies," or by "Natural Disasters," which is pretty handy. You'll also find a section of highlights listed front and center on the home page and a long list of additional Web resources.

Click on "Natural Disasters" to make your way toward drought information. You'll see a long list, dating all the way back to 1981, of disaster response information on current and archival natural disasters. The first drought-related natural disaster is "Malawi—Floods and Drought, March 2002." There's also "Afghanistan—Drought, 2002," and much, much more. Click on the Malawi link and you'll arrive at a page listing links to the latest major documents published on the Malawi drought. The list is chronological and contains information on the publisher as well as a brief description.

If you're researching drought in a particular country, look here too for the list of drought-related documents. In essence this site offers an index to documents on specific natural disasters and emergencies around the globe, and you can access the documents through a hyperlink at the site. You can't beat that for easy research. This site is also good if you want to get a better understanding of relief efforts. The National Drought Mitigation Center is focused on drought prevention, so you won't find the same kind of attention to relief efforts there.

EARTH

Best Search Engine: http://www.google.com/
Key Search Terms: Earth + geography

Enchanted Learning: The Earth
http://www.enchantedlearning.com/subjects/astronomy/planets/earth/
middle school and up

This *Enchanted Learning* site on the earth contains tons of goodies. An educational site for kids, it offers sections on how fast the earth is moving, continental drift, oceans, the atmosphere, axis tilt and seasons, inside the earth, how the earth's mass is determined, water cycle, greenhouse effect, why the sky is blue (didn't you always want to know?), geologic time charts, and more.

The introduction gives you lots of fast facts right off the bat on Earth's size, orbit, mass, density, and more. Each link provides detailed information on the subject at hand. We followed the link for "How Fast the Earth Is Moving" and learned that motion cannot be measured without a reference point and thus when we talk about the speed of Earth's movement, we have to compare it to something else, like the speed of its own axis, the Sun, the Milky Way galaxy, or our local group of galaxies. Cool graphics depict Earth's placement in the solar system, and a chart provides lots of information on the complex motion of Earth—how fast it's spinning, how fast it is revolving around the Sun, how fast the solar system is moving around the Milky Way galaxy, and many other fun facts.

Back at the home page, you'll find a list of links to earth activities, and lots of links to other pages on the *Enchanted Learning* site. You'll find pages on astronomy, oceans, and volcanoes, which may be of interest to you, too. There's also a mailing list you can join if you'd like to participate in discussions on these topics.

PlanetPals Fast Facts: Greatest Facts on Earth
http://www.planetpals.com/planet2.html
middle school and up

If you're looking for a quick reference on Earth, especially if the information you hope to find is a little off the beaten track, you should try this site. First you'll find a list of some rather expected measurements of the earth, such as its circumference, diameter, and surface area. Then you'll get a list of the chemical elements that make up the earth, complete with percentages. Another list documents how long it takes garbage to break down (this is pretty interesting!) and then the final list is where you'll find some truly unexpected information about earth, such as the fact that only 11 percent of earth's surface is used to grow food. That's surprisingly small, isn't it?

Earthwatch Global Classroom
http://www.earthwatch.org/ed/home.html
high school and up

Earthwatch is a nonprofit organization whose members strive to "improve human understanding of the planet, the diversity of its inhabitants, and the processes that affect the quality of life on Earth." The group combines both citizens and scientists in projects to maintain the earth's ecosystem. If you're ecologically-minded and looking to get involved with others in some type of earth science project, this is the site for you.

Research programs sponsored by Earthwatch that you can access through this Web site include programs in archaeology, biodiversity, cultural diversity, endangered ecosystems, global change, oceans, and world health. Some of these programs have lesson plans, photo essays, online expeditions, and other Web resources and activities linked to them. Do a little hunting to see what interests you.

The page also has sections on student awards, field research opportunities, fellowships/internships, and school partnerships. The section on the worldwide network of scientists is easily accessible and provides links to scientists broken down by their specialty. An excellent feature is the "Ask the Scientist" page where questions have been posted from students and scientists specializing in particular fields have answered them.

Earth
http://www.seds.org/billa/tnp/earth.html
middle school and up

Opening with a huge Earth photo, this page contains lots of the same facts you can find in other places, but it doesn't stop with the basics. It also gives you all kinds of quirky facts about Earth—did you know that Earth is the only planet whose English name doesn't derive from Greek/Roman mythology?—and links to sites with fascinating info on Earth, such as an entry on Copernicus that explores his realization in the sixteenth century that Earth was just another planet revolving around the Sun.

You'll find a detailed breakdown of earth's chemical composition, descriptions of the eight major plates that comprise earth's crust, a discussion of Earth's satellite, and loads of links to sites about Earth and the Moon. The bottom of the page has a little section on "Open Issues," which contains links to pages that deal with the greenhouse effect and the Gaia hypothesis. This site is both helpful and fun.

EARTHQUAKE

Best Search Tool: http://home.rmi.net/~michaelg/
Key Search Category: Earthquakes/Seismology

National Earthquake Information Center/World Data Center for Seismology
http://gldss7.cr.usgs.gov/
high school and up

Here's the *über* site for earthquake information, courtesy of the ubiquitous U.S. Geological Survey (USGS). You'll have no problem finding the data you need for your research, whether it's current earthquake news and data, near real-time earthquake data, earthquake history, general information, a regional earthquake search, or something else.

Two of the most broadly useful sections are "General Earthquake Information" (with U.S. and world data, as well as info on magnitude) and "Earthquake Information Sources" (with Web links to numerous agencies and information centers). You can even sign up for USGS's earthquake notification services—which will deliver the latest earthquake information to you pronto by e-mail.

Glossary of Earthquake Terminology
http://vulcan.wr.usgs.gov/Glossary/Seismicity/earthquake_terminology.
  html
high school and up

Here's another awesome U.S. Geological Survey (USGS) site that serves as an interactive glossary of earthquake terminology. What makes this site so user-friendly is not simply its exhaustive list of terminology, but the fact that each word—from "accelerograph" to "volcanic tremor" (okay, not quite A to Z)—is hyperlinked to more USGS info. For instance, if reading the definition of "seiche" isn't quite enough for you, just click on the word and up comes a screen with related information.

InfoPlease: Earthquakes 101
http://www.infoplease.com/spot/earthquake1.html
middle school and up

Once again, *InfoPlease* comes through as a strong resource for your preliminary research. While you won't find extensive scientific data here, you will find general information on what causes earthquakes, the difference between intensity and magnitude, the twentieth-century's largest earthquakes, and more.

At the foot of the page, you'll find links to some current factual data, such as this year's mortality rate from earthquakes. However, since the source for all of this data is the U.S. Geological Survey (USGS) National Earthquake Information Center (see above), you're probably better off going right to the horse's mouth yourself.

ECOLOGY

Best Subject Guide: http://www.lii.org/
Key Search Terms: Ecology

Ecology + education

Ecology.com
http://www.ecology.com/
high school and up

To gain a comprehensive sense of what ecology is all about, check out this slick Web site. *Ecology.com* provides a full-service selection of feature stories, news updates, expert columns, and annotated links.

Under "Feature Stories," you can read and collect information from in-depth articles on topics as varied as "The Fate of the Black Rhino" and "The Coast Redwoods of California." Each article comes complete with links to other relevant sites, graphics, and photographs. "Ecology Today" is another great section, full of topical news articles such as "The Thinning of the Arctic Ice Cap," "Tracking Air Pollution," and "The Truth About El Niño and La Niña." Again, each article is fully developed, with graphics, photos, and links to more info.

Ecology and Evolutionary Biology
http://www.esb.utexas.edu/engler/bio304/lect-outline.html
high school and up

For a more academic overview of ecology, this site—created by Dr. Helene Engler of the University of Texas at Austin—is useful. It consists of the full collection of lecture notes for an introductory course on ecology and evolutionary ecology.

Although the 28 lectures are boiled down to outline form, a wealth of topics are covered, including the scientific method, the history of evolutionary thought, the origin of life, evolution, genetics, behavioral ecology, population ecology, ecosystem ecology, biogeography, and conservation biology.

ECONOMIC GEOGRAPHY

Best Search Engine: http://www.google.com/
Key Search Term: Economic geography

Toward a Working Definition of Economic Geography
http://faculty.washington.edu/~krumme/207/concepts/ebg.html
middle school and up

While this pages deals simply with defining the discipline of economic geography, it's worth a quick visit for the wonderful way the professor explores the dynamics of defining something that has as many different subfields and related fields as economic geography. He works through a definition of economics, then one of geography, before finally arriving at a working definition of economic geography.

If you find it somewhat baffling to pinpoint what the study of economic geography entails, you'll most likely appreciate and relate to this site.

Economic and Business Geography
http://faculty.washington.edu/krumme/ebg1.html
high school and up

The home page for the *Economic and Business Geography Learning Web* in the geography department at the University of Washington, this site is probably the most comprehensive introduction to the field that you can find in one place on the Web. You'll find course materials and Web links on such subjects as "Location and Spatial Organization of Economic Activities," "Economic Geography as Spatial Interaction," "Geography of Economic Change and Development," "Regional Economic and Market Area Analysis," "Economic Geography and Information Technology," and much more.

Click on any one of the topics listed on the site and you'll be given text related to the topic as well as links to supporting Web resources.

A New Urban Geography
http://faculty.washington.edu/krumme/urban/ny01.html
high school and up

This URL takes you to yet another page at the University of Washington's authoritative site, this time a page on the new urban geography. Urban geography often falls in with economic geography, and the September 11, 2001, terrorist attacks in the United States have caused more reflection, writing, and new discussion among urban geographers than any other topic in a long while. This page is primarily an index site. It gives you a brief introduction to the topic, and then provides a list of well-organized links to articles and sites dealing specifically with the fate of cities, the future for skyscrapers, and other issues of interest to economic geographers.

ECONOMIES—COMMAND, MARKET, AND TRANSITIONAL

Best Search Engine: http://www.google.com/
Key Search Terms: Market economy

Command economy

What Is a Market Economy?
http://usinfo.state.gov/products/pubs/market/homepage.htm

This online text is focused on introducing you to the ins and outs of market economies. As the introduction notes, two types of economies have dominated the world's population—the command and market economies. The bias of this book is strongly in favor of the market economy, so keep that in mind while you're reading. Nevertheless, the information provided here makes an excellent introduction to both market and command economies.

The section of primary interest to you will be the first chapter, called "Command and Market Economies." Click on the link and you'll be taken to a concise text with sections on "Command Decision about Clothing," "The Price of Shirts," and "Markets."

Other chapters focus almost solely on market economies. They include "Consumers in a Market Economy," "Businesses in a Market Economy," "Workers in a Market Economy," "A System of Markets," "Finances in a Market Economy," and "Government in a Market Economy."

ECOSYSTEM (SEE ALSO BIOMES, ECOLOGY)

Best Search Engine: http://www.ixquick.com/
Key Search Terms: Ecosystem

Ecosystem + education

Ecosystems, Biomes, and Watersheds: Definitions and Use
http://cnie.org/NLE/CRSreports/Biodiversity/biodv-6.cfm
high school and up

This report—created for Congress and posted on a National Library for the Environment Web site—does a fantastic job of defining what ecosystems are. Although written in 1993, you'll find that most of the information here is still relevant and useful.

The report describes the meaning and applications of the word "ecosystem" and of the related terms "watershed" and "biome." It discusses the pros and cons of all three as organizing principles for land management, and the potential pitfalls for ecosystem management.

World Resources Institute
http://www.wri.org/wr2000/ecosystems.html
high school and up

Created by the World Resources Institute, this site provides excellent, in-depth reference material for your research on various ecosystems.

You can begin by tapping into basic background information on what ecosystems are, why they matter, how to sustain them, and more. To learn about individual ecosystems, simply click on the coastal, forest, freshwater, grassland, or agricultural ecosystem sections, where you'll find extensive reports and data. For instance, in the section on coastal ecosystems, there is a summary assessment, three case studies, and numerous downloadable PDF documents on topics such as coastal population and altered land cover, coral reefs, overfishing, and trawling.

ECOTOURISM

Best Search Engine:	http://www.google.com
Key Search Term:	Ecotourism

Amazon Interactive
http://www.eduweb.com/amazon.html
middle school and up

This cool site offers an ecotourism simulation game that will let you explore the many positive and negative aspects of this popular form of travel. It's based on field research into indigenous ecotourism in the Ecuadorian Amazon and is designed to illustrate the basic physical and human geography of the Amazon as well as the risks and benefits of ecotourism as a development strategy. If you'd like to learn more, you can read the research report on which these activities are based. Just click on the link for "Research Report."

The site lets you play the role of a Quechua family in the Ecuadorian Amazon. As a family, you're faced with some tough decisions concerning the role of ecotourism in your local environment and in the lives of your family and tribe. At the end of each section, you are asked a question that leads to a new set of issues. This is not a dumbed-down version of the issues either. You'll be put in just the kind of situation that ecotourism brings to many people around the world.

While at this site, you may also want to check out some of its other resources on the geography of the Ecuadorian Amazon. Head back to the home page for sections on "Where Is the Amazon?", "How Rainy Is the Rainforest?", "Making a Living," "Who Lives There?", and more.

The International Ecotourism Society: Ecotourism Explorer
http://www.ecotourism.org/
middle school and up

To learn what ecotourism is and isn't, why not go straight to the source? The ecotourists themselves will teach you all about their trade at this colorful Web site. The site offers a "Members Resource Center" and a section called "Eco-Professionals and Students" that contains links to information on research, conservation, and business. This is where you'll probably find the most helpful information. If you're researching ecotourism in a specific area, or perhaps the economic considerations of starting an ecotourism business, or a conservation issue, this is the part of the site for you.

Under the "Conservation" link in this section, you'll find information on conservation/ecotourism projects, a selection of papers on the subject of conservation and ecotourism, and a subsection devoted to the issues of parks and ecotourism.

Back at the home page, you can also find links to follow that will let you register for ecotourism short courses on the Web, search a database of eco-friendly lodges and tours, locate ecotourism speakers, and read articles about ecotourism.

EDUCATION—STATISTICS

Best Search Engine: http://www.google.com
Key Search Terms: Education + statistics

U.S. Department of Education
http://www.ed.gov/
high school and up

The U.S. Department of Education has a section on "Research and Statistics" on its Web site that offers some of the best statistical resources on education in the United States.

The section is subdivided into "Overview," "Research," "Statistics," "Evaluation," and "Assessment." If you go directly to "Statistics," you'll find the data neatly organized into the following categories: "General Information," "Survey and Program Areas," and "Publications." Under "General Information" you'll find many useful pages.

The first you'll want to look at is the "Encyclopedia of Education Stats." The encyclopedia contains links to reports on the *Condition of*

Education 2000–2001, Indicators of School Crime and Safety: 2001, and *The Digest of Education Statistics, 2000.* Also under "General Information" are links to "Fast Facts." When you get to the "Fast Facts" home page, you'll be given links to a number of fact categories. These include "Assessment," "Early Childhood," "Elementary/Secondary," "International," "Library," "Postsecondary," and more. There's also a link under "General Information" for the National Center for Education Statistics (NCES) home page. The NCES is responsible for much of the data on the U.S. Department of Education Web site, but the NCES Web site is confusing and more difficult to navigate. We recommend starting with the statistics provided here and going on to the NCES Web site if you can't find what you're looking for.

The Nation's Report Card
http://nces.ed.gov/nationsreportcard/
high school and up

This is the one part of the National Center for Education Statistics (NCES) site that we recommend you visit directly. You've probably heard in the news about the National Assessment of Educational Progress (NAEP) program. This is the program responsible for researching and compiling the Nation's Report Card, which is an invaluable tool for studying the progress of American students in various subject areas. The report card is available in the following subjects: arts, civics, geography, mathematics, reading, science, U.S. history, and writing.

The Report Card page is fully searchable and it contains a stat of the week, as well as links to other parts of the NCES Web site. You can also read the NAEP Questions Tool, which provides easy access to NAEP questions, student responses, and scoring guides that are released to the public. Other NAEP data and state profiles are also accessible from this site.

ELEVATION

Best Search Engine: http://www.google.com
Key Search Terms: Elevation + geography

Ask Yahoo!: How Do They Establish Elevation from Sea Level?
http://ask.yahoo.com/ask/19980901.html
middle school and up

At this fun Yahoo! site you can ask a question, any question, and receive what is, in this case, an authoritative and humorous response. You'll learn more than a little about establishing elevation in relation

to sea level and about determining sea level itself by reading this intriguing and relatively brief page.

Geographic Nameserver: USGS: National Mapping Information
http://geonames.usgs.gov/pls/gnis/webquery.gniswebqueryform
middle school and up

Try this site if you are looking for the elevation of a specific place or
geographic feature in the United States. There's a handy form to fill out
with information on the chosen place. Just type in the name of the
place, and a full record appears with information on latitude, longitude,
elevation, and more.

EL NIÑO

Best Search Engine: http://www.yahoo.com/
Best Search Directory: Science > Earth Science > Meteorology >
                        Weather > Phenomena

El Niño Theme Page (NOAA)
http://www.pmel.noaa.gov/toga-tao/el-nino/nino-home.html
high school and up

You could begin and end all of your El Niño research right here. What
you'll discover at this site is a rich collection of information that covers
everything from El Niño basics (what it is, why it occurs, where the
name came from, and how to recognize it), to frequently asked questions,
to the impact of El Niño and the benefits of prediction, and much more.

If your research requires actual scientific data, you'll find it here as
well. You can access drifting buoy data, sea level field analyses, real-time
data, satellite data, numerical model simulations, and 3-D animation of
El Niño temperatures. You'll find links to widely distributed information
on El Niño, including graphics, historical perspectives, and forecasts. For
additional hard science, be sure to check out the link to the Tropical
Atmosphere Ocean (TAO) project, which was designed to improve the
detection, understanding, and prediction of El Niño.

It's no surprise that the site devotes an entire section to all of the
awards and accolades it has received—including a Snap "Editor's
Choice" designation for Science and Technology, a "Times Pick" by the
Los Angeles Times, and a Four Globe Award from the *Environmental News
Network*.

NOVA: Tracking El Niño
http://www.pbs.org/wgbh/nova/elnino/
high school and up

This is another good site, with both current and historical information on El Niño. Its arrangement, however, is a bit confusing, since the names of each section do not always describe the contents adequately. Use the "Site Map" and "Search" pages to help you find specific information.

Inside a section called "Anatomy of El Niño," you'll find great material on global weather patterns that cause El Niño, as well as a Shockwave game that lets you manipulate earth's weather patterns. The section "El Niño's Reach" describes global effects and has an excellent clickable time line that explores El Niño throughout history. You'll also want to stop at the site's "Virtual Weather Station" to find current satellite images showing an infrared view of the eastern Pacific, infrared cloud cover image of the United States, and a global montage of land temperature, sea surface temperature, and cloud cover. Under "Resources," you'll find FAQs, a glossary of terms, plus suggested readings and links on the subject.

Climate Prediction Center: El Niño/La Niña
http://www.cpc.ncep.noaa.gov/products/analysis_monitoring/lanina/
high school and up

This site provides quick access to the Climate Prediction Center's comprehensive educational and scientific resources on El Niño and La Niña. The tutorial on the El Niño/Southern Oscillation (ENSO) cycle is a solid place to start for info about how sea temperatures and atmospheric conditions in the tropical Pacific affect North American weather patterns. You can also click on "Fact Sheets" or "Monographs" to get written and graphical material that explains the far-flung effects of climate patterns.

For the latest info on current El Niño conditions, you can click on "Expert Assessment" for a current diagnostic discussion or "Monitoring and Data" for a weekly update. To find historical data, click on "Previous ENSO Events," and you'll see a detailed assessment of the impact of El Niño on a regional and state-by-state basis.

ENERGY

Best Search Engine: http://www.clearinghouse.net/

Key Search Term: Energy

Energy Efficiency and Renewable Energy Network
http://www.eren.doe.gov/
high school and up

The U.S. Department of Energy's Energy Efficiency and Renewable Energy Network (EREN) has created an excellent one-stop resource for information on energy, with more than 600 links and 8,000 documents.

In the "Technologies" section, you'll find extensive information about energy efficiency for buildings, transportation, industry, and power. The "Renewable Energies" section offers resources on bioenergy, hydrogen, ocean, wind, geothermal, hydropower, and solar energy. To fine-tune your findings, you can also conduct a site search for specific keywords.

From the site's home page, you'll have access to a browsable version of the National Energy Plan. You'll also find annotated links to energy-related organizations and resources, such as federal, state, and local agencies; trade and nonprofit groups; universities and research institutions; international organizations; discussion groups; and newsletters and magazines.

Energy and Environment Resources on the Web
http://www.weea.org/sampler/
high school and up

The World Energy Efficiency Association put together this Web site, which will definitely speed up your research into energy issues. You can use the drop-down menu to access annotated links to information resources in the following categories: U.S. government agencies, U.S. national laboratories, other governments, international organizations, universities, corporations, electric/gas utility industries, nonprofit organizations/professional associations, libraries/bibliographies/collections, electronic lists/conferences, and newsgroups. You'll appreciate the obvious time and effort that went into writing the reviews of every energy-related Web site posted under these categories.

ENVIRONMENTAL GEOGRAPHY

Best Search Engine: http://www.google.com/
Key Search Term: Environmental geography

Exploitation, Conservation, Preservation: A Geographic Perspective on Natural Resource Use
http://www.wiley.com/college/geog/cutter018104/resources/Index.htm
high school and up

This is the Web site created by a geography professor as an accompaniment to his Introduction to Environmental Geography course. You'll find it to be a virtual gold mine for all types of resources.

The site is structured like the textbook used in the course, so you'll see 15 different chapter titles—"Natural Resources: Thoughts, Words, and Deeds," "Ecologic Perspectives on Natural Resources," and so on. Click on any one of these chapters, and you'll gain access to a glossary for the chapter, a featured Web link complete with suggested activities for students, additional Web resources, and links to news items related to the chapter's material.

If this isn't enough for you, click on the professor's name—James Hayes-Bohanan—and fly through cyberspace to his personal home page, where an eclectic mix of environmental geography articles, projects, links, and other cool stuff awaits.

EQUATOR (SEE ALSO LATITUDE AND LONGITUDE)

Best Search Engine: http://www.webscout.com/

Key Search Term: Equator

The Equator, Hemispheres, Tropic of Cancer, and Tropic of Capricorn
http://geography.about.com/science/geography/library/misc/blequator.htm
middle school and up

Created by *About.com*'s geography expert, this site concisely defines three significant, imaginary lines that run across the surface of the earth: the equator, the Tropic of Cancer, and the Tropic of Capricorn. You'll learn where the equator is positioned on the earth; which countries it runs through; how many miles long it is; how the Northern, Southern, Western, and Eastern hemispheres are determined; and more.

For additional information, check out *About.com*'s "Coordinate Systems" or "Physical Geography" links.

EQUINOX

Best Search Engine: http://www.ixquick.com/

Key Search Term: Vernal and autumnal equinox

Vernal and Autumnal Equinoxes
http://windows.arc.nasa.gov/cgi-bin/tour_def/the_universe/uts/equinox.
   html
middle school and up

Developed for the *Windows to the Universe* Web site by the University Corporation for Atmospheric Research (UCAR), this page on the vernal and autumnal equinoxes offers a brief introduction to the topic. You can choose to view the beginner, intermediate, or advanced page for information on equinoxes. (Make yourself feel like Alfred Einstein by choosing "advanced," since—to be honest—we didn't notice much difference between the three.) Be sure to check out the site's highlight—a diagram showing how the sun moves through the sky on an equinox.

InfoPlease: Equinox
http://www.infoplease.com/spot/equinox1.html
middle school and up

InfoPlease comes through with an encyclopedic explanation of what vernal and autumnal equinoxes are. To gather more background data, you can click on the hyperlinked words—such as "celestial sphere" and "ecliptic"—that are sprinkled throughout the text. One of these links—to "procession of the equinoxes"—provides information that's actually difficult to find at other Web sites. You might also appreciate the fact that *InfoPlease* nudges you to look at other relevant *InfoPlease* sections on the planets and the seasons.

EROSION (SEE ALSO GEOMORPHOLOGY, SOIL TYPES, WEATHERING)

Best Search Engine: http://www.dogpile.com/
Key Search Terms: Erosion + geography
                        Erosion + geology + education

Soil Erosion Tutorial
http://soils.ecn.purdue.edu/~wepphtml/wepp/wepptut/jhtml/intro.html
high school and up

This tutorial does a good job of describing erosion processes, as well as ways to predict and control erosion. You'll find top-notch descriptions of how wind erosion and water erosion occur and how they are controlled. You'll also learn about soil erosion prediction technology—in particular, the Water Erosion Prediction Project (WEPP). WEPP, which is shaping up to be the gold standard in water erosion prediction technology, is being developed for use by the Soil Conservation Service, the U.S. Forest Service, the Bureau of Land Management, and other major organizations involved in soil and water conservation.

Soil and Sediment Erosion/Wind Erosion
http://www.gcrio.org/geo/soil.html and http://www.gcrio.org/geo/erosion.html
college level

Written by the U.S. Global Change Research Information Office, these two Web pages—one focusing on soil and sediment erosion and the other on wind erosion—provide excellent overviews on the subject. You'll find brief factual data about erosion processes, the significance of erosion, human and natural causes, methods and frequency of measurement, and more.

ESTUARY

Best Search Engine: http://www.ixquick.com/
Key Search Term: Estuary

National Estuary Program
http://www.epa.gov/owow/estuaries/
high school and up

In the section of the National Estuary Program's (NEP) site called "About Estuaries," there's an excellent introduction to the topic. You'll learn what estuaries are, why they are important, and why they need protection. The "Challenges" section presents information on specific issues, such as nutrient overloading, pathogens, toxic chemicals, habitat loss and degradation, introduced species, alteration of natural flow regimes, and declines in fish and wildlife populations.

To learn about specific NEP estuaries, click on "Program Profiles" or "Success Stories." Each profiled estuary provides you with summary information, maps, highlights, and more.

Exploring Estuaries
http://www.epa.gov/owow/estuaries/kids/
middle school

This pretty site from the Environmental Protection Agency will teach you all about estuaries, which are the places where freshwater streams and rivers flow into the ocean and mix with seawater. You can read about estuaries, take a virtual tour of two different estuaries, play games and activities, find other Web resources on estuaries, and look up estuary-related words in the glossary. The text on each of the tours is focused on exploring the pollution threats to these estuaries and what can be done to help protect and restore water quality in these areas.

You might want to start with "About Estuaries," which gives a good introduction, then click on "Take a Tour," which is located under one of the flying bird's wings, to explore some of our country's most fascinating estuaries. There are two estuary tours to choose from. You'll find out what makes these places so special and meet some of the plants and animals that live there. You'll also learn about some of the challenges the estuaries are facing along with how the local communities are working to protect them for the future.

The Barataria-Terrebonne estuary, located west and south of New Orleans, is a web of bays, lagoons, marshes, and swamps that covers a vast amount of land. On your tour of this special place, you'll encounter brown pelicans, alligators, and blue crabs, read about how wetlands benefit the people of south Louisiana, and learn what people are doing to preserve this endangered place.

The other estuary you can tour at this wonderful site is the Long Island Sound. After an introduction where you learn about the basic geography of the sound, you'll meet the winter flounder, bluefish, and oysters that the sound is famous for; learn about pollution issues in the sound; and discover a link to *Long Island Sound Study Online,* where you can find fact sheets, maps, posters, and more about this estuary.

Once you've toured, you might want to search other resources or play some of the water games found here. Or maybe you're ready to find a way to get active and support the preservation of these estuaries or an estuary near you. If so, check out the following site for young activists.

Estuarine Research Foundation
http://www.erf.org/
high school and up

This site for the Estuarine Research Federation (ERF), an international organization that promotes research in estuarine and coastal waters, provides some excellent resources for your research.

The site's "Education" center offers information about the science and management of estuaries, lagoons, and bays along coasts worldwide. In addition to reading a text overview about estuaries, you can utilize the site's E-ReFs database (a Web-based version of the *Estuarine Science Reference Series*). E-ReFs provides access to literature on important topics related to estuarine and coastal ocean science, divided into categories that include "Bivalves," "Carbon Cycling," "Ecological Risk Assessment," "Marine Biodiversity," "San Francisco Bay," "Tidal Wetland Restoration," and more.

ETHNIC GROUPS (SEE ALSO IMMIGRATION)

Best Search Engine: http:www.google.com

Key Search Terms: Ethnic groups

Or names of individual ethnic groups of interest

Countries of the World
http://www.countryreports.org/
middle school and up

This terrific site, selected as one of the best sites on the Web for teachers, is also one of the best sites for students. Basic research on ethnic groups from all over the world is easy and quick. Go to the home page and click on "World Countries" for a comprehensive database of the world's countries with extensive demographic information on each one. Once you choose a country, you'll be given a menu of the following: "Economy," "Defense," "Geography," "Government," "People," "National Anthem lyrics," and "Related Links." Pick "People."

Among many other statistics, you'll find a breakdown of the population by ethnic group, including the percentage of the population belonging to each group. Other really helpful information here includes age structure, population growth, religious affiliations, languages spoken, literacy, and more.

You won't get detailed information on individual ethnic groups at this site. You'll have to continue your search for that elsewhere. But you will get accurate information on just which ethnic groups are found in a particular country.

Multicultural Pavilion: Multicultural Paths
http://curry.edschool.virginia.edu/go/multicultural/sites1.html
high school and up

This is the links page for the University of Virginia's award-winning *Multicultural Pavilion* Web site, and it's an excellent place to look for resources if you're interested in American ethnic groups. You won't find too many international links here, but you will find well-screened links to Web sites on American ethnic groups, as well as general resources for ethnic and multicultural studies.

Links on the page are divided into the following categories: "General Multicultural Paths," "Multicultural Education: Subjects and Fields," "Multicultural Education: Teaching and Learning," "Equity in Education," and "Multicultural Education: Historic Collections."

Try looking under the "Social Studies and History" link in the "Subject and Fields" category for a wonderful collection of links to sites on African Americans, Asian Americans, Hispanic Americans, and Native Americans.

Race, Ethnicity, and Identity
http://cfdev.georgetown.edu/cndls/asw/aswsub.
    cfm?head1 = Race%2C%20Ethnicity%2C%20and%20Identity
high school and up

For more international resources and for resources categorized by name of ethnic group, try this Georgetown University Web site. It's from the *American Studies Web* at Georgetown, and it's a tremendously comprehensive list of Web resources.

You can find Arab American, Eastern European American, Filipino American, Italian American, Slavic American, South Asian American, and many other ethnic groups here. There's even a section of resources on Whiteness Studies.

The menu at the left side of the page contains many other subject pages of interest. Browse the list, and you just might find a topic that relates to your specific research.

ETHNOCENTRISM

Best Search Engine: http://www.yahoo.com/

Key Search Term: Cultural anthropology

Anthro.Net
http://www.anthro.net/
high school and up

Although it's possible that you'll find other Web sites with more specific information about ethnocentrism on your own, you'll appreciate this site's unique anthropology-specific search engine. It turned up a whopping 21 relevant Web sites when we searched for the term "ethnocentrism"—far more *relevant* sites than the mainstream search engines. The *Anthro.Net* database contains thousands of reviewed Web sites and bibliographic references relevant to the study of anthropology and archaeology.

Ethnocentrism: Key Anthropology Concepts
http://www.iupui.edu/~anthkb/ethnocen.htm
high school and up

This wordy site delves into a number of questions about ethnocentrism. The author asks—and answers the following questions: What is ethnocentrism? Why are people ethnocentric? What can we do about it? If you're looking for a broad and impassioned overview of the subject, you'll find it here. Keep in mind, however, that this site, while affiliated with a university, is clearly a personal exploration into the subject.

EUROPEAN UNION

Best Search Engine: http://www.google.com/

Key Search Term: European Union

EuroInternet
http://eiop.or.at/euroint/
high school and up

This is grand central for European Union (EU) information resources on the Web. It's a great big index site, so you'll need to treat it as such. Use the menu at the left side of the page to browse the main categories of information. These include "Writings," "EU Institutions," "Research Institutions," "Teachings," "Databases and Documents," "People," "Newsgroups and Lists," "Events and Conferences," "Eurosceptics," "Subjects," "Area-Specific Information," and more.

If you're interested in a specific institution within the European Union, you'll find it under "EU Institutions." Browse the subjects to look for more specific topics, and try the "Research Institutions" section if you're looking for information on a specific country within the EU. There's a research institute for each country. Otherwise, try the search engines under "Writings" or the databases under "Databases and Documents."

History of European Integration
http://www.let.leidenuniv.nl/history/rtg/res1/index.htm
high school and up

Leiden University's History Department maintains this page on the history of European integration. If your topic is historical in scope, you might want to try looking here. You'll find the usual sections for the most part: archives, Brussels, Cold War sites, discussion groups, European Union institutions, Eurospeak, federalism, historical documents, histories, journals, oral histories, time lines, statistical sources, and more.

European Union for Young People
http://www.eurunion.org/infores/teaching/Young/EUYoungPeople.htm
middle school and up

This page is part of the *European Union in the U.S.* Web site and it contains some fun and accessible resources for kids who are studying

European integration. Sections include "Fun," "Traveling in Europe," "Studying in Europe," "Studying about Europe," "For Europeans Only," and "Working in Europe."

Don't be put off by the less-then-impressive graphics on the home page. The resources are abundant here, and the Web technology improves. Under "Fun" you'll find links to resources on the "Environment for Young Europeans," "Euro at School," "Euro Quiz," "Eurodesk," "Euromyths," and more. The "Eurodesk" site lets you ask specific questions about the European Union and access an online database. Links to kid-friendly pages at the various embassies of European Union member states might be of interest to you if you're interested in issues involving one or more particular countries, or if you would just like to explore these countries. You can access a page on the Vikings at the Danish Embassy site, Irish travel stories at the Irish Embassy site, or the royal palaces of Spain at the Spanish Embassy site.

The other sections of the site are focused on more specific topics. If you're hoping to travel, study, or work in Europe, go to the appropriately named page for a long list of links to Web sites that can help you turn your plans into reality.

FAMINES

Best Search Engine: http://www.google.com/

Key Search Terms: Famine + geography

United Nations World Food Programme
http://www.wfp.org/index2.html
high school and up

The World Food Programme of the United Nations (WFP) is a good one-stop resource on world hunger. The menu at the left side of the page contains pages on "About WFP," "Newsroom," "Appeals," "How to Help," "Operations," "Policies," and more. On the right you'll see an "Alert" column with information on immediate crises. At the time of our visit, these included "Afghan Crisis: Relief to Recovery," "Hunger Warning for Eastern and Southern Africa," "Bangladesh Slums: Eyewitness."

There's also a tiny little map of the world on the home page, where you can click on a continent to access hunger information for that region of the world. The country briefs for Asia included information on Afghanistan, Armenia, Azerbaijan, Bangladesh, Bhutan, Cambodia, China, DPR Korea, and East Timor. Each country brief contains an overview, a description of WFP activities in the country, a list of links to other resources on the country, and contact information for the World Food Programme in that country.

If you're interested in helping with food relief, check the "Appeals" section of the site, which will tell you how you can contribute money through the flash donor alert initiative. It also contains information on current shortfalls and projected needs.

USAID Famine Early Warning System Network
http://www.fews.net/
high school and up

At the *Network*, you can access famine information by clicking on one of the links to region and country centers, choosing a supplemental report on a topic such as desertification and climate change, picking a resource out of the toolkit, say a link on hazard monitoring and remote sensing, or connecting with another famine-related organization.

Some of the text at the country centers section of the site is not available in English, but this is noted right upfront on the main menu. There are also few country centers outside of Africa, so if you want information on Africa, this is a good page, but if you're researching another continent, this may not be your best source. That said, the articles you can retrieve through these country center links are wonderfully detailed and comprehensive without being unintelligible to the general reader. They come complete with color-coded maps, useful tables, and other resources.

If you're researching climate, vegetation, flooding, weather, markets/prices, or other typical geography concepts as they relate to famine, you'll want to go to "Resources and Toolkit," which has separate links on each of these topics under the broader topic of "Hazard Monitoring and Remote Sensing."

You'll also find lots of resources on "Contingency and Planning," "Capacity Building," and other famine-related topics at this excellent U.S. government site.

FERTILITY RATES (SEE ALSO VITAL STATISTICS)

Best Search Engine: http://www.google.com/
Key Search Term: Fertility rates

Countries of the World
http://www.countryreports.org/
middle school and up

This terrific site, selected as one of the best sites on the Web for teachers, is also one of the best sites for students. Basic demographic research on people from all over the world is easy and quick. Go to the home page and click on "World Countries" for a comprehensive database of the world's countries with extensive demographic information on each one. Once you choose a country, you'll be given a menu of the following: "Economy," "Defense," "Geography," "Government," "People," "National Anthem lyrics," and "Related Links." Pick "People."

Among many other statistics, you'll find an overall fertility rate given for the female population. Other really helpful information here includes age structure, birth rate, infant mortality rate, population growth, religious affiliations, languages spoken, literacy, and more.

You won't get detailed information about the fertility rate here. You'll have to continue your search elsewhere for that. But you will get accurate information to start you on your way.

Overpopulation.com
http://www.overpopulation.com/faq/basic_information/total_fertility_rate/
middle school and up

If you're studying fertility rates, you probably already know that they are the single greatest indicator of future population. As a result, those concerned with overpopulation pay close attention to these numbers around the world.

Overpopulation.com is just such an entity. You'll find its page on total fertility rates informative and useful if you're just beginning to research overpopulation issues and fertility rate. The article presents a good overview of total fertility rates around the world, complete with some useful charts comparing rates over time.

At the bottom of the page, you can link to total fertility rate statistics by region and country. If you want to explore other overpopulation topics, head back to the home page (just use the menu at the left to get you back) and you'll find articles on a wide variety of topics.

Population World Reference Bureau
http://www.prb.org//content/NavigationMenu/Other_reports/2000–2002/
    2001_world_population_data_sheet.htm
middle school and up

The *Population World Reference Bureau* offers a great site for finding population stats and overviews of population issues. You'll find the "2001 World Population Data Sheet," with links to all kinds of specific data. The drop-down menu of topics includes "Environment," "HIV/AIDS,"

"Population Trends," "Reproductive Health," "Education," "Employment," "Family Planning," "Fertility," and more. There are also menus for regions of the world and for other *Population Reference Bureau* sites.

FLAGS

Best Search Engine: http://www.google.com/

Key Search Terms: Flags + geography

Flags of All Countries
http://www.geographic.org/flags/flags.html
middle school and up

This flags page is part of a larger site called *Geographic.org*, where you can get all kinds of cool geography info on countries worldwide. At the flags page, you'll have access to a link for every country you can come up with and all its flags, like Ashmore and the Cartier Islands, China (including the flags for Hong Kong, Taiwan, Macao, and Tibet), Guernsey, and everywhere else.

Click on the link for the country of you choice, and the page that pops up will display a nice image of the country's flag and provide further links to "Country Facts," "Climate," "Geography," and "Maps." There's also a "Flag Identifier" page, where you can see groupings of flag designs—those with solid backgrounds, those with vertical stripes, and so on.

This site also contains the data from the 1999 CIA *Factbook* Country Ranks, with rankings of countries by numerous different geographic, economic, population, and military criteria. This doesn't have much to do with flags, but perhaps you'll find it interesting anyway.

World Flags
http://www.enchantedlearning.com/geography/flags/
middle school and up

Although this *Enchanted Learning.com* site doesn't contain nearly as many flags as the comprehensive site listed above—*Geographic.org*—it's worth the visit if you'd like to find printouts of flags to color, information and help in designing your own flag, or want to learn more about marine signal flags, which are used to communicate at sea. There's also an entire section of the site devoted to U.S. national and state flags, which you won't find at the previous site.

You can search for flags by continent, by the A to Z listing of countries, or by type, such as bicolor, couped cross, crescent, and star.

FLOODS

Best Search Engine: http://www.google.com

Key Search Terms: Floods + geology

Significant Floods in the United States during the Twentieth Century—USGS Measures a Century of Floods
http://ks.water.usgs.gov/Kansas/pubs/fact-sheets/fs.024–00.html
middle school and up

This U.S. Geological Survey (USGS) fact sheet compiled in March 2000 is a comprehensive look at some of the biggest and most damaging floods of the twentieth century. If you are interested in the history of-floods in particular regions, or in researching a particularly infamous flood from the last century, or a particular type of flood, such as storm-surge floods or dam- and levy-failure floods, you'll want to check out this excellent site.

The table of contents includes the following sections: "USGS Flood Measurements"; "Significant Floods of the Twentieth Century"; "Regional Floods"; "Flash Floods"; "Ice-Jam Floods"; "Storm-Surge Floods"; "Dam- and Levee-Failure Floods"; "Debris, Landslide, and Mudflow Floods"; "Flood Information on the Internet"; "Other Internet Sites"; and "Flood Facts."

Click on "Significant Floods" for an overview of floods covered in this fact sheet and a nice atlas with interpretive table showing all of the floods discussed and providing information on the date of the flood, the number of deaths that resulted, the uninflated financial costs of the flood, and specific comments.

Other Web resources with links from this page include a site on flash flood safety (did you know that flash floods are responsible for most deaths from flooding?), one on river forecast centers, and one on dam safety.

USGS: Floods and Flood Plains
http://water.usgs.gov/pubs/FS/OFR93–641/index.html
middle school and up

This is another general U.S. Geological Survey (USGS) site on floods and flood plains. It makes a great first stop if you're just beginning to research the subject of floods. It's a basic introduction to the social and ecological impacts of flooding, as well as the basic causes of flooding. You'll get a good overview here of the problems floods cause and how they are viewed from a natural hazard perspective.

A brief introduction covers the economic and human costs of floods, as well as presenting statistics on frequency in the United States. This is followed by a brief section on weather patterns and how they determine when floods occur; a section on very large floods; one on flood plains; a section on zoning restrictions; and finally a section on the role of dams and levees in reducing flooding.

FOLK GEOGRAPHY

Best Search Engine: http://www.google.com
Key Search Term: Folklife

Louisiana Folklife Program: Defining Terms
http://www.crt.state.la.us/folklife/main_defining_terms.html
middle school and up

Folk geography is a subcategory of cultural geography. Specifically, it is the study of folk culture. What exactly is folk culture, you may ask? This page from the Louisiana Folklife Program's Web site will give you a wonderful overview of folklore, folklife, and folk culture by defining what they are and what they are not.

You'll find fascinating reading just on defining the subject, as well as links to other pages on the Web site that go into detail about Louisiana's "Living Traditions." Go there to explore the Creole State Exhibit, a virtual tour of the vast folklife exhibition permanently housed at the state capitol building, or a detailed essay on Louisiana's traditional cultures, or maps that detail ethnic and folk regions in the state.

Try the "Links" section if you want to explore other Louisiana-related resources, such as a site called *Good for What Ails You: Secrets of the Louisiana Bayou Healers* and another site that offers an online *Encyclopedia of Cajun Culture*. You'll also find links to some of the best national resources on folklife, including sites for the American Folklore Society and the American Folklife Center at the Library of Congress (see below for a full review).

American Folklife Center, Library of Congress
http://lcweb.loc.gov/folklife/
middle school and up

This is folklife central for the United States, and if you're intrigued by the study of folklife, you'll absolutely love this comprehensive site from the Library of Congress. Created by Congress in 1976 to preserve and present American folklife, the American Folklife Center offers information on just about every folklife topic you could imagine.

The table of contents right on the home page gives you an idea of the scope here. You've got the "Index to Site Contents," which is huge. Click on that link and you'll be given an A to Z listing of all the resources housed on this site, things like an "Archive of American Folk Culture Collections," numerous essays on archival practice, a link to an online collection called "Buckaroos in Paradise: Ranching Culture in Northern Nevada, 1945–82," guides, educational materials, The Endangered Music Project, and so much more.

If you manage to get out of the "Index" and come back to the home page for this site, you'll see that other sections of the site include "Published Recordings," "The September 11 Documentary Project," "Links to Ethnographic Resources," and much more.

If you're really into the study of folk geography, you could probably hang out at this Web site for a year or more and not tire of the resources. Not that we recommend it, but just be forewarned that you'll find much to captivate you here.

FOOD CHAIN

Best Search Engine: http://www.directhit.com/
Key Search Term: Food chain

MadSci Network: What Is a Food Chain?
http://madsci.wustl.edu/posts/archives/mar98/889129527.En.r.html
middle school and up

This site gives you a quick notion of what a food chain is, as explained by a zoologist at the University of Minnesota. Set in a question-and-answer format, it's clearly geared toward a student audience. Although it's only five paragraphs long, it's a worthwhile place to begin exploring the subject of food chains and food webs.

"Food Web" (Microsoft Encarta Online Encyclopedia 2000)
http://encarta.msn.com/find/Concise.asp?z=1&pg=2&ti=0177C000
high school and up

As part of *MSN Encarta Encyclopedia*, this article on food webs was written by a professor of wildlife biology. The article explains what ecosystem food chains and food webs are and distinguishes between grazing food webs and detrital food webs. The article also examines how food webs can be broken into trophic (nutritional) levels, and there is an explanation of the energy flow within the different levels of a food web.

The nice thing, as always, about this *Encarta* article is the highlighted links to related articles. For instance, just click on the words "ecosystems" or "ecology" to gain a broader perspective on the subject of food chains.

FORCED MIGRATION

Best Search Engine: http://www.google.com/

Key Search Term: Forced migration

Forced Migration Review
http://www.fmreview.org/
high school and up

This is the Web site of the in-house journal of the Refugee Studies Centre in Oxford, England. Published three times a year in English, Arabic, and Spanish, it is dedicated to providing a forum for debate on the most immediate issues facing refugees and internally displaced people and those working with them. You'll find articles, research abstracts, conference reports, and news items all geared toward uniting the efforts of academics, practitioners, refugees, and others interested in forced migration issues.

Click on "Latest and Back Issues" to access an electronic archive of the journal, complete with descriptions of articles within each edition. It's easy to find topics of interest, but remember that these journals are geared toward academics and professionals and do not offer good introductory resources, but should be consulted for more in-depth research on specific topics.

If you are hunting for information on refugee issues in a specific country, try the "Links" page at this site. There is a link for "Country-Specific Information." Click on it for a page titled "Displacement, Conflict, Countries Hosting Refugees," and you'll find dozens of countries, including Azerbaijan, Burkina Faso, Kosovo, Myanmar, Uzbekistan, and just about every country you can name that has any sort of refugee crisis at hand. The resources for each country vary. You may also find information of interest in the "News/Events/Resources" section of the site.

Brookings—CUNY Graduate Center: Project on Internal Displacement
http://www.brook.edu/dybdocroot/fp/projects/idp/idp.htm
high school and up

The Project on Internal Displacement seeks to improve the international community's response to the global crisis of internal displacement by supporting the mandate of the Representative of the UN Secretary General on Internally Displaced Persons. You'll find presentations, reports, studies, articles, and other resources designed to do just that . . . support the United Nations as it seeks to support those in the international community who are working to help internal refugees.

The table of contents includes a section on documents and resources, which archives policy briefs, books, articles, UN reports, commentary, and foreign policy studies. Another offering of interest is the books that you will find at the bottom of the page. These include "Masses in Flight: The Global Crisis of Internal Displacement," "Exodus Within Borders," and "The Forsaken People: Case Studies in Internal Displacement." Click on any of these links and you'll be taken to a summary of the book, as well as a link for reaching the entire text of the book online.

Other parts of the site include a "What's New" section where you can locate a variety of types of resources on the most recent forced migration topics. At the time we visited, there were quite a few resources on the displacement crisis in Afghanistan. These included press releases, *New York Times* articles, United Nations briefings, and a transcript of an online chat with Roberta Cohen, Senior Fellow at the Brookings Institution.

FORESTS

Best Search Engine: http://www.google.com/
Key Search Terms: Forests + geography

Forest Information Service
http://www.wcmc.org.uk/forest/data/
high school and up

This page from the World Conservation Monitoring Centre Web site is a wonderful resource for global forest information. It's a simple site, where you can research individual countries and see national maps and country-specific statistics, including data on forest diversity and conservation status. The data comes from a variety of national and international sources. You can also access a general world forest map, which might be helpful if you want to visually compare the amount of forest in different parts of the world.

In addition to the forest information, there are other pages on this site that focus on habitats, species, regions, climate change, conventions and agreements, and protected areas. Some of these may also be of interest. Use the menu at the bottom of the page to access these other sections of the site.

National Geographic: Explore the Fantastic Forest
http://www.nationalgeographic.com/forest/
middle school

Here's a fun, interactive forest site from National Geographic. Be your own guide as you learn about a variety of different forest habitats by clicking on the forest map. Take the path and then use the colorful arrows at the bottom of the picture to see what's to the left, center, and right of the path. Interpretive text pops up as you click and make your way through this virtual landscape. And be sure to listen carefully. There are many different sounds in the forest, too.

The home page includes links for downloading Netscape Navigator, Shockwave, and QuickTime VR if you need any of these programs to optimize your listening and viewing experience.

World Wildlife Fund: Forests for Life
http://www.panda.org/forests4life/
middle school and up

Here's a great activist site for kids. You'll like the colorful graphics on this page and the easy access to information about protecting, certifying, and restoring forests. Part of *The Living Planet Campaign* site, the *Forests for Life* page includes the following forest-friendly sections: "Newsroom," "Fieldwork and Policy," "Partnerships," "Publications," and "Photo Galleries." There are also links to "Protect," "Certify," and "Restore" the forest.

Click on "Protect" and you'll read a page called "Forests Are Essential to the Web of Life." From here there's a link to "Help Protect the Forests," which tells you how to become involved in an Internet campaign to save forests and provides descriptions of how consumers, businesses, governments, investors, and forest owners can each make a difference in their own way.

Click on "Certify" to learn all about the forest certification process, which is meant to track where timber comes from to ensure that products made of wood come from forests that are well managed. The Forest Stewardship Council oversees the forest certification process, and you can access their Web site through a link on this page.

If you want to learn about what the World Wildlife Fund (WWF) is doing to restore forests around the world, click on "Restore." You'll also find links to other landscape restoration sites on the Web.

Back at the main menu, try the "Newsroom" for up-to-date articles and press releases on forest issues or go to "Fieldwork and Policy" to read about WWF's involvement in specific forest policy issues.

Forest Types of the World
http://forestry.about.com/library/tree/blwrldx.htm?once = true&
middle school and up

Here's another global forest site, but this one is focused more on tree identification than on conservation, like the *Forest Information Service* site. At this *About.com* site, you'll get maps and data on the world's forests, broken down into sections organized by continent. So you can explore "Africa Forest Types," "Asia Forest Types," "Europe Forest Types," "North and Central America Forest Types," "Oceania Forest Types," and "South America Forest Types."

Once you choose your continent, you'll be given a list of countries and then you'll be able to access information on specific forests within a country. You'll also be given the country location of the five largest forests on the continent. A drop-down menu will give you countries to choose from. If you pick Sweden, for example, you'll get a detailed article on forest resources, management, and products and trade, complete with graphs and maps that illustrate the text. Links to specific geographic information on Sweden's forests, forest cover statistics, and vegetation information are also available.

FRONTIER

Best Search Engine:	http://www.google.com/
Key Search Terms:	Frontier + geography

The Geography of Frontier America
http://www.nal.usda.gov/ric/richs/frontierinventory.htm
middle school and up

You may think of the Old West when you hear the term "frontier," but explore this site and you'll learn that the frontier is not a thing of the past, nor does it refer strictly to an unpopulated landscape. Geographers talk about the technology frontier, the economic frontier of a certain group in society, or the agrarian frontier, for example.

This site from the Frontier Education Center in Ojo Sarco, New Mexico, deals with the American frontier, simply defined as the most remote and sparsely populated regions of the country. It examines this frontier and provides lots of research data on a variety of issues, but before it gets into the nitty-gritty, it explores a more complex definition of the term "frontier."

Under "Definition of Frontier," you'll find sections on "Historical Background," "Using Consensus to Develop a New Definition," "Testing the New Definition," and "Alaska, Hawaii, and the Trust Territories." Once you have read all this on defining the word "frontier," you'll have an excellent introduction.

The sections of the site that follow will take you into more depth on specific frontier issues. These include "Process of Gathering Frontier Data," "Health Resources in the Frontier," "Land Ownership in the Frontier," "The Frontier Economy," and "Projecting the Future." The report is written with the intent of helping the Frontier Education Center advocate for better health care and other resources for those living in the frontier.

FUELS—ALTERNATIVE

Best Search Engine:	http://www.google.com
Key Search Terms:	Alternative + fuels
	Electric + cars
	Ethanol + automobiles

Alternative Fuels Data Center
http://www.afdc.nrel.gov/
high school and up

This U.S. Department of Energy site is the place to look for just about every alternative fuel resource you could dream of. As the site describes itself, "it's a one-stop shop for all your alternative fuel and vehicle information needs." When you see the more than 3,000 documents in its database, the interactive fuel station mapping system, listings of available alternative fuel vehicles, and links to related Web sites, you'll agree.

Use the menu at the left side of the home page to find the pages within the site that you need. Sections include "Alternative Fuels," "Alternative Fuel Vehicles," "Refueling Sites," "Frequently Asked Questions," "Resources and Documents," "What's Now?", "Upcoming Events," "Related Web Sites," and more. The site has an easy-to-use search function, also, in case you have a specific topic you want to research.

If not, try the "Alternative Fuels" section to learn just which fuels are classified as alternative and to read excellent general information on each of these. The alternative fuels include biodiesel, electricity, ethanol, hydrogen, methanol, natural gas, propane, P-series, and solar energy. General stats you'll find on each of these fuels includes a description of what the fuel is, how it's made, the market for it, benefits of using it,

FAQs, research and development on the fuel, and other resources about it. In addition, for each fuel, you'll find a section called "Standards, Codes, and Legislation," "Training and Safety," "Fuel Supply Information," and "Papers, Publications, and Presentations."

If you're interested in vehicles per se, go to "Alternative Fuel Vehicles." You'll find information on buying them, converting your vehicle to alternative fuel, and a grand collection of other miscellaneous resources. There are also a few links to information on advanced technology vehicles.

The "Refueling Site" is just what it sounds like—the place where you can view maps of locales around the country that offer alternative fuel stations. This might be a good thing to know before you head out on a cross-country, or even crosstown, trip in your alternative fuel vehicle.

If you are conducting heavy-duty research, try the "Resources and Documents" page, which includes links to resources about alternative fuel and alternative fuel vehicle (AFV) technologies, programs, funding, regulations, contacts, and more.

> *Alternative Transportation Fuels and Clean Gasoline: Background and Regulatory Issues*
> http://cnie.org/NLE/CRSreports/Air/air-6.cfm
> high school and up

This is an issue brief for Congress on alternative fuels. Consequently, it deals with many of the legal and policy issues concerning fuels, transportation, and pollution. A hyperlink table of contents allows you to jump to any part of the article that interests you. Try reading the summary first. If you want to go more in-depth after that, pick from among the following sections: "Most Recent Developments," "Background and Analysis," "Legislation," "Congressional Hearings," "Reports and Documents," and "Additional Reading." The "Background and Analysis" section contains the most detailed information. You'll find a discussion of vehicle emission controls, alternative fuels and clean vehicles, proposed national energy strategy, and more.

This site is designed purely to relay information, and you can expect the reading to be somewhat dry. But there are goodies to be found, especially if you're interested in the subject from the perspective of the government's involvement.

FUELS—FOSSIL

Best Search Engine: http://www.northernlight.com/
Key Search Terms: Fossil fuels + education

Fossil Energy (U.S. Department of Energy)
http://www.fe.doe.gov/
high school and up

The U.S. Department of Energy's *Fossil Energy* Web site is a must-visit for any student researching fossil energy. The education section of the site is a good place to begin: just click on "For Students" to read an intro to energy and to read units on coal, oil, and natural gas. The education section also sports a stellar glossary of terms and a good frequently asked questions section.

Back at the site's home page, click on "Publications" to access scores of downloadable publications and reports on coal and electric power, petroleum reserves, and oil and gas. You can also go to "R and D Projects" to locate online fact sheets about current and completed fossil energy projects. Finally, the site's frequently updated "In-Depth Profiles" section offers detailed timely articles on interesting topics, such as a new coal-purifying bacteria, the nation's energy oil stockpile, clean coal technology, President Bush's national energy policy, and carbon sequestration.

LinkCenter: Fossil Fuels
http://www.bydesign.com/fossilfuels/links/
high school and up

This site—with its outstanding selection of links to relevant sites—provides a starting point for learning about how North America uses fossil fuels.

The site is organized in a straightforward fashion, with five major sections: "Fossil Fuel," "Oil," "Coal," "Natural Gas," and "Electricity." Click on "Fossil Fuel" to find a general overview page, as well as pages that describe fossil fuels' benefits and environmental aspects. Inside the "Oil," "Coal," "Natural Gas," and "Electricity" sections, you can click on tutorials to learn about each fuel's history, creation, processing, use, transport, and more. Each tutorial offers numerous links to other Web sites with related information.

GEOGRAPHIC INFORMATION SYSTEMS (GIS)

Best Search Engine: http://www.yahoo.com/
Key Search Term: GIS

A Guide to GIS Resources on the Internet
http://sunsite.berkeley.edu/GIS/gisnet.html
high school and up

With a subject as huge and as widely covered on the Web as GIS, you'll definitely want to utilize subject directory sites to narrow your search. This one—*A Guide to GIS Resources on the Internet*—was created by the well-respected Berkeley Digital Library SunSITE, an organization known for building stellar digital collections and services.

This site's vast collection of well-annotated Web sites is organized into four broad divisions: "Directories," "Data Resources," "Tools and Training," and "Other." Under "Directories," you'll find "General Directories," "Special Topics" (conferences, software, etc.), and "Related Topics" (GPS, remote sensing, etc.). Look under "Data Resources" to find "Global Listings," "U.S. Federal Data," "U.S. State Data," and "Country-Specific Data" (such as GIS data for Nepal!). In the "Tools and Training" area, you'll find "Tutorials," "User Assistance," "Tools and Utilities," and "Terminology."

GIS Lounge
http://gislounge.com/
high school and up

GIS Lounge is another great Web site that not only catalogs other GIS-related Web sites, but provides original content as well. No matter what your level of expertise on GIS is—from wet-behind-the-ears to expert—you're sure to find good material for your research here.

If you're a newbie, start in the section called "About GIS." You'll find an expansive answer to the question "What Is GIS?" complemented by comments from other GIS giants, such as the U.S. Geological Survey, the Environmental Systems Research Institute, and the National Aeronautics and Space Administration. The "Learning GIS" section can help you sort out the array of learning approaches, from structured curriculums to distance learning to online tutorials. Other useful sections you'll find at the *GIS Lounge* Web site include "Data," "Events and Conferences," "GPS," "Mobile GIS," "Programming and OS," "Remote Sensing," "Software," "Women in GIS," and "Industry News."

If you're further along in your GIS studies, check out the "Career" section; it's one of the best that you'll find. It includes information on building a career, surviving a GIS job interview, salary surveys, job descriptions, internship and job search sites, GIS recruiters, and reviews of other GIS-related job sites.

GEOLINGUISTICS

Best Search Engine: http://www.google.com
Key Search Terms: Geolinguistics + definition

Geolinguistics
http://georoots.org/Articles/geolinguistics.htm
high school and up

This *GeoRoots* site offers a fascinating and poetic description of geolinguistics, including a detailed discussion of why geologists study words. While the site is focused on geologists, the discussion is equally relevant for geographers. After the introduction, the author goes into some rather detailed comparisons of the word for "earth" in different languages. She uses this to show how geologists learn about the earth from words in much the same way that they learn about the earth from rocks.

Don't expect any hard facts or impressive statistics at this site. This is just an enjoyable and enlightening read.

The Language Geography Connection
http://www.buffalo.edu/reporter/vol29/vol29n22/n4.html
middle school and up

This is an article from the University at Buffalo *Reporter*. It's based on an interview with a geography professor there who is interested in the way language and meaning relate to our understanding of geologic features and spatial concepts. This branch of study within geography, which crosses disciplines with linguistics quite a bit, is just one of the many areas in which language is studied by geographers, but it's an interesting one.

We include this little article because the professor's explanation of his research interests provides such an accessible introduction to the field of geolinguistics. Read it to get a start, then go on to the other sites, which delve deeper into the complexities of the field.

American Dialect Society
http://www.americandialect.org/
high school and up

Studying dialects is a core concern of geolinguists, who try to discern how the language and the geography of a place are interconnected. The Web site of the American Dialect Society is a great place to acquaint yourself with the professional study of dialects. It is, in its own words, "dedicated to the study of the English language in North America, and of other languages, or dialects of other languages, influencing it or influenced by it." Got that?

You'll find the standard sort of offerings for an academic professional organization here. There is an e-mail discussion list you can browse or even join if you want to participate, a section on words of the year, which takes a long hard look at words that cropped up after the September 11, 2001, terrorist attacks (these folks voted "9-11," in its various configurations, as the word of the year), and sections on publications, reference, and news. If you're researching a specific geolinguistic topic, you might try browsing the news section. There is no easy way to search this site.

There's also a list of links to language articles elsewhere, and a list of other Web resources, which is chock-full of great linguist links.

Terralingua
http://www.terralingua.org/
high school and up

If you're ecologically minded and also have an interest in languages, you'll love what Terralingua is up to. Terralingua (TL) is an international, nonprofit organization concerned about the future of the world's biological, cultural, and linguistic diversity. Its focus is to support the perpetuation and continued development of the world's linguistic diversity and explore the connections between linguistic, cultural, and biological diversity through research, applied work, and advocacy.

From the home page, you'll want to choose "Learn about Terralingua," where you can read a detailed description of the organization's structure and philosophy. For your research, check out the "Resource List" on language endangerment, survival, and revitalization. There's also an interesting article on "Indigenous and Minority People's Views of Language." "Current Projects" will inform you about Terralingua's work. And the "Frequently Asked Questions" page addresses such topics as "How many languages are there?", "How many speakers do certain languages have?", and "Where are the languages?" There's also a brief glossary of terms on this page, with terms like "diglossia," "mother tongue," "linguistic genocide," and others.

GEOMORPHOLOGY

Best Search Engine: http://www.metacrawler.com/
Key Search Term: Geomorphology

Virtual Geomorphology
http://main.amu.edu.pl/~sgp/gw/gw.htm
high school and up

This Web site is impossible to ignore if you're researching a subject in geomorphology on the Internet. It contains links to hundreds of pertinent Web sites, encompassing every academic branch of geomorphology. Here's just a sampling of the site's subject index: "Geomorphological Systems," "Theoretical Geomorphology," "Structural Geomorphology," "Dynamic Geomorphology," "Global Changes in Geomorphology," "Biogeomorphology," "Historical Geomorphology," "Planetary Geomorphology," "Regional Geomorphology," "Applied Geomorphology," "GIS in Geomorphology," and more. For each of these subject areas, you'll find a lengthy list of hyperlinks to Web sites.

Geomorphology (Microsoft Encarta Online Encyclopedia 2000)
http://encarta.msn.com/index/conciseindex/69/06913000.
   htm?z = 1&pg = 2&br = 1
high school and up

This *MSN Encarta Encyclopedia* article provides a concise overview of geomorphology, the branch of science that fuses physical geography and geology. Written by a professor of geology, this article offers an introduction to geomorphology, along with sections describing historical geomorphology, process geomorphology, underlying dynamics, and weathering and erosion. As always with *Encarta Encyclopedia* articles, there are links to related articles.

Images Illustrating Principles of Geomorphology (Vanderbilt University)
http://geogweb.berkeley.edu/GeoImages/Wells/wells.html
high school and up

Want to actually see photographs of what other Web sites merely describe? This site is a collection of hundreds of photos illustrating geomorphological phenomena, grouped under headings such as "Alluvial Plain Deposits and Human Transformations of Land Surfaces"; "Dunes"; "Coastal Zones and Volcanoes"; "Glaciers and Valleys"; "Desert Pavement/Varnish and Weathering Features"; "Flood Deposits"; "Coasts and Rain"; "Tidal Flats"; and "Erosion and Rivers."

It's easy to find what you're looking for here; under broad topic headings, there are quick links to individual photographs capturing, say, braided channel and terraces, braid bars with varnish, alluvial fill and terraces, or prehistoric fields and canals.

GEOSPHERE (SEE LITHOSPHERE/GEOSPHERE)

GEOTHERMAL ENERGY

Best Search Engine: http://www.askjeeves.com/
Key Search Term: Geothermal energy

Geothermal Education Office
http://geothermal.marin.org/
grade school and up

The Geothermal Education Office's Web site provides an ideal introduction to geothermal energy. You'll find information geared for both introductory levels and advanced levels, including a glossary of geothermal and related terms, an online slide show, and grade-specific educational packets and materials.

A highlight of the site is the interactive worldwide map, which provides information on how specific countries and geographic regions are using geothermal energy. You'll also find a lengthy list of useful Web sites about geothermal energy.

Geothermal Energy
http://www.eren.doe.gov/RE/geothermal.html
high school and up

The U.S. Department of Energy's Energy Efficiency and Renewable Energy Network (EREN) has created an excellent one-stop resource for information on geothermal energy.

Under "Geothermal Energy Topics," you'll find expansive sections on exploration, drilling, direct use, heat pumps, electricity production, advanced production, and environment. Each of these sections offers introductory material, technical reports, fact sheets, links to related sites, and more. To fine-tune your findings, you can also conduct a site search for specific keywords.

On the home page, you'll also find annotated links to other geothermal organizations and resources, such as federal, state, and local agencies; trade and nonprofit groups; universities and research institutions; international organizations; discussion groups; and newsletters and magazines.

GLACIATION (SEE ALSO GLACIER, ICE AGE)

Best Search Engine: http://www.google.com/
Key Search Terms: Glaciation

Glacier + geomorphology

Ice Core Project (U.S. Geological Survey)
http://id.water.usgs.gov/projects/icecore/
high school and up

The Ice Core Project Web site does a great job of making ice core research quite relevant and interesting to students and the average Joe.

Studying thousand-year-old ice to determine what the earth's climate was like in the past, researchers then apply that knowledge to modern global climactic change research.

Click on the U.S. Geological Survey (USGS) fact sheet, "Global Ice Core Research: Understanding and Applying Environmental Records of the Past," to get an overview of the subject. For info on specific glaciers that USGS scientists have studied, such as the Galena Creek Rock Glacier in Wyoming or the Inilchek Glacier in Kyrgyzstan, click on those links. There are also excellent links to other good glacier studies Web sites, and e-mail links to the scientists conducting this project.

GLACIER (SEE ALSO GLACIATION, ICE AGE)

Best Search Engine: http://www.northernlight.com/

Key Search Terms: Glacier + education

Glacier
http://www.glacier.rice.edu/
high school and up

You'd be hard pressed to find a better general educational Web source on glaciers than this one. From the home page, you can enter the following sections: "Introduction," "Expedition," "Global Connections," "Weather," "Ice," and "Oceans." To answer most of your questions about glaciers, you'll want to visit the "Ice" section. Here, you'll find information on ice shapes and sizes, ice movement, glaciers' effect on the landscape, the Antarctic ice sheet, interglacial cycles, and the Ice Age.

For information focusing on Antarctica, visit the "Weather" and "Oceans" sections. You may also want to check out the site's annotated "Polar Resources" and extensive "Bibliography" sections.

All about Glaciers (National Snow and Ice Data Center)
http://nsidc.org/glaciers/
high school and up

This excellent site from the National Snow and Ice Data Center (NSIDC) is broken into broad sections, making it an ideal place to begin your research.

Look under "Data and Science" to find data and imagery, publications, project links, and relevant organizations. Inside "General Information," you'll discover a question and answer section, glossary, gallery of historic photos, quick facts, and more. For the latest media coverage related to glaciers and glacier research, go to "Glacier News." Click on the handy, alphabetized "Site Map" for pinpointing specific information.

GLOBALIZATION

Best Search Engine: http://www.scout.cs.wisc.edu/index.html

Key Search Term: Globalization

Berkeley Labor Guides: Globalization
http://www.iir.berkeley.edu/~iir/library/blg/global.html
high school and up

For a topic as far reaching and widely debated as globalization, you can use all the research help you can get. This outstanding directory from the Institute of Industrial Relations Library, University of California, Berkeley provides a selective list of key resources on this topic. Here, you'll find a collection of links (many of them annotated) to relevant publications, videos, organizations challenging globalization, organizations supporting globalization, policy-making institutions, and Web directories on globalization. Be sure to make this site one of your first research stops.

Center for Economic Policy and Research: Globalization
http://www.cepr.net/globalization/maihome.html
high school and up

The Center for Economic and Policy Research (CEPR) was established to promote democratic debate on important economic and social issues. The issue of globalization merits its own section at the CEPR Web site, as do issues such as social security, intellectual property and patents, and the stock market.

Within the "Globalization" section, you can access the full text of recent briefings and publications from a range of sources. (Hot tip: In the list of publications, be sure to look for CEPR's excellent "Globalization Primer.") For specialized aspects of your research, you may want to click on "International Monetary Fund/World Bank," "World Trade Organization (WTO)," "Multilateral Agreement on Investment (MAI)," or the "Free Trade Area of the Americas (FTAA)" to read background information, reports and articles, overview materials and analysis, and more.

GLOBAL WARMING (SEE ALSO CLIMATE, GREENHOUSE EFFECT, ICE AGE, OZONE LAYER)

Best Search Engine: http://www.shell.rmi.net/~michaelg/

Key Search Terms: Global warming

Climate change

Environmental Protection Agency: Global Warming
http://www.epa.gov/globalwarming/
high school and up

The Environmental Protection Agency (EPA) has created a comprehensive resource for gathering both general information and scientific data on global warming. We're not the first ones to notice it—the site has received awards and recognition from such places as Lightspan's *StudyWeb*, the *Scout Report*, the Institute for Scientific Information, and *USA Today*.

The site is handily broken into four broad sections: "Climate," "Emissions," "Impacts," and "Actions." In the "Climate" section, you'll find information on climate trends, atmospheric changes, and future climate. The "Emissions" section provides info on greenhouse gases, emissions inventory reports, and sinks, and offers detailed emissions data and links for international, national, state, local, and individual levels. As you'd expect, the "Impacts" section delves extensively into how global warming affects health, water resources, polar regions, mountains, forests, rangelands, deserts, nontidal wetlands, coastal zones, agriculture, fisheries, birds, national parks, states, and other nations. The "Actions" section looks at how various industries, countries, and governmental agencies are working to lessen global warming.

In addition to the major sections described above, this site has other resources for you to draw on, such as online greenhouse gas calculators, case studies of greenhouse gas emissions reduction projects, position papers, and conference reports.

Climate Change Campaign
http://www.panda.org/climate/
high school and up

The spotlight here at this World Wildlife Federation (WWF) site is on climate change and global warming. To educate yourself, click on the subject heading "Causes," "Impacts," or "Solutions." Each of these sections contains excellent information, with highlighted text linked to more detailed data.

The "Newsroom" section is a good resource for WWF's timely press releases on climate change and related events in the news. For other publications, go to "Publications," where you can access publications prepared for WWF by independent scientists and researchers. Also, be sure to check out the section called "Cutting Edge," with its bimonthly climate change news reports and links to related sites. For background information and photos from an international summit held in Hague, Holland, in November 2000, click on "Climate Summit."

Hot Planet: The Weather Channel Special Report
http://www.weather.com/newscenter/specialreports/hotplanet/index.html
high school and up

The home page for the Weather Channel's *Hot Planet* site provides an evenhanded overview of the issue of global warming. From here, you can spring off into the sections "Man vs. Nature," "Accurate Predictions," and "Possible Impact" to explore the topic in detail. Throughout the site, you'll find sound factual data, along with compelling observations and quotes by scientists and researchers.

If you're looking for a current assessment of global warming in a specific region of the country, look no further. The *Hot Planet* site provides a link to a recent federal study—the *National Assessment of the Potential Consequences of Climate Variability*—conducted by a consortium of experts from government, universities, industry and nongovernmental organizations. Here, you can explore the research results by reading the full assessment report or by clicking on an interactive U.S. map.

GREENHOUSE EFFECT (SEE ALSO GLOBAL WARMING, ICE AGE)

Best Search Engine: http://www.metacrawler.com/

Key Search Term: Greenhouse effect

The Warming of the Earth (Woods Hole Research Center)
http://www.whrc.org/globalwarming/warmingearth.htm
high school and up

This online guide to global warming is organized into six sections: "The Greenhouse Effect," "Scientific Evidence," "The Culprits," "Potential Outcomes," "What the Skeptics Don't Tell You," and "The Kyoto Protocol." Each section briefly explains an aspect of global warming and includes links to other resources.

Under "The Greenhouse Effect," you'll find a scientific (*not* a dumbed down) overview of the effect greenhouse gases have on the environment. Read the "Potential Outcomes" section, which draws largely on a report by the Intergovernmental Panel on Climate Change (IPCC), for information on changes to sea level, temperature, hydrologic cycle, human health, food production, and ecosystems.

Greenhouse, Green Planet (NOVA Online)
http://www.pbs.org/wgbh/nova/ice/greenhouse.html
high school and up

This page—part of NOVA's *Cracking the Ice Age* site—explains how greenhouse gases trap the sun's heat on our planet, the role each gas plays, and how modern society may be enhancing the greenhouse effect. It's a limited overview, but a worthwhile site to visit early in your research efforts.

GREEN REVOLUTION

Best Search Engine: http://www.looksmart.com/
Key Search Term: Green revolution

Lessons from the Green Revolution
http://www.fao.org/docrep/003/w2612e/w2612e6a.htm
college level

Written by the Food and Agricultural Organization of the United Nations (FAO) for the World Food Summit in 1996, this site's text provides crystal clear information about the green revolution.

Be sure to read the "Executive Summary," which provides a wonderfully concise overview of the green revolution's history, the present-day situation, and surrounding issues. You'll also find sections that focus on improving food security for the poor, productivity objectives, sustainability objectives, target areas for the green revolution, and new tools in the green revolution.

The Green Revolution
http://www.orst.edu/instruction/bi301/greenrev.htm
high school and up

Thanks to this Web site, you'll be privy to the study guide and discussion notes for an excellent 300-level biology course (Human Impacts on the Ecosystem) at Oregon State University. This portion of the site focuses on the green revolution and offers information on history, trends in acreage and yields, resource limitations (i.e., water, land), fossil fuels and agriculture, and problems with green revolution–style agriculture (i.e., human population, diminished crop diversity, fertilizers).

You can also access other topics covered in the course, such as pesticides in agriculture, land degradation related to agriculture, and prospects for sustainable agriculture. In addition, there's a handy link to the Leopold Center for Sustainable Agriculture, based at Iowa State University, where you'll find more information on research in sustainable agriculture.

GROSS DOMESTIC PRODUCT (SEE ALSO GROSS NATIONAL PRODUCT)

Best Search Engine: http://www.google.com

Key Search Terms: Gross domestic product + definition

The State of the Economy
http://www.harcourtcollege.com/econ/state.html
middle school and up

To get the current macroeconomic indicators, try this easy-to-read site from Harcourt College Publishers. You'll find national income, personal income and gross savings, labor market, price index, exchange rates, and much more. The topic at hand, gross domestic product, is the first statistic listed under national income.

This site won't interpret or analyze the figures for you, but it will get you started by providing the raw numbers. For more in-depth research, try the sites listed below.

White House Economics Statistics Briefing Room
http://www.whitehouse.gov/fsbr/output.html
high school and up

The *White House Statistics Briefing Room*, part of the White House Web site, provides up-to-date stats with fancy charts and slick graphics. You can find just about any economic statistic you want if you know how to use the site. For gross domestic product (GDP), you have to go to the part of the site called "Output." (The URL provided takes you directly to "Output.") And you'll get a basic description for the most recent quarter. In other words, the site doesn't give you the exact dollar figure for gross domestic product. Rather, it tells you how much it increased or decreased compared to the previous quarter. It also provides a chart showing the changes in GDP between 1995 and 2001.

For the hard-core dollar amounts for GDP or any of the other indicators provided here, click on the statistic and you will be taken to the Bureau of Economic Analysis, which is not a pretty or slick site but which does contain all the background numbers that went into calculating the percentages you see on the White House page.

FactMonster: Gross National Product
http://www.factmonster.com/ce6/bus/A0821928.html
middle school and up

You can always rely on *FactMonster* for good accessible definitions, and although this is officially the *FactMonster's* entry on gross national product, you'll find the definition for gross domestic product embedded in the definition for gross national product. So kill two birds with one stone, and learn about both.

GROSS NATIONAL PRODUCT (SEE ALSO GROSS DOMESTIC PRODUCT)

Best Search Engine: http://www.google.com/

Key Search Term: Gross national product

FactMonster: Gross National Product
http://www.factmonster.com/ce6/bus/A0821928.html
middle school and up

You can always rely on *FactMonster* for good accessible definitions. You'll learn exactly what gross national product is and how it relates to gross domestic product. The entry here also provides a link to the International Bank for Reconstruction and Development, which in 1995 created a new system for measuring total national wealth based on the value of natural and mineral resources. This would make interesting further reading if your research relates to the topic of national wealth.

GULF STREAM

Best Search Engine: http://www.ixquick.com/

Key Search Term: Gulf stream

The Gulf Stream
http://fermi.jhuapl.edu/student/phillips/
high school and up

Despite its clunky design, this is a useful reference site, created by a U.S. Naval Academy midshipman and a researcher at Johns Hopkins University's Applied Physics Laboratory.

The Gulf Stream topics covered in surprising detail include Gulf Stream history (sixteenth century through the twentieth century), climate and weather influence, eddies and rings, instruments for Gulf Stream observations, satellite observations, and naval applications.

The Gulf Stream Voyage
http://k12science.ati.stevens-tech.edu/curriculum/gulfstream/
middle school and up

This site offers an online educational project utilizing both real-time data and primary source materials to understand the science and history of the Gulf Stream. You'll find project instructions, eight activities using real-time data, links to reference material and current satellite images—all designed to help you investigate this particular ocean current and how it affects the Atlantic Ocean.

Under "Reference Material," you'll find a list of links to sites with basic information about the Gulf Stream and ocean currents, online projects about the Gulf Stream, online databases, and more.

The Gulf Stream
http://coolspace.gsfc.nasa.gov/outreach/activity/gulf.html
high school

Although very limited in scope, this site was developed as a classroom launching point for study and research activities about the Gulf Stream. It offers a research project designed for grades 9–12. You'll find background info on the Gulf Stream, links to satellite images, and suggested study activities.

HEALTH

Best Search Engine: http://www.google.com/
Key Search Terms: Health + geography

FirstGov for Kids: Health
http://www.kids.gov/k_health.htm
middle school

If you're working on developing your own research interest within the field of health geography, you might find it useful to take a look at this collection of annotated links to health sites designed for kids. There's a wide range of topics to explore here, and you'll find the descriptions of links useful in helping you decide which ones to check out.

There are Web sites that deal with drugs, including alcohol and tobacco, environmental health issues, mining safety, food safety, and many other health issues.

Just Another Medical Geography Page
http://www.geocities.com/Tokyo/Flats/7335/medical_geography.htm
high school and up

You'd never know from the deprecating title of this Web site what a stellar resource it is! *Just Another Medical Geography Page* is a comprehensive resource containing, in Part 1, a nice introduction to the field of medical (or health) geography, a section on the "Geography of Disease," and a section called "Examples of Current Research," which gives information about some of the most popular areas of research within the field of medical geography. All of this text comes complete with hyperlinks to sites that discuss specific issues in more detail. You'll find links to the World Health Organization, to pages on medical cartography, to a page on someone's research into the spread of wildlife rabies, and many other fascinating topics and institutions.

At the bottom of the page follow the link for Part 2, "Geography of Health." Again you will be given an excellent overview, as well as sections with more detailed information on "Human Health and Environmental Restructuring" and "The Geography of Health Care." Links take you to pages on ozone layer depletion, low birth weight babies, and to an exhibit on hospital discrimination in Detroit in the 1950s, among other topics.

Part 3 is on "GIS, Remote Sensing, and Health," and you can access that by clicking on the link at the bottom of Part 2. Hyperlinks on this page take you on an exploration of the use of GIS in research on Lyme disease in northeastern United States and Filariasis in the Nile Delta. You'll also find links to many useful articles and institutions.

HEMISPHERE

Best Search Engine: http://www.google.com/
Key Search Term: Hemisphere

The Equator, Hemispheres, Tropic of Cancer, and Tropic of Capricorn
http://geography.about.com/library/misc/blequator.htm
middle school and up

This concise *About.com* article explains in accessible terms the imaginary lines that crisscross the earth, dividing it into four separate hemispheres—north, south, east, and west. In addition to learning how these lines are determined and what their significance is, you'll run across links to other *About.com* pages on such related topics as climate, solstices, the international date line, longitude, and latitude.

HINDUISM

Best Search Engine: http://www.google.com/

Key Search Term: Hinduism

Hindu Resource Center
http://www.hindunet.org/
high school and up

There's a lot of information (and clutter) to sort through here in order to find the good stuff. But there's a lot of good stuff here, and we'll do our darndest to explain to you how to find it. Begin under the "Channels" section by clicking on "Hindu Resources." Here, you'll find frequently asked questions about Hinduism, a vast resource center on every aspect of Hindu life, and introductions to Hindu Dharma, Jain Dharma, Sikh Dharma, and Buddha Dharma.

From this point, go ahead and delve into the "Hindu Universe Resource Center," which contains information on Hindu arts; scriptures; history; gods, sages, and gurus; customs; social and contemporary issues; and—unbelievably—quite a bit more.

A Study of Hindu Religion
http://freeweb.pdq.net/bnaiyer/sadhana.html
high school and up

If you can get past the psychedelic look of this Web site, you'll discover a wealth of research information. The site offers an introductory course in Hindu religion in which you'll learn about Hindu religion, philosophy, devotional practice, and the four yogas.

There's also a more comprehensive tutorial offered at the site for those of you looking for more in-depth information. This tutorial is divided into seven chapters that cover the principles and practice of the faith, the essentials of Hindu traditions, a historical overview, and information on religious texts, rituals, customs, traditions, and conflicts.

Hinduism
http://www.bbc.co.uk/religion/religions/hinduism/history/index.shtml
middle school and up

This BBC site provides a stellar introduction to the long and complex history of Hinduism. The coverage is comprehensive, beginning with prehistoric religion in India—Hinduism dates back as far as 3000 B.C.E.—and continuing through preclassical religion, when the Vedas were written, the rise of Jainism and Buddhism, the arrival of Islam, and more. There's even a section on the International Society of Krishna Consciousness. In addition to the history, you can read about Hinduism beliefs, customs, worship, and holy days, too. If you just want a simple overview, go to "Features," where you'll find "The Bare Essentials of Hinduism."

History of India: Hinduism and Transition (600 B.C.–322 B.C.)
http://www.historyofindia.com/hinduism.html
middle school and up

This page on Hinduism is part of a larger *History of India* site, which means that you can easily expand your research by following links to other parts of the site. Click on the question, "What Is Hinduism—Religion or Culture?" at the bottom of the page to explore this pervasive question.

HISTORICAL GEOGRAPHY

Best Search Engine: http://www.google.com/

Key Search Term: Historical geography

T-O Map
http://geography.about.com/library/weekly/aa082597.htm
high school and up

Historical geography is concerned with individual and collective understandings, experiences, and interpretations of places in the past. As a result it is interested in reconstructing the geographies of places, including mental and material cultural geographies. Historic maps figure prominently in the research of geographers researching within this discipline. And the T-O map is one of the common historical maps geographers study when their research involves the Middle Ages.

The highly stylized T-O map was developed in the Middle Ages and represented the world view of many people at that time. It's a very simple one-dimensional circle, representing the known universe, with the universe divided into three continents—Asia, Europe, and Africa. Look for yourself at the drawing of a T-O map on this page and read the brief but enlightening article. If your research involves the Middle Ages, when the church dominated all aspects of life, including cartography, you'll not want to overlook T-O maps, but even if it doesn't you'll probably be fascinated by what the T-O map tells us about human perspectives and how they evolve.

Historical Atlas of the Twentieth Century
http://users.erols.com/mwhite28/20centry.htm
high school and up

Historical Atlas of the Twentieth Century is a huge and wonderful historical maps site divided into four main sections—"The Basics," "General Trends," "Specific Places and Events," and "Sources." If your area of interest lies within the twentieth century, and it's something that could be mapped, then you're likely to find it here.

Under "The Basics," you can find out how to best use the site and explore a section called "Keeping the Turn of the Century in Perspective," which contains such rankings as the best people, events, and achievements, of the twentieth century, as well as rankings for the most overrated in these categories.

"General Trends" has maps that show socioeconomic trends, populations, wars, art, and religion, among other subjects. "Specific Places and Events," which is likely to be your focus, contains links to maps and information on Europe, North and South America, Asia, Africa, and "International Relations," which contains maps on the First and Second World War, the Cold War, natural disasters, and world governing bodies like the United Nations.

These are beautiful maps and they don't take forever to load, so you can browse until your heart's content and your brain has a grasp on what China looked like during the era of the warlords, for example, or what political violence in America in the twentieth century looks like when you put it on a map.

HOUSING

| Best Search Engine: | http://www.library.uu.nl/geosource/ |
| Best Subject Directory: | Academic subjects > Urban Geography, Housing, and Planning |

Housing Information Gateway
http://www.colorado.edu/plan/housing-info/menu0.html
high school and up

This site serves as a gateway to other Web sites with housing resources. You'll find it particularly useful for research on international housing issues. Simply click on "List by Location" to find housing resources specific to continents and countries. For instance, under "Latin America," we were able to quickly locate descriptions of six organizations working on housing issues in Latin America. You'll also find the site's list of relevant listservs and conferences quite helpful.

Habitat for Humanity
http://www.habitat.org/how/why.html
high school and up

Habitat for Humanity has long been an advocate of affordable, safe housing. You might be surprised, however, at the wealth of solid research data provided on its Web site. This page features articles and statistics exploring the need for housing, as well as links to other organizations addressing housing and homelessness issues.

You'll find well-written articles from a variety of documented sources, recent U.S. and international statistics on housing, and government reports and documents.

HUMAN GEOGRAPHY (SEE CULTURAL GEOGRAPHY)

HUNGER (SEE ALSO AGRICULTURE, SUSTAINABLE DEVELOPMENT)

Best Search Engine: http://www.google.com/
Key Search Terms: Hunger + education

FoodFirst
http://www.foodfirst.org/
high school and up

Food First/The Institute for Food and Development Policy is a nonprofit think tank focusing on issues of hunger, food, poverty, agriculture, trade, and rural development. Its Web site offers a number of excellent tools to help with your research on hunger. Start with the "Resource Library," where you'll find links to organizations and research resources on the Web, broken into the categories of "Hunger/Poverty/Food Security," "Human Rights," "Environment," "Labor," "Social and Economic Justice," "Sustainable Agriculture," "Biotech," and "International Development/Globalization."

Another worthwhile resource here is the "Media Quik Stop," with press release, op-eds, interviews, and more. To find carefully researched analyses on hunger issues and excellent action plans, visit the "Take Action" section.

Hunger Notes (World Hunger Education Service)
http://www.worldhunger.org/
high school and up

Hunger Notes, a Web site created by the World Hunger Education Service, is a good place to turn for basic information on hunger and poverty issues. The organization aims at integrating ethical, religious, social, economic, political, and scientific perspectives on hunger and poverty. At the Web site, you'll find useful sections—with source material and links to other sites—on Africa, Asia, the United States, and "Global." There's also a forum for relevant book reviews, and a section focusing on "Nutrition, Health, and Population."

United Nations World Food Programme
http://www.wfp.org/index2.html
high school and up

The World Food Programme of the United Nations (WFP) is a good one-stop resource on world hunger. The menu at the left side of the page contains "About WFP," "Newsroom," "Appeals," "How to Help," "Operations," "Policies," and more. On the right you'll see an "Alert" column with information on immediate crises. At the time of our visit, these included "Afghan Crisis: Relief to Recovery," "Hunger Warning for Eastern and Southern Africa," and "Bangladesh Slums: Eyewitness."

There's also a tiny little map of the world on the home page, where you can click on a continent to access hunger information for that region of the world. The country briefs for Asia included information on Afghanistan, Armenia, Azerbaijan, Bangladesh, Bhutan, Cambodia, China, DPR Korea, and East Timor. Each country brief contains an overview, a description of WFP activities in the country, a list of links to other resources on the country, and contact information for the World Food Programme in that country.

If you're interested in helping with food relief, check the "Appeals" section of the site, which will tell you how you can contribute money through the flash donor alert initiative. It also contains information on current shortfalls and projected needs.

Center on Hunger and Poverty
http://www.centeronhunger.org/
high school and up

Here's an excellent site for information on hunger within the United States. Established in 1990, the Center on Hunger and Poverty conducts research and policy analysis, disseminates analytic information on poverty and hunger, carries out education initiatives, and provides assistance to policy makers and organizations.

For national facts and figures, state data, and a guide to recent studies on food insecurity and hunger, tap into the center's "Food Security Institute" (FSI) section. Here, you'll also find information on how food security is measured by the U.S. Department of Agriculture. Within "FSI Publications," you can download relevant reports and summaries. To find more information, look under "Resource Links" for links to other national hunger organizations, sites with food security information, and asset development resources (i.e., academic and policy research/advocacy).

HUNTING AND GATHERING

Best Search Engine: http://www.askjeeves.com/

Key Search Terms: Pastoral

Hunting and gathering

Agricultural Revolution: Hunting and Gathering
http://www.wsu.edu/gened/learn-modules/top_agrev/3-Hunting-and-
    Gathering/hunt-gathering1.html
high school and up

This site, a learning module on the agricultural revolution, will supply you with a basic grasp of hunting and gathering. Intended for students in a freshman world civilizations course at Washington State University, the seven topics covered in this module provide information to help you understand the sharp contrast between the ancestral way of life (hunting and gathering) and sedentary agriculture. Along with the page specifically focusing on hunting and gathering, you'll have access to topics such as "Earth as a Solar-Driven System," "Soil: The Fundamental Resource of a Civilization," "Emergence of Agriculture," "Technology," "Domestication," and "Social Consequences."

Hunting and Gathering (Mesa Community College)
http://www.mc.maricopa.edu/academic/cult_sci/anthro/lost_tribes/hg_ag/
    hg1.html
high school and up

Here's an excellent Web site, created by an instructor of a course called "Buried Cities, Lost Tribes." Drawing judiciously from other academic Web sites, this site has a somewhat meandering layout that takes some time to comb through.

You'll find information on the social systems within a hunting and gathering community, their knowledge of plants and food sources, division of labor between the sexes, egalitarianism vs. individualism, and child-to-adult ratio and other population characteristics. Be sure to click on a link to "Lifestyles of Hunters and Gatherers" to visit a University of California, Davis Web site, with an outstanding list of suggested readings and further links to case studies of contemporary hunters and gatherers (i.e., Aborigines in Australia, Kung Bushmen in southern Africa, Inuit of northern America).

HURRICANE

Best Search Engine:	http://www.ixquick.com/
Key Search Terms:	Hurricane
	Hurricane + education

Hurricanes (National Oceanic and Atmospheric Administration)
http://hurricanes.noaa.gov/
high school and up

There's no question about where to look on the Web for comprehensive hurricane information. It's right here at the National Oceanic and Atmospheric Administration's (NOAA) National Hurricane Center.

You'll find daily color satellite imagery; news releases and a news archive; and hot topics such as "Hurricane Basics," "Storm Names," "Tracking Models," "Hurricane Hunters," "Hurricane Dynamics," and a chronological list of hurricanes. You can also access popular NOAA products, including "Story Ideas," "Frequently Asked Questions," "Preparedness Guide," and a "Media Center." Each resource at this site goes above and beyond to provide you with accurate data and information and relevant Web links.

Hurricane Hunters
http://www.hurricanehunters.com/welcome.htm
high school and up

True hurricane buffs are behind this lively and educational site. Created by the 53rd Weather Reconnaissance Squadron (better known as the Hurricane Hunters of the Air Force Reserves), this site follows the folks who fly airplanes right into the eyes of hurricanes.

You'll find information about the current and past hurricane and winter storm seasons, experience a cyberflight into the eye of a hurricane, learn how to read and interpret weather reconnaissance aircraft reports, access fact sheets and frequently asked questions, and utilize the "Homework Help" and "Links" sections. You can also use the "Ask a Hurricane Hunter" section to ask your own questions and read previous questions and answers.

Hurricane Information Guide (USA Today)
http://www.usatoday.com/weather/whur0.htm
high school and up

Created and frequently updated by *USA Today*, this site provides excellent information on hurricanes. Its particular focus, as you might expect from a daily newspaper, is on the current hurricane season. Within those sections, you'll find predictions and wrap-ups (depending upon the season) and other up-to-date news. There's also a nice collection of satellite images (visible, infrared, and water vapor) and safety and preparation guides. Click on the section called "Hurricane Basics" to learn about hurricanes' causes, life cycles and surges, and to see an animation of hurricane development.

HYDROLOGIC CYCLE

Best Search Engine: http://www.northernlight.com/

Key Search Term: Hydrologic cycle

The Hydrologic Cycle
http://ceed.wsu.edu/watersheds/Watershed_Education/hydrologic_cycle.
   htm
high school and up

This page is part of the Center for Environmental Education's module on watersheds. In the educational module, you learn about watersheds, the hydrologic cycle, groundwater, free flowing rivers, stream and river classifications, erosion, and biomonitoring. The section on the hydrologic cycle is an in-a-nutshell explanation of the cycle's four parts: precipitation, runoff, evapotranspiration, and storage.

The Hydrologic Cycle (Online Meteorology Guide)
http://ww2010.atmos.uiuc.edu/(Gh)/guides/mtr/hyd/home.rxml
high school and up

The University of Illinois's excellent series of online instructional modules pulls it off again. As a section within the *Meteorology Guide,* the "Hydrologic Cycle" module is organized into the following topics: "Earth's Water Budget," "Evaporation," "Condensation," "Transport," "Precipitation," "Groundwater," "Transpiration," "Runoff," and "Summary and Examples."

The site is well designed, with excellent diagrams and animations interspersed throughout the text. Thanks to a toolbar on the left side of the page, the site is easy to navigate. Highlighted text link to a glossary of terms and relevant case studies. And unlike other online courses that cater to students with lightening-fast computers, it's available in both graphics and text-only versions.

The Hydrologic Cycle
http://csd.unl.edu/esic/pamphlets/hydro-cycle/hydro-cycle.html
middle school and up

This little page contains a nice overview of the world's hydrologic cycle with a graphic illustration. It describes the cycle as a natural machine, a constantly running distillation and pumping system. It contains lots of fun facts about water and where it goes, as well as a table of water equivalents in case you just happen to need to know how much a gallon of water weighs, for example, or how many acre-feet of water per day is produced when you have a rate of flow of 1,000 gallons per minute. Could be handy.

HYDROSPHERE

Best Search Engine: http://www.google.com/

Key Search Terms: Hydrosphere + geography

The Four Spheres
http://geography.about.com/library/misc/blsphere.htm
middle school and up

This brief *About.com* article defines earth's four spheres for you—the atmosphere, lithosphere, biosphere, and, yes, the hydrosphere. Get the basics and then proceed to the following sites for more in-depth research.

Earth's Water
http://ga.water.usgs.gov/edu/mearth.html
middle school and up

This page from the United States Geological Survey *Water Science for Schools* site is chock-full of things you might want to know about the earth's hydrosphere. Click on the following sections to take you on a comprehensive tour: "Where Is Earth's Water?", "How Much Water Is There?", "The Water Cycle," "Water on the Earth's Surface," "Water in the Ground," "Rain," and "Glaciers and Icecaps." This site doesn't miss much.

Head back to the home page for information on "Water Basics," "Special Topics," a "Glossary of Water Terms," an "Activity Center," and more.

The Sea
http://www.the-sea.org/main.htm
high school and up

Although this is a personal page, written and maintained by a sea admirer, it contains reliable information that is presented in a pleasing format. One quirk, however, is that you will need to use the menu at the bottom of the page to access any pages once you leave the home page. It's a tiny little menu, but it's your ticket to lots of great info on the world's oceans.

Try "Oceans Map" where you can click on an ocean to read a detailed but accessible description of the ocean's geography. There's also a table that gives you all the seas connected to each ocean.

Other sections of this site include "Sea Creatures," "Hurricanes," "Currents and Waves," "Tides," and "Ocean Links" for other related Web sites.

NOAA Ocean Explorer
http://oceanexplorer.noaa.gov/
high school and up

Although the *Ocean Explorer* site is only in its first year, it already houses an impressive collection of information on the National Oceanic and Atmospheric Administration's (NOAA) major ocean exploration efforts.

Here, you can follow ocean explorations in near real-time, learn about ocean exploration technologies, observe remote marine areas through multimedia technology, review NOAA's 200-year history of ocean exploration, and discover additional NOAA resources in a virtual library.

To learn about NOAA's recent ocean expeditions, go to the "Explorations" section. Here, you can read each expedition's mission plan, summaries and observations, daily updates, and more. Visit the site's "Gallery" for a collection of images, audio, and video. The "Technology" section offers photos and descriptions of the various technologies used in ocean exploration.

How NASA Studies Water
http://kids.mtpe.hq.nasa.gov/water.htm
middle school and up

You may think only of space exploration when you think of the National Aeronautics and Space Administration (NASA), but NASA's work involves studying and monitoring all aspects of the earth as well, including earth's water. This cool site will explain to you how NASA missions collect data on the earth's global water cycle and connect you with three different sites that each involve studying the hydrosphere.

Links will take you to the SeaWifs Project, which is designed to provide earth scientists with information on earth's fertility, the Tropical Rainfall Measuring Mission, which does just what it says—measures rainfall in the tropics—and an El Niño site that will tell you about just how El Niño affects you and why it's important.

Both the SeaWifs Project and the Rainfall Measuring Mission pages contain lots of in-depth information on the specific bodies of water being studied as well as specifics about the NASA equipment and technology being used.

ICE AGE (SEE ALSO GLACIATION, GLACIER, GLOBAL WARMING, GREENHOUSE EFFECT)

Best Search Engine: http://www.dogpile.com/

Key Search Terms: Ice Age

                       Ice Age + education

Ice Ages
http://www.museum.state.il.us/exhibits/ice_ages/
middle school and up

This online museum exhibit about the Ice Age gives you a glimpse of what the midwestern United States might have looked like over 16,000 years ago.

To use this site, you can simply click and wander through the exhibits to find out more about the environments, plants, and animals of the midwestern United States at that time. However, the most expedient way to use the site for research is to click on the "List of Topics" page. Here, you can select the portion of the tour that's pertinent to your research. You'll see that there are separate sections for late Pleistocene landscapes, plants, animals, and extinctions. The emphasis throughout the site is on the Midwest, which helps to bring the notion of the Ice Age into an interesting perspective (especially for those of us who have spent time in the flyover states and seen nary a dinosaur).

NOVA Online: Cracking the Ice Age
http://www.pbs.org/wgbh/nova/ice/
middle school and up

As always, the PBS NOVA series has done a good job of deciphering science into text, photographs, and graphics that we can all understand.

The most in-depth section of this site is entitled "Big Chill," where you'll find a long article discussing the cyclical pattern of major global cooling periods—or ice ages—dating back 600 million years ago to pre-Cambrian times. The article explores theories for these climate changes. The section called "Greenhouse—Green Planet" explores the greenhouse effect, and "Continents" examines the movement of continents and how it can be measured.

Under "Links," you'll find some other excellent Web resources, broken into topic areas that include "Ice Age and Early Climate," "Ice Core Drilling," "Geology of the Himalayas," "General Climatology," and "Plant Fossil Guides."

Glacier
http://www.glacier.rice.edu/
high school and up

You'd be hard pressed to find a better general educational Web source on glaciers than this one. And if your subject is the Ice Age, you certainly need to know about glaciers. From the home page, you can enter the following sections: "Introduction," "Expedition," "Global Connections," "Weather," "Ice," and "Oceans." To answer most of your questions about glaciers, you'll want to visit the "Ice" section. Here, you'll find information on ice shapes and sizes, ice movement, glaciers' effect on the landscape, the Antarctic ice sheet, interglacial cycles, and the ice ages.

Once you've familiarized yourself with glaciers, click on "What Causes Ice Ages?" to get the bigger picture. This is a great overview of earth's different ice ages. You'll find information on the land at the Poles, tectonic events, Earth's orbit, and other factors that combine to produce or reduce glaciation.

For information focusing on Antarctica, visit the "Weather" and "Oceans" sections. You may also want to check out the site's annotated "Polar Resources" and extensive "Bibliography" sections.

IGNEOUS PROCESSES

Best Search Engine:	http://www.google.com/
Key Search Terms:	Igneous processes
	Volcanoes

How Volcanoes Work
http://www.geology.sdsu.edu/how_volcanoes_work/
high school and up

If you're into volcanoes, you probably already know about this grand site from San Diego State University's Department of Geological Sciences. It describes the science behind volcanoes and volcanic processes and is intended as an educational resource. In fact, it's intended for a fairly advanced student, but the material is certainly accessible to those without much background. Just navigate through the site contents sequentially, taking the links in the order that they are provided so that you don't miss crucial background information.

"Eruption Dynamics," "Volcanic Landforms," "Eruption Products," "Eruption Types," "Historical Eruptions," and "Volcanism on Other Worlds" are your main areas for exploration. There's also a volcano crossword, volcano links, and more than 250 volcano images throughout the site, including a volcano animation if you have QuickTime installed.

Expect detailed academic information here, and remember that if you just want some basic information, you should start at the beginning of a section and read from there. At the end of each section, you can test yourself with a handy quiz.

Types of Volcanoes
http://volcano.und.nodak.edu/vwdocs/vwlessons/volcano_types/index.
   html
middle school and up

This section of the colossal *Volcano World* site offers a classification system for volcanoes. The six types covered here are shield volcanoes, stratovolcanoes, rhyolite caldera complexes, monogenetic fields, flood basalts, and midocean ridges. For each type, simply click on the name to read a brief text description and view photos illustrating that type of volcano.

To view the rest of the *Volcano World* Web site, just click on the icon at the bottom of any page. From the home page, you can choose many excellent sections, including "Ask a Volcanologist" FAQs, "Interviews with Volcanologists," "Teaching and Learning Resources," "Today in Volcano History," and a powerful internal search engine.

Igneous Processes and Volcanism
http://www.tmm.utexas.edu/npl/mineralogy/Mineral_Genesis/
    IgneousProcessesVolcanism.htm
high school and up

This site offers a very useful description of igneous activity on earth that occurs due to volcanism. Igneous processes can also result from plutonism, but you won't find that covered here. Topics covered at this site include divergent boundaries, convergent boundaries, hot spots, and igneous minerals.

Several nice graphics help to illustrate the text, and references to specific volcanoes provide examples of the general concepts. If you are researching the cause of igneous processes or the formation of gemstones, you'll find excellent and concise information here; just be prepared to concentrate. There's nothing lightweight or froufrou here.

ILLITERACY

Best Search Engine:	http://www.google.com/
Key Search Terms:	Illiteracy + world
	Illiteracy + statistics

Indicators on Literacy
http://www.un.org/Depts/unsd/social/literacy.htm
high school and up

This site presents data collected by the United Nations Educational, Scientific, and Cultural Organization (UNESCO) from nearly every nation in the world. You'll find rates of illiteracy among people aged 15–24 and people 25 and older. Be sure to read the relevant footnotes and technical notes for the country you're researching, as they offer some interpretation of the statistics.

International Literacy Explorer: A Teacher Training Tool for Basic Information
http://www.literacyonline.org/explorer/
college level

This comprehensive Web site will give you a broad understanding of literacy and basic education issues in an international context. Use the "Overview" section to become familiar with some general literacy concepts. Next, move into the "Literacy Projects" section, which takes you on a virtual tour of literacy projects throughout the world, complete with QuickTime movies. The projects are presented in the context of five themes: "Language and Culture," "Gender and Development," "Teaching and Learning," "Quality and Innovation," and "Technology for Learning." Another section of this site focuses on "Statistics." In it, you'll learn how to find statistical information about literacy and basic education levels in just about any country.

IMMIGRATION

Best Subject Directory: http://www.clearinghouse.net/

Key Search Term: Immigration

Immigration and Naturalization Service (INS)
http://www.ins.usdoj.gov/
high school and up

Although the INS Web site appears less conducive to student research than some other government agencies, there's still plenty to be found here. In fact, if you're searching for statistics on immigration (or confirming numbers from another Web source), you'd be downright foolhardy to overlook this site.

To tap into INS statistics from the home page, simply click on "Statistical Reports." (You'll go to http://www.ins.usdoj.gov/graphics/about ins/statistics/index.htm.) You'll find monthly statistical reports; fiscal year end statistical reports; and fact sheets, reports, and definitions of immigrants, refugees, asylees, parolees, naturalizations, illegal immigrants, and more. From INS's home page, you can also delve into a section called "Teacher and Student Resources." Here, you'll find an offering of historical and sociological resources on immigration and the INS.

Immigration Index
http://www.immigrationindex.org/
high school and up

This site's motto—"The Immigration Resource Directory on the Net," sums it up pretty well. The *Immigration Index* contains an incredible collection of news and information about immigration worldwide.

You'll save yourself a good deal of Web searching by using this collection of annotated and categorized links. The resources are organized into the following categories: "Asylum," "Conflict," "Country Data," "Deportation," "Detention," "Discrimination," "E-mail Lists," "Funding," "Gender," "Government," "Human Rights," "Trafficking," "Legal," "Migration," "News," and "Studies."

Center for Immigration Studies
http://www.cis.org/
high school and up

The Center for Immigration Studies (CIS) is an independent, nonpartisan, nonprofit research organization devoted to the research and policy analysis of the economic, social, demographic, fiscal, and other impacts of immigration on the United States. You'll find CIS's well-designed Web site easy to use for your research.

On the home page, headlines from current news and articles are compiled on a toolbar—just click on the headline to go directly to a full article. Another toolbar provides a list of common topics in immigration studies, such as assimilation and citizenship, refugee resettlement and asylum, guest workers, current numbers, and more. Click on a topic to read about it, access relevant reports prepared by CIS, and find links to other useful Web sites.

IMPERIALISM

Best Search Engine: http://www.ixquick.com/
Key Search Term: Imperialism

Encarta: Imperialism (Microsoft Encarta Online Encyclopedia 2000)
http://encarta.msn.com/find/Concise.asp?ti = 01ABF000
middle school and up

Want to read a general introduction to imperialism? This encyclopedia article is concise and to the point, but it covers everything you need for a good overview. Sections include "Introduction," "History," "Explanations of Imperialism," and "The Effects of Imperialism."

Internet Modern History Sourcebook: Imperialism
http://www.fordham.edu/halsall/mod/modsbook34.html
college level

The *Internet Modern History Sourcebook* is part of a Web enterprise designed to serve the needs of teachers and students in college survey courses in modern European history, American history, modern Western civilization, and world cultures. The site's sourcebook on imperialism is divided into the following sections: "Analyses of Imperialism," "Motives and Attitudes," "Celebrations and Objections to Imperialism," "China and the West," "India under the British," "Africa," "The Middle East," "The Japanese Exception," and "American Imperialism."

Each section is composed of links to a number of copy-permitted essays and Web sites about the particular topic. For instance, within the "Analyses of Imperialism" section, you'll find essays on "The Economic Basis of Imperialism" and "The Sociology of Imperialism." Look in the broad section on "Africa," and you'll find links to the *South African War Virtual Library*, as well as links to essays on the diamond fields of South Africa, the French in West Africa, and more.

History of Imperialism
http://members.aol.com/TeacherNet/World.html
middle school and up

This AOL gateway site on imperialism covers all parts of the world and spans all time periods. It's neatly organized, too, so that you don't spend all day trying to locate your specific topic. The table of contents at the top of the page contains hotlinks to all the entries, and these include sections on Africa, Asia, India, and Latin America, as well as sections on maps, cartoons, and other miscellaneous topics.

Online History of the United States: The Age of Imperialism
http://www.smplanet.com/imperialism/toc.html
college level

Developed by Small Planet, in association with The History Channel, this site provides excellent information on imperialism as it existed during the late nineteenth and early twentieth centuries in the United States.

During this time period, the United States pursued an aggressive policy of expansionism, extending its political and economic influence around the globe. Each section of the site covers a broad topic, such as "Expansion in the Pacific," "Spanish-American War," "Boxer Rebellion," "Panama Canal," "U.S. Intervention in Latin America," lesson plans and unit tests (intended for teachers, but extremely useful for students as well), and an excellent bibliography of printed reference materials. Throughout each section, you'll find links to relevant background material, maps, online museum exhibits, biographical info, historical time lines, encyclopedia articles, and photographs—all of which will enrich your understanding of U.S. imperialism.

INDUSTRIALIZATION

Best Search Engine: http://www.infind.com/
Key Search Term: Industrialization

Internet Modern History Sourcebook: Industrial Revolution
http://www.fordham.edu/halsall/mod/modsbook14.html
high school and up

The *Internet Modern History Sourcebook* is part of a Web enterprise designed to serve the needs of teachers and students in college survey courses in modern European history, American history, modern Western civilization, and world cultures. The site's sourcebook on the industrial revolution is divided into the following sections: "Industrial Revolution," "Social and Political Effects," and "Literary Response."

Each section is composed of links to a number of copy-permitted essays and Web sites about the particular topic. For instance, within the "Industrial Revolution" section, you'll find essays on "The Industrial Revolution in England" and "The Origin of Power Loom Weaving." Look in the section on the "Social and Political Effects," and you'll find information on the lives of workers, new social classes, and social reformism.

General Resources on the Gilded Age and Progressive Era
http://www2.h-net.msu.edu/~shgape/internet/index.html
high school and up

Collected by the Society for Historians of the Gilded Age and Progressive Era, this set of links provide an excellent launch pad for research into industrialization in the United States.

The links—although not annotated—are nicely divvied into logical subject areas. Under "General Resources," you'll find about a dozen links to excellent Web sites on nineteenth-century American history, the Progressive Era, the Gilded Age, and more. Look under "Political Leaders" to find links with information about countless politicians, leaders, and political movements. The sections focusing on "The Rise of Big Business and American Workers" and "New Immigration and Urban America" may be the biggest gold mines for your research. Other relevant links are sorted into sections, which include "Transformation of the West," "Literary and Cultural Resources," "Crisis of the 1890s," "War with Spain," "Progressive Reform," and "The Great War."

The Fabulous Ruins of Detroit
http://detroityes.com/home.htm
middle school and up

When we think of industrialization in the United States, the automobile quickly comes to mind, and no one place in this country had more to do with the automobile than Detroit. In the early twentieth century, the development of massive industrial structures changed the face of Detroit and heralded a second industrial revolution. This awesome site will take you on a tour of those abandoned automobile plants and company headquarters. Many of the pictures were taken during the destruction of the buildings, so you'll witness the detonation of the smoke stacks above an electricity plant and the crumbling of bricks as a factory folds in on itself.

The text accompanying the photos illuminates not only the historical significance of the structures but also the current status of the buildings (some survive and are seeking supporters to keep them alive). In addition to the industrial ruins featured here, you can tour ruins of nineteenth-century residences, ruins of downtown Detroit, and neighborhood ruins. There's also a section called "The City Rises," where you can see images of a resurgent Detroit. Lauded as a Yahoo! Pick of the Year in 1998 and given four stars by *Encyclopedia Britannica*, this is a one-of-a-kind site.

If your interest in industrialization focuses on urban geography and the affects of industrialization on urban landscapes, people, and structures, you will surely find this site loaded with useful text and thought-provoking images.

INFANT MORTALITY (SEE ALSO VITAL STATISTICS)

Best Search Engine: http://www.google.com/
Key Search Term: Infant mortality

Countries of the World
http://www.countryreports.org/
middle school and up

This terrific site, selected as one of the best sites on the Web for teachers, is also one of the best sites for students. Basic demographic research on people from all over the world is easy and quick. Go to the home page and click on "World Countries" for a comprehensive database of the world's countries with extensive demographic information on each one. Once you choose a country, you'll be given a menu of the following: "Economy," "Defense," "Geography," "Government," "People," "National Anthem Lyrics," and "Related Links." Pick "People."

Among many other statistics, you'll find infant mortality rate. Other really helpful information here includes overall fertility rate, age structure, birth rate, population growth, religious affiliations, languages spoken, literacy, and more.

You won't get detailed information about the infant mortality rate here. You'll have to continue your search elsewhere for that. But you will get accurate information to start you on your way.

Infant Mortality 1900s
http://users.erols.com/mwhite28/inf-mort.htm
middle school and up

If your research requires that you get a historical overview of infant mortality throughout the twentieth century, you'll want to check out this page of maps. It shows the world and the infant mortality rates for 1900, 1930, 1960, and 1994. You'll be able to visually trace trends around the world.

The page is part of the *Historical Atlas of the Twentieth Century*, which contains maps of all kinds of interesting data, some of which may also be of interest to you. The infant mortality maps are located in the section of the site called "General Trends" under "Living Conditions" in a little subsection called "Socio-Economic Trends." That's where you can also locate maps on life expectancy, literacy, telephones, and agricultural workforce in case any of those figure into your research as well.

National Center for Health Statistics
http://www.cdc.gov/nchs/fastats/infmort.htm
high school and up

For detailed information on infant death in the United States, this page is great. You'll find the leading causes of infant death and comprehensive data on infant deaths organized by age, race, and sex, as well as by 61 different causes of death. There's also a page on linked birth and infant death data, which is a valuable tool for monitoring and exploring the complex interrelationships between infant death and risk factors present at birth. In the data found on this page, the information from death certificates of infants under one year of age is linked with information from the birth certificates. You'll find this page under "Related Links" on the home page. There are also links to the Centers for Disease Control and Prevention and the National Institute for Child Health and Human Development, both of which sponsor research on infant mortality.

INTERNATIONAL DEBT

Best Search Engine: http://www.google.com/

Key Search Term: International debt

Social Development and World Peace: United States Conference of Catholic Bishops
http://www.nccbuscc.org/sdwp/international/debtindex.htm
high school and up

This international debt/foreign aid page highlights the issue of relieving debt for poor countries. It contains the following sections: "Action Alerts," "Statements/Letters," "Important Debt Reduction Legislation," "Catholic Campaign on Debt Educational Resources," and "Archives."

At this site you can trace the efforts of this organization and many others to get debt relief legislation passed during the Clinton administration, read letters and statements from members of this organization and others on all aspects of international debt relief for poor countries, including "Background on Debt and Foreign Aid." You can also read a summary of new debt legislation.

Under the section called "Catholic Campaign on Debt Educational Resources," you'll see a link for "Educational Resources." Click here and gain access to several excellent articles on the subject, including "What Is the International Debt Crisis?" and "Who Is Affected by International Debt?" You'll want to take a look at both of these as they provide excellent background information on the subject.

The "Archives" also have useful historical information including letters, statements, press releases, congressional testimony, and conference summaries.

The Third World Debt Crisis
http://www2.gol.com/users/bobkeim/money/debt.html
middle school and up

This page is a great introduction to the crisis of international debt for developing countries. It answers such questions as "What Is the Third World Debt Crisis?", "How Did It Start?", "Why Does It Keep Growing?", and "What Can We Do?"

The page is an excellent resource for students just beginning to study international debt. It defines terms like "debt," "crisis," "hard currency," "soft currency," "commodity," and others and provides a link to a list of countries that are considered to be developing countries.

The menu at the bottom of the page contains links for "Learners," "Teachers," and "Interactivities." Under "Learners" you'll find articles on numerous issues that go beyond international debt. The articles are sorted into the following categories: "Globalization," "Human Rights," "War and Peace," and "The Environment." Also on this page are quizzes on landmines and poverty, vocabulary quizzes derived from the articles on Iraq, Disney, money and debt, and other topics, and "Quick-Checks," which are question-and answer sites that will help you make sure you understand what you've read in the articles on the page. You'll see the "Quick-Check" features as you read the article on international debt, so give it a try if you want to test yourself and insure that you're understanding the concepts.

DebtChannel.org
http://www.debtchannel.org/
high school and up

DebtChannel describes itself as the global portal on international debt. Look here for a wide variety of information. Some of the highlights of this site are the features that allow you to search for debt by country and by topic. There are sections of the site devoted to news and to campaigns to relieve debt, and there's a "Beginner's Guide to Debt," which goes into quite a bit more detail than the articles at the *Third World Debt Crisis* site. If you want to get into the specific plans and initiatives that have been proposed to relieve debt or if you want to understand definitions of different kinds of debt, this is the place to look. It's more than an overview, but the language is still accessible to those without a background in the subject.

You can also access a section of the site called "Views" that provides in-depth reports on debt and related issues, as well as a discussion forum.

IRRIGATION

Best Search Engine: http://www.google.com/

Key Search Term: Irrigation

World Wide Virtual Library: Irrigation
http://www.wiz.uni-kassel.de/kww/projekte/irrig/irrig_i.html
high school and up

This subject directory, part of the *World Wide Virtual Library on Agriculture*, contains hundreds of categorized and annotated links that will facilitate your research into the field of irrigation.

Look through the site's index to locate the specific area of irrigation you're researching. These categories include irrigation and soil-water relationship, irrigation and drought management, scientific online journals, online articles on irrigation, irrigation projects, irrigation statistics, irrigation standards, irrigation policy, irrigation and water experts, water resources, hydrology, and more.

AquaStat
http://www.fao.org/WAICENT/FAOINFO/AGRICULT/AGL/AGLW/
    aquastatweb/main/html/aquastat.htm
high school and up

Developed by the Land and Water Development Division of the Food and Agriculture Organization (FAO), *AquaStat* offers global information on water and agriculture. The site will be able to provide you with statistical information on the state of agricultural water management throughout the world, with an emphasis on developing countries and countries in transition.

Use the site's "Country Profiles" or "Regional Overviews" to find in-depth information and charts on a country or region's geography and population, climate and water resources, irrigation and drainage development, and trends in water resource management.

ISLAM

Best Search Engine: http://www.lii.org/search/
Key Search Term: Islam

Al-Islam
http://al-islam.org/
high school and up

This well-designed site offers excellent Islamic resources on the history, law, practice, and society of the Islamic religion and the Muslim peoples. It's the handiwork of the Ahlul Bayt Digital Islamic Library Project (DILP), a nonprofit group working to digitize and present high-quality Islamic information.

For general research, click on "Beginner's Guide" to read an introduction, frequently asked questions, and common misperceptions. Another good general section is called "About Islam," where you'll find information on basic beliefs, as well as links to other educational materials, community resources, and publications. For more in-depth research, tap into any of the following sections: "Beliefs and Practices," "History and Current Events," "The Infallibles," or "Allah and the Holy Qur'an." You can also use the site's subject index or search engine to fine-tune your search for information.

Islamic Server
http://www.usc.edu/dept/MSA/
high school and up

This extensive collection of Islamic resources, created by the Muslim Students Association at the University of Southern California, will satisfy much of your research appetite. You'll find a general introduction to the fundamentals of Islam, three translations of the Qur'an, and introductions to the Sunnah and Hadith of Muhammad.

The site also covers special topics as they relate to Islam, including economics, history, human relations, law, politics, and women. The section called "What Is Not Islam" discusses the Nation of Islam, the Ahmadiyya/Qadiani Movement, and the International Community of Submitters. Other tools here include a glossary of Islamic terms and concepts and searchable databases of the Hadith and Qur'an.

Islamic Philosophy, Scientific Thought, and History
http://www.arches.uga.edu/~godlas/history.html
middle school and up

This gateway site on Islamic history will let you choose among many different topics. The site is divided into four sections, each of which contains numerous annotated links. The sections are "General Essays," "Islamic Philosophy," "Islam and Science," and "Islamic History."

Each section contains many different types of resources. You'll find maps, dictionary entries, personal memoirs, historical essays, scholarly articles, brief biographies, and much more.

Islam: Empire of Faith
http://www.pbs.org/empires/islam/faithkoran.html
middle school and up

This interactive, multimedia PBS site deals more with Islam the religion than it does with Islamic civilization. You'll find sections on "The Koran and Tradition," "The Five Pillars," "People of the Book," and "Islam Today," for example. Click on any of these for superbly written introductions to the faith.

LABOR FORCE

Best Search Engine: http://www.google.com/
Key Search Term: Labor force

Labor Force Statistics
http://www.census.gov/hhes/www/laborfor.html
high school and up

This page on labor force statistics from the United States Census Bureau contains links to the following reports: "Reasons People Do Not Work, 1996"; "Dynamics of Economic Well-Being, Labor Force, 1992–1993: A Perspective on Low-Wage Workers"; "Dynamics of Economic Well-Being, Labor Force, 1991–1993"; and "Dynamics of Economic Well-Being: Labor Force and Income, 1990 to 1992."

Each of these reports has numerous tables attached to it, so when you click on a report you will be given a list of links to tables that break down the data into more specific categories. For the first report, for example, on low-wage workers, you'll find tables of data on average hourly earnings sorted by months of low-wage employment and persons with earnings sorted by age-sex groups, among others.

There are also links to other sources of labor force data, including the Bureau of Labor Statistics. Click back to the home page to find these links.

Economagic
http://www.economagic.com/blslf.htm
high school and up

This *Economagic* page lets you search for data from the Bureau of Labor Statistics (BLS), which is highly preferable to searching for data at the BLS Web site.

Economagic does a super job of organizing the data into logical categories, making it easy to determine just what you need and making it quick to access.

You can search for information using a number of different criteria, including occupations and industries, sex, age, race, and class of worker. The search form at the bottom of the page is slightly complicated, but the instructions are excellent and include an example of how to use the form, so just follow the example and you should be fine.

The Library of Congress Country Studies
http://lcweb2.loc.gov/frd/cs/
middle school and up

If you're interested in international labor force information, try the *Country Studies* from the Library of Congress. You'll find 101 countries and regions covered, with notable omissions including Canada, France, the United Kingdom, and other Western nations, as well as a number of African nations. The date on which information for each country was posted appears on the title page for each country and at the end of each section of text.

These books are excellent sources of information for many basic topics. They present a description and analysis of the historical setting and the social, economic, political, and national security systems and institutions of countries throughout the world. They also examine the interrelationships of those systems and the ways they are shaped by cultural factors.

These country studies are completely available online, and you can search in two ways. You can browse the table of contents for each country book, or you can search for keywords in all country books or across a certain continent.

LAKES

Best Search Engine: http://www.google.com/

Key Search Term: Lakes

Lakes on the Internet
http://www.lakesusa.com/asp/Frameset.asp?Page = /areas/maps/gamap.
   htm&Keys = /areas/f_keys/main_key.htm
middle school and up

If you're looking for lake information for the United States, this nifty site is your ticket. At present it covers all lakes in Alabama, Georgia, Mississippi, South Carolina, and Tennessee and a few of the largest lakes that are in other states, like Lake Powell in Arizona. To keep you up to date, there is a lake status report that tells you which states are next, as well as a "New Additions" section, where you can see the latest lakes to go online. At present, Texas, Kentucky, and North Carolina are slated for completion, but I expect that by the time you read this, many more states will have their lakes online, too.

What do you find for those lakes that are online? Maps galore, including 3-D maps, fishing information, lake weather, lake level graphs, navigation charts, satellite images, lake news, lake discussion groups, and much more.

Large Lakes of the World
http://www.factmonster.com/ipka/A0001777.html
middle school and up

This is a *FactMonster Almanac* page. It lists dozens of the largest lakes in the world, with information on area (in square miles and kilometers), length, and depth. The lakes are organized in the chart from largest to smallest. The Caspian Sea starts out the list (it's landlocked and thus technically considered a sea by geographers) with 152,239 square miles, and the list ends with the Koko-Nor Lake in China, which covers 1,630 square miles.

The World's Water
http://www.worldwater.org/
high school and up

For information on the world's freshwater resources, try this site, which is based on a book of the same name. You'll navigate through sections on "Water Data," "Water Conflict Chronology," "Water Links," and "The Books."

"Water Data" is devoted to tables, figures, and maps taken from the book. There are tables and charts on total renewable freshwater supply by country, access to safe drinking water in developing countries, and many other diverse topics. You'll also find a couple of maps and documents.

The "Water Conflict Chronology" gives you an introduction to the subject of water conflict in history, then a link at the bottom of the page takes you to the chronology itself. It starts in 1503 and runs up to 1999–2000. The chronology is really neat. It gives you the date of the conflict, the parties involved, the basis of the conflict, whether is was violent or nonviolent, a description of the conflict, and the sources used to compile the data.

The list of "Water Links" is huge and nicely organized into the following sections: "Government and Intergovernmental," "Nongovernmental Organizations and Associations," "University and Educational," "Commercial," "Water Publications," "Articles and Reports," "Discussion Lists," and a few other miscellaneous categories.

LAND COVER

Best Search Engine:	http://www.google.com/
Key Search Terms:	Land cover
	Earth statistics

The Land Atlas
http://www.epa.gov/ceisweb1/ceishome/atlas/nationalatlas/landatlas.html
high school and up

Here you'll find links to many different maps of the United States that feature specific aspects of the U.S. land environment. The home page opens with a little chart that lists issues on the left and maps on the right. Just scroll down the list of issues for something that strikes your fancy, then click on the map located to the right of the issue.

The four issues listed include "Land Resources," "Land Use and Cover," "Threats to Human and Ecological Health," and "Health of the People on the Land." The maps provided under "Land Use and Cover" include "Predominant Cover," "Agricultural Lands," and "Human Settlement." Each section contains numerous maps on specific issues that relate to the category. You can click on the map for a larger image and on the caption for the text link to the complete original document.

This *Land Atlas* page is part of a larger atlas site that contains all kinds of maps and information for the United States as a whole and for individual states. Just use the menu at the left to access other information.

World Land Areas and Elevation
http://www.factmonster.com/ipka/A0001763.html
middle school and up

This *FactMonster Almanac* page is once again a great source for information on land cover. The table gives the land area for each continent (there's also an entry in the chart for the whole world) in square kilometers and square miles, its percentage of the total land area of the earth, and its highest and lowest elevations.

Global Land Environments
http://www.esd.ornl.gov/projects/qen/nerc.html
high school and up

Lots of colorful historical maps of land cover is what you'll find on this page. And by historical, we mean a long time ago. The first map shows forest and desert coverage on earth 18,000 years ago. Then there is a series of ecosystem maps of Ice Age earth. Each map is accompanied by an in-depth detailed article. Just click on the link to access the text. The series includes Europe, Eurasia, Africa, Australasia, North America, and South America.

The bottom of this page contains a long list of links to other sites that deal with past environments, such as "A Quick Background to the Pliocene," "The Onset of Northern Hemisphere Glaciation," "A Siberian Mega-Lake at the Last Glacial Maximum," and "Carbon Storage in Ecosystems: Past, Present, and Future" just to name a few.

LAND DEGRADATION (SEE ALSO DESERTIFICATION)

Best Search Engine: http://www.google.com/
Key Search Term: Land degradation

Land Degradation and Desertification Website
http://www.nhq.nrcs.usda.gov/WSR/Landdeg/papers.htm
middle school and up

This site is part of the Working Group on Land Degradation and Desertification of the International Union of Soil Sciences. Its agenda is derived from the United Nations Conference on Environment and Development, which proposed a wide range of activities to address land degradation in general and desertification in particular. It's an excellent source for international information on land degradation.

If you're just beginning your research, you'll be happy to see the little question at the top of the page that asks, "Want to know what land degradation is?" Just click at the end of that question for an excellent introduction to the topic. You'll get solid definitions of both degradation and desertification, a list of causes, and another list of results, all in a fancy self-scrolling box.

Further down the page, "Land Degradation News and Views" provides links to different articles, newsletters, and conference reports on the topic. Along the way, you'll spot quite a few resources on soil science. Even though the focus of these resources is broader, they might also have information of interest to you.

Drylands Home Page
http://www.iied.org/drylands/index.html
high school and up

The *Drylands Programme Home Page* of the International Institute for Environment and Development offers up some excellent resources on land degradation and activist projects aimed at preventing it. The group's focus is Africa, so if you're looking for information specifically on Africa, you're in the right place. But even if you're looking for general information on land degradation, you're going to find much of value here.

In its own words, "The Drylands programme aims to promote the sustainable, equitable, participatory, and decentralized management of natural resources in dryland Africa, through policies and institutions, thereby contributing to improved livelihoods, poverty reduction, and long term ecological and economic sustainability." You can search for information on the group's activities in the following categories: "Land Rights and Tenure," "Pastoral Resources and the Common," "Making Decentralization Work," "Participatory Soils Management," "Poverty and Livelihoods," "Desertification: Assessing the Convention," and "Information and Networks."

This is kind of hodgepodge, but you'll learn a lot about activist programs in Africa by browsing here, particularly in the soils management section of the site.

Desertification
http://www.fao.org/desertification/default.asp?lang = en
high school and up

This United Nations multimedia Web site from the Food and Agriculture Organization (FAO) contains technical and scientific data and information, as well as links to a number of highly informative Web sites on desertification. Choose your language preference from the left side of the page—English, Spanish, French, or Arabic to start.

The site is most useful to those who've already narrowed their research focus. In the "Documents" section, for instance, you can locate FAO documents about desertification by selecting a region (Africa, Asia, Europe, Latin America, the Near East, North America, or Pacific); theme (crop production; forest and rangelands management; land and water management; knowledge, information and communication; environmental conventions and cross-sector issues; and sustainable development); document category (maps and statistics, photos, text, and videos); and/or document type (field manual, success story, scientific/technical paper, etc.).

For more general information, click on "Institutions" to find links to international organizations carrying out desertification-related activities and other groups working in the field. The "Activities" section offers reports, strategy outlines, and other news about FAO's program to combat desertification.

LANDFORMS

| Best Search Engine: | http://www.google.com/ |
| Key Search Term: | Landforms |

Color Landform Atlas of the United States
http://www.fermi.jhuapl.edu/states/states.html
middle school and up

Types of landforms include rain forest, tundra, desert, forest, grasslands, oceans, waterfalls, canyons, reefs, mountains, volcanoes, and many others. Each landform has unique characteristics, some of which you will find on maps and some of which you won't.

This color landform atlas of the United States gives you a variety of features on different maps. Just click on any one of the states—they're all listed—and you'll be given a list of links to various maps for that state. These include a shaded relief map, a county map, a black-and-white map, a satellite image, and sometimes other resources. There are also dozens of links to external sites given for each state . . . places like *Environmental Protection Agency Watershed Info* and *Roadside America*, both of which provide additional info on the state, although the information may or may not be related to landforms in the state.

The list of links to other U.S. sites is short but excellent.

Illustrated Glossary: Landforms and Bodies of Water
http://www.enchantedlearning.com/geography/landforms/glossary.shtml
middle school and up

This is a terrific landforms resource from one of our favorite educational sites—*Enchanted Learning.com*. It's set up as a glossary but a glossary with graphics for every entry, and it includes bodies of water.

You can find definitions and pictures of the following landforms: canyon, cave, delta, hill, mesa, mountain, valley, volcano, and more. When you're all done exploring these landforms, take the landforms quiz to see just how many of it's special features you can remember.

Landforms of the World
http://www.geocities.com/monte7dco/
middle school and up

This *Geocities* site provides a more comprehensive list of landforms with definitions, complete with pictures for each one and a couple of examples of the landform. Go to "Forest" and you will find out the two main characteristics that make up a forest, as well as the names of two different forests—Olympic National Forest and the rain forests of Brazil.

You won't find a landforms quiz here, but there are lesson plans for teachers. And if you are searching for information on a specific landform, try the "Links" page, which contains links to sites that address particular landforms. There's a Great Plains site, a site about deserts of the world, and a site about the forests and landscapes of Minnesota, just to name a few.

Landforms on Topographic Maps
http://www.csus.edu/indiv/s/slaymaker/Geo110L/landforms.htm
middle school and up

For high-power fun with landforms, try this site, which will connect you with topographic maps illustrating the landforms of your choice.

To quickly reach a topic on the list, click on one of the following categories: "Geologic Structures," "Igneous Activity," "Mass Movement," "Streams," "Underground Water," "Glaciers," "Wind," and "Waves and Currents." Under each of these, you'll find dozens of specific landforms that you can view on a topographic map. Under "Glaciers, for example, you can view crevasses, cirques, drumlins, eskers, finger lakes, hanging valleys, kame terraces, kettles, moraines of various types, tarns, and other features. And that's just the "Glaciers" section!

These are nice maps, too. They load fairly quickly and each contains a large red arrow pointing at the feature of choice so you can't miss it, even if you're totally unfamiliar with the landform.

LAND USE

Best Search Engine: http://www.google.com/

Key Search Term: Land use

The Land Atlas
http://www.epa.gov/ceisweb1/ceishome/atlas/nationalatlas/landatlas.html
high school and up

This site is listed above under the topic of land cover, but it's equally good if you're researching land use issues. You'll find links to many different maps of the United States that feature specific aspects of the U.S. land environment. The home page opens with a little chart that lists issues on the left and maps on the right. Just scroll down the list of issues for something that strikes your fancy, then click on the map located to the right of the issue.

The four issues listed include "Land Resources," "Land Use and Cover," "Threats to Human and Ecological Health," and "Health of the People on the Land." The maps provided under "Land Use and Cover" include "Predominant Cover," "Agricultural Lands," and "Human Settlement." Each section contains numerous maps on specific issues that relate to the category. You can click on the map for a larger image and on the caption for the text link to the complete original document.

This *Land Atlas* page is part of a larger atlas site that contains all kinds of maps and information for the United States as a whole and for individual states. Just use the menu at the left to access other information.

Natural Resources Conservations Service: State of the Land
http://www.nhq.nrcs.usda.gov/land/home.html
high school and up

If you're looking for numbers and analysis of numbers on land use, this site should help. It describes itself as providing "data and analysis on land use, soil erosion and soil quality, water quality, wetlands, and other issues regarding the conservation and use of natural resources." The menu at the left side of the simply designed home page offers you these options—"What's New," "Agriculture and the Environment," "Maps," "Facts and Figures Index," "GIS and Data," "About Us," and "Site Map." You'll also see links for "Analysis on the Health of America's Non-Federal Lands and Water Quality Issues," and the "National Resources Inventory," which are the site's primary resources for data.

Click on "Agriculture and the Environment," and you can explore soil erosion, water quality, wetland conservation, grazing lands, people on the land, and land use, among other topics. The "Land Use" section of the site is where you will want to go first for an introduction to the importance of studying and understanding land use. "Maps, Facts and Figures" will give you numerous tables and maps that show broad land cover and land use by state, wetlands by broad land cover and land use by state, broad land cover and land use by land resource region, dominant cover/use types, grazing land by land cover/use, and much more. There's even a graphic called "How Our Land Is Used" from 1997.

If you're interested in the use of GIS technology in analyzing and solving land use problems, you'll find great resources in the GIS section of this site as well. The "Links" page hosts all kinds of organizations interested in land use issues—from government agencies to conservation groups to cartography sites.

Center of Excellence for Sustainable Development
http://www.sustainable.doe.gov/landuse/luintro.shtml
high school and up

This land use site is oriented more toward urbanization issues and grappling with land use consideration within the context of urban growth. The site contains sections on "Key Principles," "Strategies," "Civic Participation," "Success Stories," "Codes/Ordinances," "Articles/Publications," "Educational Materials," and other topics.

For a good introduction, go to "Key Principles" where you'll find a number of different links to sites that offer guidance on land use. There's "Principles for Better Land Use Policy" (put out by the National Governors' Association), "New Urbanism/Neo-Traditional Planning," and "Land Use Agenda for the Twenty-First Century America," among others.

The "Strategies" section contains land use planning strategies. Here you can read about transit-oriented design, mixed use strategies, urban growth boundaries, infill development, greenways, Brownfield redevelopment, open space protection, urban forestry, and other topics that are hot among urban planners.

If you need to learn about the codes and ordinances that govern land use decisions in towns and cities, go to the page of the same name. You'll find links to sites all around the country—places like Burlington, Vermont, the state of Maryland, Scottsdale, Arizona, Napa, California, and other places that have literally shaped their communities through the thoughtful work they have done on land use codes and ordinances.

You'll enjoy the excellent planning that went into this great little site. It's packed with extremely useful information that's been organized in a logical and easy-to-access way.

LANGUAGE

Best Search Engine: http://www.google.com

Key Search Term: World languages

Fifty Most Widely Spoken Languages in the World
http://www.factmonster.com/ipka/A0774735.html
middle school and up

FactMonster comes up with the best charts, and this one is no exception. If you want to know how many people speak a certain language and where those people live, you'll love this handy page. Starting with the most widely spoken language—can you guess it?—that's right, Mandarin Chinese, and ending with Sindhi, which is spoken in Afghanistan, Pakistan, India, and Singapore, this chart provides rank, names of all the countries where the language is spoken, and the number of people who speak it.

You'll find source information at the bottom of the chart, as well as links to other amazing *FactMonster* pages on language. There's one called "Amazing Language Facts," another called "Speaking of Language," and another called "Person Speaking a Language Other than English at

Home." "Speaking of Language" is just the *FactMonster* home page for all things related to language. So you'll find the other two pages listed there, as well as numerous other resources on language, both English and languages from all around the world. For fast, fun language information, *FactMonster* is worth a look.

Ethnologue: Languages of the World
http://www.ethnologue.com/web.asp
middle school and up

This is one of the Web's premiere world language sites, with loads of stellar information. You'll find a country index with language maps, language names, language codes, language families, an overview of the site, and a search function for the site.

The "Country Index" gives you a map of the world. Click on the name of the continent you want to explore, and a list of countries opens up. Choose your country, and a page devoted to the languages of that country opens. You'll get an introduction to the languages, then a list of the spoken living languages with detailed information on each, and a list of extinct languages. Under Egypt, for example, you'll find five types of Arabic, Domari, Greek, Kenuzi-Dongola, Nobiin, Sivvi, and under extinct languages, Coptic.

If you're interested in language families, try the page of the same name. You'll get a list of all language families in the world with links to pages that explore each language within the language family.

The section "Language Names" lists some 6,800 languages, so if you want to browse the alphabetical listings in the database, go here. Remember that you can also use the search function if you know the name of the language you want to find.

Geonative: Put Minority and Native Languages on the Map
http://www.geocities.com/Athens/9479/
middle school and up

This is such a cool site. It offers up so much information about minority and native languages around the world and it does it in those native languages, so that you can actually see what they look like on the page. In the main part of the site, found by searching the "Main Table Index," the information on any given language is given in English on one side of the page and in the particular language on the other side of the page.

Start out on the home page by clicking on the language of your choice, and an introduction in that language opens up. You'll be given the choice of viewing the "What's New Page," browsing the "Main Table

Index," using the site's search function, or trying out links to external sites.

The "Index" is where you access the heart of the site. It's an A to Z listing of contents that begins with Ainu, Alsace, and Aragon, and ends with Wales, Yiddish, and Zimbabwe. You'll find dozens and dozens of links in between. Click on "Quechua," which is located under "P" for Peru, and you'll find text about Quechuan, written in English on one side of the page and in Quechuan on the other side of the page. You'll also find information on Inga, the northernmost form of Quechua, and on Aymara, which is also spoken in Peru but is the main native language spoken in Bolivia.

The "Links" page provides a good annotated list of other language sites, so check it out if you want more resources when you're done at *Geonative*.

LA NIÑA (SEE ALSO EL NIÑO)

Best Search Engine: http://www.ixquick.com/

Key Search Term: La Niña

Climate Prediction Center: El Niño/La Niña
http://www.cpc.ncep.noaa.gov/products/analysis_monitoring/lanina/index.
    html
high school and up

This site provides quick access to the Climate Prediction Center's comprehensive educational and scientific resources on El Niño and La Niña. The tutorial on the El Niño/Southern Oscillation (ENSO) cycle is a solid place to start for info about how sea temperatures and atmospheric conditions in the tropical Pacific affect North American weather patterns. You can also click on "Fact Sheets" or "Monographs" to get written and graphical material that explains the far-flung effects of climate patterns.

For the latest info on current conditions, you can click on "Expert Assessment" for a current diagnostic discussion or "Monitoring and Data" for a weekly update. To find historical data, click on "Previous ENSO Events," and you'll see a detailed assessment of the impact of El Niño and La Niña on a regional and state-by-state basis.

National Academy of Sciences: El Niño and La Niña
http://www.nationalacademies.org/opus/elnino/
high school and up

You'll be impressed by this online article on El Niño and La Niña, "Tracing the Dance of Ocean and Atmosphere," written for the National Academy of Sciences' Office on Public Understanding of Science. Its comprehensive sections include "Of Weather and Climate," "Starting with the Atmosphere," "A Meteorologist Looks at the Sea," "Ocean-ography's Perspective," "Wakeup Call," "Need for More Comprehensive Data," and "The Power of an Interdisciplinary Approach."

Each section offers a thorough examination of the topic, with hyper-linked text to related information. For instance, within "A Meteorologist Looks at the Sea," you can click on scientists' names to link to bio-graphical information and publications lists. The site also offers a good time line of events in the history of understanding El Niño/La Niña, as well as annotated links to a handful of select Web sites.

LATITUDE AND LONGITUDE

Best Search Engine: http://www.infind.com/

Key Search Term: Latitude and longitude

About Geography: Latitude and Longitude
http://geography.about.com/science/geography/library/weekly/aa031197.htm
high school and up

It can't hurt to initiate your latitude and longitude research with a visit to an overview site like this one. Here, you'll learn all of the basics, such as when and why the latitude and longitude system was developed and how it is noted on maps. Plus, you can easily link to *About.com's* excellent picks of related Web sites, which include general resources about coordinate systems; conversion of decimal degrees into degrees, minutes, and seconds; atlas and time zone databases; and online data-bases for finding quick latitude, longitude, and elevation readings.

Great Outdoor Recreation Pages (GORP) Hiking Skills: Latitude and Longitude
http://www.gorp.com/gorp/activity/hiking/skills/navigation/lat_lon2.htm
high school and up

This site offers a refreshingly hands-on approach to learning about latitude and longitude. Along with providing historical info on the lat-itude and longitude system—which is essentially the foundation for Global Positioning Systems (GPS)—this site helps you explore the sub-ject with your own maps and GPS device.

This Web site's seven-part series offers an introduction to GPS, an explanation of the difference between magnetic and true north, information on calculating global position, guidelines for route planning, and more.

LIFE EXPECTANCY (SEE ALSO VITAL STATISTICS)

Best Search Engine: http://www.google.com

Key Search Terms: Life + expectancy + statistics

Countries of the World
http://www.countryreports.org/
middle school and up

This terrific site, selected as one of the best sites on the Web for teachers, is also one of the best sites for students. Basic demographic research on people from all over the world is easy and quick. Go to the home page and click on "World Countries" for a comprehensive database of the world's countries with extensive demographic information on each one. Once you choose a country, you'll be given a menu of the following: "Economy," "Defense," "Geography," "Government," "People," "National Anthem Lyrics," and related links. Pick "People."

Among many other statistics, you'll find life expectancy at birth. Other really helpful information here includes overall fertility rate, age structure, birth rate, infant mortality rate, population growth, religious affiliations, languages spoken, literacy, and more.

You won't get detailed information about life expectancy here. You'll have to continue your search elsewhere for that. But you will get accurate information to start you on your way.

Life Expectancy 1900s
http://users.erols.com/mwhite28/life-exp.htm
middle school and up

If your research requires that you get a historical overview of life expectancy throughout the twentieth century, you'll want to check out this page of maps. It shows the world and the life expectancy for different parts of the world for 1900, 1930, 1960, and 1994. You'll be able to visually trace trends around the world.

The page is part of the *Historical Atlas of the Twentieth Century*, which contains maps of all kinds of interesting data, some of which may also be of interest to you. The life expectancy maps are located in the section of the site called "General Trends" under "Living Conditions" in a little subsection called "Socio-Economic Trends." That's where you can also locate maps on infant mortality, literacy, telephones, and agricultural workforce in case any of those figure into your research as well.

National Center for Health Statistics
http://www.cdc.gov/nchs/fastats/lifexpec.htm
middle school and up

For detailed information on life expectancy in the United States, this page is great. Two reports of comprehensive data are available here and can be downloaded—one on life expectancy at single years of age and the other on life expectancy at birth, sorted by race and sex.

Quick stats available right on the home page include life expectancy at birth, life expectancy at 65, males at birth and at age 65, and females at birth and at age 65.

Links to the National Institute on Aging, the American Association of Retired Persons, and the Centers for Disease Control and Prevention appear on this page. Each of those organizations has life expectancy information as well.

LITERACY RATES

Best Search Engine: http://www.google.com/

Key Search Term: Literacy rates

National Center for the Study of Adult Learning and Literacy
http://gseweb.harvard.edu/~ncsall/pdrn.htm
high school and up

This is the center's "Practitioner Dissemination and Research Network" page. The menu at the left will take you to "Research," "Publications," "Teaching and Training Materials," "Scholarship Info," and "Links." "Research" contains studies, reports, occasional papers, research briefs, and other material that may be of interest to you.

There is no easy way to search the site, so you'll just have to browse to find what you're looking for, but there are many useful things under "Research Briefs." These three-page summaries of the longer reports include study findings and implications for practice, policy, and research. "The Outcomes and Impacts of Adult Literacy Campaigns in the United States," "Changes in Learners' Lives One Year after Enrollment in Literacy Programs," and "Who Benefits from Obtaining a GED?" are just a few of the report titles we ran across when browsing this part of the site.

International Literacy Network
http://www.theiln.org/
middle school and up

For an overview of what's going on in the world of international literacy campaigns, try this site. The *International Literacy Network* contains "Success Stories," where you can read about the latest achievement in international literacy, "What You Can Do," which contains suggestions for getting involved as a volunteer, parent, teacher, librarian, or businessperson, news about literacy issues, and a FAQ section, where you can find answers to commonly asked questions.

The network is made up of numerous organizations concerned with literacy, like the American Library Association, the Center for Applied Linguistics, USAID, and the World Bank. Check out any of their home pages here by clicking on their names.

Countries of the World
http://www.countryreports.org/
middle school and up

This terrific site, selected as one of the best sites on the Web for teachers, is also one of the best sites for students. Basic demographic research on people from all over the world is easy and quick. Go to the home page and click on "World Countries" for a comprehensive database of the world's countries with extensive demographic information on each one. Once you choose a country, you'll be given a menu of the following: "Economy," "Defense," "Geography," "Government," "People," "National Anthem Lyrics," and related links. Pick "People."

Among many other statistics, you'll find the literacy rate for people age 15 and older. Other really helpful information here includes overall fertility rate, age structure, birth rate, infant mortality rate, population growth, religious affiliations, languages spoken, life expectancy, and more.

You won't get detailed information about literacy here, but you will get a breakdown of the literacy rate for males and females, in addition to the figure for the total population. You'll have to continue your search elsewhere for more in-depth information.

Life Expectancy 1900s
http://users.erols.com/mwhite28/life-exp.htm
middle school and up

If your research requires that you get a historical overview of literacy throughout the twentieth century, you'll want to check out this page of maps. It shows the world and the literacy rates for different parts of the world for 1900, 1930, 1960, and 1994. You'll be able to visually trace trends around the world.

The page is part of the *Historical Atlas of the Twentieth Century*, which contains maps of all kinds of interesting data, some of which may also be of interest to you. The literacy maps are located in the section of the site called "General Trends" under "Living Conditions" in a little subsection called "Socioeconomic Trends." That's where you can also locate maps on infant mortality, life expectancy, telephones, and agricultural workforce in case any of those figure into your research as well.

LITHOSPHERE/GEOSPHERE
(SEE ALSO PLATE TECTONICS)

Best Search Engine:　　http://www.google.com/

Key Search Term:　　Lithosphere

The Four Spheres
http://geography.about.com/library/misc/blsphere.htm
middle school and up

This brief *About.com* article defines earth's four spheres for you—the atmosphere, lithosphere, biosphere, and hydrosphere. Get the basics and then proceed to the following site for more in-depth research.

USGS: Inside the Earth
http://pubs.usgs.gov/publications/text/inside.html
middle school and up

This page, *Inside the Earth,* is part of the U.S. Geological Survey's *This Dynamic Earth* publication, which explains how plate tectonics impacts all geological processes. You'll find well-written text and a terrific cut-away view of the earth's layers, including the lithosphere.

LONGITUDE (SEE LATITUDE)

MAGNETIC POLE

Best Search Engines:　　http://www.metacrawler.com/ and http://www.askjeeves.com/

Key Search Term:　　Magnetic pole

Ask the Space Scientist: Earth—Magnetic Field
http://image.gsfc.nasa.gov/poetry/ask/amag.html
high school and up

As part of the National Aeronautics and Space Administration's (NASA) Ask-the-Space-Scientist program, this Web site offers superb information about magnetic poles. We'd be surprised if you can't find the information you need in the 32 questions that are answered by Dr. Sten Odenwald.

You can learn about the relationship between Earth's rotation and its magnetic fields, the number of magnetic poles (surprise—the answer isn't two!), the movement of the magnetic field, the effect of the magnetic field on El Niño cycles, and much more.

Tracking the North Magnetic Pole
http://www.geolab.nrcan.gc.ca/geomag/e_nmpole.html
high school and up

This site was developed by Canada's National Geomagnetism Program, an organization that monitors and predicts the changing magnetic field in Canada. Interestingly, Canada has the most complex pattern of magnetic declination of any country in the world; therefore, keeping track of its position and motion is critical to Canadian cartography.

At this mostly text-filled site, you'll read about how the idea of north and south magnetic poles was first developed in the sixteenth century. You will also find basic definitions of magnetic poles and magnetic declination, information on historical and modern-day efforts to determine the precise location of the north magnetic pole, data exploring how and why the magnetic pole moves, and information on the navigational significance of the north magnetic pole.

MAP PROJECTIONS (SEE ALSO CARTOGRAPHY)

Best Subject Directory: http://www.mercatormag.com/
Key Search Term: Map projections

Map Projection Home Page
http://everest.hunter.cuny.edu/mp/index.html
college level

Created and maintained by the geography department at Hunter College, this site houses a good collection of information on map projections. Click on "The Basics" to find information on the history of map projections, choosing a projection, projection distortion, and types of projections (conic, cylindrical, and planar). Elsewhere in the site, you'll find book reviews of texts dealing with map projections, software, related links, and bibliographies.

Map Projections
http://www.colorado.edu/geography/gcraft/notes/mapproj/mapproj_f.html
college level

Developed for the Geographer's Craft Project at the University of Colorado, Boulder, these materials provide an in-depth explanation of map projections. The introductory section discusses how map projections attempt to portray the surface of the earth on a flat surface, resulting in some distortions of conformality, distance, direction, scale, and area. You can see this result for yourself in the site's deft use of graphics.

The site is composed of sections of the different types of projections, such as cylindrical, conic, azimuthal, and miscellaneous. In each section, you'll get text and graphic information about what these projections are and how they're used.

MAPS—HISTORICAL (SEE ALSO CARTOGRAPHY)

Best Subject Directory: http://directory.yahoo.com/Science/Geography/
                            Cartography/

Key Search Term: Historic maps

Perry-Castañeda Library Map Collection: Historical Maps
http://www.lib.utexas.edu/maps/historical/index.html
high school and up

The Perry-Castañeda Library Map Collection at the University of Texas at Austin is widely recognized as one of the Web's best information resources on maps. This section of the site lives up to that reputation, offering hundreds of historical maps of continents, regions, and countries across the globe.

In addition to giving you access to the maps preserved (in JPEG format) at the Perry-Castañeda Library itself, you'll be directed to other Web sites with maps for the region or country you're researching. For instance, when we clicked on "Historical Maps of Russia and the Former Soviet Republics," we found six relevant maps at this site, as well as at least a dozen links to other Web sites.

Map Collections 1500–1999
http://memory.loc.gov/ammem/gmdhtml/gmdhome.html
high school and up

This is another fantastic site for historical maps. The Geography and Map Division of the Library created *Map Collections 1500–1999* for the small fraction of their 4.5 million items that have been converted to digital form. With a focus on Americana, the site is organized into seven major categories: "General Maps," "Cities and Towns," "Conservation and Environment," "Discovery and Exploration," "Cultural Landscapes," "Military Battles and Campaigns," and "Transportation and Communication."

There are several ways to access this collection, which makes it a breeze to use for research. You can browse each of the seven categories; search the site by keyword; or browse by geographic location, subject, title, or creator.

MAPS—POLITICAL

Best Search Engine: http://www.google.com/

Key Search Term: Political maps

Atlapedia Online: Political Maps
http://www.atlapedia.com/online/map_index.htm
high school and up

Atlapedia Online contains full-color physical and political maps, as well as key facts and statistics on countries of the world. Use the "World Maps" section to find political maps for particular countries. In the "Countries A to Z" section, you'll find some extra goodies, including figures and statistical data on geography, climate, people, religion, language, history, and economy.

World Sites Atlas: Interactive Political Maps
http://www.sitesatlas.com/Atlas/PolAtlas/polatlas.htm
high school and up

Similar to the *Atlapedia* site reviewed above, this page by *World Sites Atlas* offers political maps of world regions. Simply click on the interactive map to see a detailed political map for that area or choose from a list of countries at the bottom of the page. Then use the site's map legend to determine what each type style and/or map color indicates in terms of political status.

MAPS—TOPOGRAPHICAL

Best Search Engine: http://www.ixquick.com/

Key Search Terms: Topography

                        Topographic maps

Maps 101: Topographic Maps, The Basics
http://maps.nrcan.gc.ca/maps101/
high school and up

The Centre for Topographic Information, Natural Resources Canada, has created a wonderful site based on information originally in a brochure by the same name. Information is easy to locate here, thanks to a good navigation toolbar, but it's worth your time to browse a bit as well.

Start with the frequently-asked-questions section, where many of your own queries might have already been answered. Using the toolbar, you'll also find material describing the various grid reference systems, magnetic declination, map scales, contours, and map symbols. There's also some good tips on using topographic maps, such as how to find compass bearings and grid bearings, how to orient a map, and a list of mapping terminology. Be sure to check out the extensive links to map libraries and other mapping sites as well.

Hands-On Topographic Maps
http://earthview.sdsu.edu/trees/topohans.html
high school and up

This is an educational site from San Diego State University's Earthview project. It provides an overview of how contour lines are used in topography and walks you through the process of constructing a topographic map using 2-D and 3-D data. Do you have a spare shoebox sitting around your house? Two of the most interesting projects described here involve building topographic maps out of shoeboxes.

Be sure to click on the "Webquest on Topography" link at the bottom of the page, which takes you to a page with lessons linked to topographic images of Puget Sound, the Rio Grande Rift, the greater Los Angeles area, and more.

Topographic Map Symbols
http://mac.usgs.gov/mac/isb/pubs/booklets/symbols/
middle school and up

Leave it to the U.S. Geological Survey (USGS) to create an excellent online resource for geography students and other users of topographic maps. Along with a brief introduction on what a topographic map is and how to read one, this site provides clear charts for map symbols in six different categories.

If you need to know the designated map symbols for elevation, boundaries, land surface features, water features, buildings, roads, and railroads, this site has the goods. Under "Topographic Map Information," there's also a handful of links to related mapping sites and to map dealers who can supply you with topographic maps from USGS's collection of nearly 70,000 titles.

MARRIAGE RATES

Best Search Engine: http://www.google.com/
Key Search Term: Marriage rates

Divorce Rates and Marriage Rates—What Happened
http://www.divorcereform.org/rates.html
middle school and up

Wow. If you want info on marriage and divorce rates plus the analysis that goes along with them, you'll love this in-your-face collection of data and articles.

It's part of the Divorce Statistics Collection from Americans for Divorce Reform, and it contains these statistics computed and compiled from just about every angle you can imagine. Material here includes "Statistics on Why Divorce Rates Increased," "Divorce Rates in Families with Children," "Divorce Rates for Specific U.S. States and Localities," "Report on Current Marital Status of Adults and Composition of Households," "State-Level Statistics on Current Marital Status," "Facts about Marital Distress and Divorce," the "2002 Census Bureau Report on Marriage and Divorce," and much more.

Crude Marriage Rates for Selected Countries
http://www.infoplease.com/ipa/A0004385.html
middle school and up

For about 20 Western countries, you can view the marriage rates for four years—1990, 1997, 1998, and 1999. Links will take you to a similar chart that shows divorce rates for basically the same group of countries.

MEDICAL GEOGRAPHY

Best Search Engine: http://www.ixquick.com/
Key Search Term: Medical geography

Just Another Medical Geography page
http://www.geocities.com/Tokyo/Flats/7335/medical_geography.htm
high school and up

This interesting—although somewhat disjointed—site provides you with an understanding of what medical geography is and its relation to other disciplines, such as medical anthropology, medical sociology, and health economics. You'll uncover historical information, dating back to Hippocrates, on how medical geography has matured as an academic specialty. Be sure to delve into the pages on the "Geography of Disease," where you'll find good links to sites related to epidemiology and health statistics. Another page focuses on the "Geography of Health," approaching health issues from a geographic perspective.

The site's author has collected a number of additional resources on medical geography, such as links to articles and published studies, online health atlases, researchers and research centers, discussion groups, and a conference calendar. He has also assembled excellent links to sites in closely related fields, including climate and health, emerging infectious diseases, epidemiology, geostatistics, rural health, and tropical medicine.

Geography Exchange: Medical Geography Resources
http://www.zephryus.demon.co.uk/geography/links/medi.html
high school/college level

While you won't find any original content here, this site by the *Geography Exchange* offers a good collection of links to Web sites that are relevant to the field of medical geography. Selected and annotated by teachers, this list of 20-plus sites can help direct you to some useful information.

For instance, you could link from here to the *Atlas of Health Care* in the United States, a useful Web resource for advanced researchers seeking statistics and detailed information. Or you could link to the World Health Organization's (WHO) site on emerging communicable diseases to learn about the spread of cholera, hemorrhagic fevers, rickettsial diseases, spongiform encephalopathies, and more.

MEGAPOLIS

Best Search Engine: http://www.google.com/
Key Search Terms: Megapolis
                    Megalopolis

Megalopolis
http://geography.about.com/library/weekly/aa021599.
   htm?terms = megalopolis
middle school and up

This *About.com* article defines the megalopolis known as BosWash, the Boston to Washington, D.C., corridor that French geographer Jean

Gottman studied in the 1950s and wrote about in a book called *Megalopolis*.

The article goes into some depth about BosWash with interesting statistics on the area, while also providing an overview of the term and concept. You'll even get a link to the small ancient Greek city of the same name.

MIGRATION

Best Search Engine: http://www.google.com/

Key Search Terms: Migration + geography

Migration + demographics

Center for Migration Studies
http://www.cmsny.org/index.htm
high school and up

The Center for Migration Studies (CMS), founded in 1964, is the only institute in the United States devoted exclusively to understanding and educating the public on the causes and consequences of human mobility at both origin and destination countries. If you are looking for research material that touches on sociodemographic, historical, economic, political, or legislative aspects of human migration, you'll find a number of excellent resources at the CMS Web site.

The absolute highlight of this site is CMS's searchable and browsable library and archives, which constitutes one of the most comprehensive libraries on migration, refugees, and ethnic groups in the world. You can also use the site's "Publication" section to access CMS publications, which include two journals, a newsletter, and various reports on migration, refugees, and ethnic groups.

AmeriStat (Migration)
http://www.prb.org/AmeristatTemplate.cfm
high school and up

Population Reference Bureau's *AmeriStat* site, which bills itself as a "one-stop source for U.S. population data," offers some excellent resources on domestic and international migration.

Alongside other population-related topics such as fertility, labor, and mortality, you'll find an entire section devoted to migration. Here, you can click on headlines to read articles and reports, view statistical charts and graphs, and locate original source materials. To give you a taste of what you might find here, we've noted the headlines of some of the site's recent reports, including "U.S. Foreign-Born Drawn to Eight States," "Migration to the South Brings U.S. Black Full Circle," and "Twenty-Somethings Move the Most."

MONSOON

Best Search Engine: http://www.google.com/

Key Search Terms: Monsoon + education

                             Monsoon + climate

Program for the Advancement of Geoscience Education: Links: Monsoon
http://www.page.ucar.edu/pub/education_res/presearch/met/monsoon.htm
high school and up

Created by the Program for the Advancement of Geoscience Education (PAGE), this site offers links to Web information on monsoons—information that's surprisingly elusive on mainstream search engines. Here, you'll be directed to several Web sites with general monsoon information, as well as sites specific to certain geographic areas affected by monsoons. Some of the links are accompanied by brief text descriptions, while others you'll have to click and see for yourself.

Encylopedia.com: Monsoon
http://www.encyclopedia.com/articles/08690.html
middle school and up

Aren't you just hankering for a simple definition of a monsoon? If so, this site will appease you. It provides an encyclopedia-style definition, as well as offering monsoon-related journal and newspaper articles from the *Electric Library* (a fee service).

MORAINE (SEE ALSO GLACIER)

Best Search Engine: http://www.google.com/

Key Search Terms: Moraine + geography

                             Glacier + moraine

Glacial Deposition: Glacial Moraine
http://www.zephryus.demon.co.uk/geography/resources/glaciers/moraine.
    html
middle school and up

This quickie site provides short descriptions and photographs of eight types of moraine. The six types that create recognizable, lasting landforms are ground, lateral, medial, push, recessional, and terminal. Two other types—superglacial and englacial—exist only while the glacier itself is in existence.

About Geography: Glacial Depositions and Moraines
http://geography.miningco.com/library/weekly/aa053199.htm
middle school and up

This straightforward site simply tells you about the different types of glacial and ice sheet depositions. You'll find brief definitions of the following: glacial flour, till, terminal moraine, recessional moraine, ground moraine, lateral moraine, medial moraine, push moraine, ablation moraine, and glacial erratics.

All about Glaciers (National Snow and Ice Data Center)
http://nsidc.org/glaciers/
college level

This excellent site from the National Snow and Ice Data Center (NSIDC) is broken into broad sections, making it an ideal place to begin your research.

Look under "Data and Science" to find data and imagery, publications, project links, and relevant organizations. There's a "World Glacier Inventory," where you can get specific details about many of the world's glaciers, including parameters such as location, area, length, orientation, elevation, and classification of morphological type and moraines. There are also numerous links that will take you to collections of images of glaciers, including one site dedicated to photos of Alaskan glaciers and another focused on Norwegian glaciers.

Go to "General Information" for a definition of moraines and a list of some pretty fascinating glacier facts. In addition to the glossary and quick facts, you'll discover a Q&A, a gallery of historic photos, and more. For the latest media coverage related to glaciers and glacier research, go to "Glacier News." Click on the handy, alphabetized "Site Map" for pinpointing specific information.

MORTALITY RATES (SEE ALSO DEMOGRAPHICS, POPULATION, VITAL STATISTICS)

Best Search Engine: http://www.google.com
Key Search Terms: Mortality + rates

Countries of the World
http://www.countryreports.org/
middle school and up

This terrific site, selected as one of the best sites on the Web for teachers, is also one of the best sites for students. Basic demographic research on people from all over the world is easy and quick. Go to the home page and click on "World Countries" for a comprehensive database of the world's countries with extensive demographic information on each one. Once you choose a country, you'll be given a menu of the following: "Economy," "Defense," "Geography," "Government," "People," "National Anthem Lyrics," and related links. Pick "People."

Among many other statistics, you'll find death rate. Other really helpful information here includes overall fertility rate, age structure, birth rate, infant mortality rate, population growth, religious affiliations, languages spoken, literacy, and more.

You won't get detailed information about the death rate here. You'll have to continue your search elsewhere for that. But you will get accurate information to start you on your way.

Cancer Mortality Maps and Graphs Web Site
http://www3.cancer.gov/atlasplus/
high school and up

Medical geographers study mortality rates for many different diseases, but cancer is probably one of the diseases looked at most frequently, and this site from the National Cancer Institute provides some excellent resources on geographic patterns and time trends for cancer mortality in the United States.

Your menu options include an atlas of cancer mortality in the United States for the years 1950–94; interactive mortality charts and graphs; customizable mortality maps; and links to related U.S. and international sites.

The site contains information on more than 40 cancers, and it's organized so that you can easily download geographic and mortality data in accessible spreadsheet formats. The files are compressed to make the downloading quicker, so you'll just need to uncompress them once they are on your computer. If you need to create charts or graphs of your own, you might find this download feature particularly helpful.

MOUNTAINS

Best Search Engine: http://www.google.com/
Key Search Term: Mountains

Mountains of the World
http://www.btinternet.com/~nigelspencer/mountain-world.htm
middle school and up

Even though this is a personal home page, created by a couple of mountain enthusiasts and climbers to document their trips and climbs, this digital tour of the world's great mountains will wow with you with beautiful pictures and educate you about the mountains' special features. Following in the footsteps of your tour guides, you'll visit Mount Kinabalu in Borneo, about a dozen peaks in the Alps of Europe, the high Atlas mountains of Morocco, Mount Whitney in the United States, Mount Kilimanjaro in Africa, Mount Everest in Nepal, and several other high places of the earth.

Mountains of the World is just one part of this mountain site, however. You can also visit the mountains of Scotland and the mountains of England and Wales. Head to the bottom of the page for the "Mountaineering Site Map," where you'll get an index of all the mountain pages on the site. The site map lists links to every peak you can visit here.

Don't expect information in a scientific format, but do expect to learn about elevation, vegetation zones, geographic location, climate, history of people climbing the mountain, and a day-by-day recounting of your tour guide's experience on the mountain.

Peakware World Mountain Encyclopedia
http://www.peakware.com/encyclopedia/index.htm
high school and up

This site bills itself as the world's premiere mountain and mountaineering Web site, and it just might be right if you're looking for a site that focuses on human interaction with the mountains. You'll find a wealth of wonderful mountain information—much of it created by those who visit the site. (The site is set up to allow visitors to add information about specific peaks and submit favorite mountain photos.)

More than 1,700 peaks are catalogued here. Find them by browsing the index or by using the search function found in the menu at the top of the page. The index allows you to choose a continent and then organize the peaks on that continent by various combinations of name and elevation. Each peak name is a link to a page with detailed information on the best times to climb the mountain, best routes to take, elevation, location, and more. The "Photo Gallery" allows you to search for specific mountain photos (or add ones of your own).

Although the previous sections of the site provide good resources, it's the section on highest peaks that will probably be the most valuable in your research. It's an extensive database of information that will answer all the most commonly asked questions about the world's tallest mountains, as well as some of the more obscure questions. You'll find tables on the "8,000 Meter Peaks" (tallest mountains in the world), the "Seven Summits" (tallest mountain on each continent), "Highest Unclimbed Peaks," "Fifty State High Points," "Colorado Fourteeners" (peaks in Colorado that top 14,000 feet, "California Fourteeners" (same thing in California), "Alpine 4,000 Meter Peaks," "Highest Active Volcanoes," and "Deadliest Volcanic Eruptions in the Twentieth Century."

The site also contains maps, links, and a page called "Eco" that covers sound environmental practices when hiking and climbing in the mountains. Read this if you have any questions about what it means to tread lightly on the earth.

NATIONAL ANTHEMS

Best Search Engine: http://www.google.com/
Key Search Term: National anthems

Country Reports: National Anthems
http://www.countryreports.org/
middle school and up

Odds are you didn't even know the country of Tuvalu *existed,* let alone that it had a national anthem. If you haven't bumped into the *Country Reports* Web site already, you'll be thrilled by it now. Its extensive collection of historical, economic, and geographical information on hundreds of countries around the world has earned kudos from the National Education Association, *Forbes* magazine, Ziff-Davis, and others.

To listen to the national anthem of your choice, simply click on a country and then click on "National Anthem." You can also read the lyrics, which—lucky for you—are translated into English.

NATIONS IN TRANSITION

Best Search Engine: http://www.google.com/
Key Search Term: Nations in transition

Nations in Transition
http://www.bcpl.net/~sullivan/modules/nationsgr9/
middle school and up

This educational Web site, geared toward teachers and students, will not only introduce you to the issues faced by nations in transition, it will also give you some excellent tips on conducting and presenting your own research.

After a brief introduction to defining the term "nations in transition," the site presents a research assignment to help you explore the issues faced by nations in transition and by those who work with them. Following this assignment, you'll find instruction on the various stages of conducting a research project—questioning; planning; gathering; sorting and sifting; synthesis and evaluation; refined gathering, sorting, and sifting; and final synthesis and evaluation.

Go to "Gathering, Sorting, and Sifting," which is where you'll find resources to help in your research on this topic.

The subsection called "Nonprint Resources" contains a long list of questions and topics, each of which is a link to an essay at this site. You'll find, for example, "Problems with German Reunification," "Western Europe Needs the U.S. and NATO," "China in Transition," "Capitalism in Russia," "South Africa in Transition," "The Balkans for Beginners," and many more useful links.

Chances are you'll find plenty of helpful information here. And if you need help when you get ready to write up your research paper, try the link at the bottom of this page called "Guide to Writing a Basic Essay."

Center for Nations in Transition
http://www.hhh.umn.edu/centers/cnt/
high school and up

Although the work of this center focuses on central and eastern Europe, you'll find lots of good general resources as well. And if your own topic relates to the countries of central and eastern Europe, you'll find a wealth of specific information.

The menu at the left side of the page contains links to an environmental indicators study, a database on economies in transition, and other resources. If you are interested in environmental issues for nations in transition, you'll want to take a look at the environmental indicators study. It analyzes many different statistics on the environment over a period of time for six different central and eastern European countries to determine if the movement of the indicators as a collective whole indicate a society that is becoming more sustainable or less sustainable.

The database on economies offers information on central European countries, the Baltics, the Balkans, and numerous other European and Asian countries, including China, Mongolia, and Vietnam. Data includes stats in the following areas: population and surface area, gross national product and gross domestic product, inflation, external debt,

trade, resource flows, health, commercial energy use, land use, urbanization, forest, production, investment, and macroeconomic indicators.

NATION-STATE

Best Search Engine: http://www.google.com/
Key Search Term: Nation-States

States, Nations, and Nation-States
http://www.countrywatch.com/@school/state_or_nation.htm
middle school and up

Understanding "nation-states," as opposed to "nations" and "states,"
can be a bit confusing, but this *Countrywatch.com* page does an excellent
job of teasing out the differences between nations, states, and nation-
states. In addition to a brief overview, you'll get a list of the criteria
used to determine a country's status as a state and examples of countries
that, like the United States, are considered to be both states and nation-
states.

NATURAL RESOURCES

Best Search Engine: http://www.google.com/
Key Search Term: Natural resources

SpeakOut
http://www.speakout.com/Issues/
high school and up

This section of the *SpeakOut* Web site is designed to help you—the
latent activist—find information on topics ranging from international
affairs to food and farming to the environment. Although the site has
an activist bias, you'll find that the information provided here on the
environment is evenhanded and legitimate as a research source.

Click on the "Environment" button to see a selection of natural
resource-related topics, including endangered species; oceans, lakes, and
rivers; forests, deserts, and wilderness; and recycling and waste. Within
each topic, there are neatly organized issues and subtopics. For instance,
look inside "Oceans, Lakes, and Rivers" and click on "Should Old Dams
Be Torn Down?" As with every subtopic, you'll get background information, history, and facts, as well as lucid on the one hand and on the
other hand summaries. In this instance, the impressively diverse sources
for information includes American Rivers, Trout Unlimited, and the

National Hydropower Association. You'll also find good links to relevant organizations, as well as links to editorials and feature articles from other news sources.

Natural Resources Conservation Service
http://www.nrcs.usda.gov/
high school and up

The U.S. Department of Agriculture's (USDA) *Natural Resources Conservation Service* Web site is a gem if you're looking for a good general overview of natural resource topics in the United States. Menu items include "Earth Team," "General Information," "Media Information," "Teachers and Students," "Science and Technology," and more.

If you are looking for an opportunity to get involved in conservation programs, go to "Earth Team," where you can learn all about volunteering with this organization in one of its many programs to reduce soil erosion, conserve our water and improve its quality, and develop pride in our country's natural resource heritage.

Under "General Information," you can locate resources on "Home and Garden Tips," "Backyard Conservation," "Fact Sheets," "Tidbits for Teachers," "Living in Harmony with Wetlands," and other topics.

For information on any of the USDA's many conservation programs, try the "Programs" link. Click on the name of any program here, and you'll be taken to a page with detailed information on the program. There's the Farmland Protection Program, the Flood Risk Reduction Program, the Forestry Incentive Program, Soil Survey Programs, Wetlands Reserve Program, and many others.

The "Science and Technology" section of the site gives you access to, among other things, "Natural Resources Inventories and Databases," "Natural Resources Assessments," "Soil Survey Data," "Maps," "Facts and Figures," and many other useful reports.

Finally, you should browse the list of feature topics on the right side of the home page for topics related to your area of research. Current features when we visited included "Defending Against Drought," "Animal Feeding Operations," Conservation Buffers," and the "Snow Survey and Water Supply" among others.

Introduction to Sustainability: SD Gateway
http://sdgateway.net/introsd/
high school and up

This site, developed by the Sustainable Development Communications Network, provides a powerful overview of what sustainable development is and why it is important. The site contains a time line of sustainable development history, background material on important aspects of the concept, and suggestions for further exploration.

Inside the "Definition" section, you'll read about how various groups and organizations describe sustainable development, and you'll find a searchable database, with access to the full text of many reports and articles on sustainable development. You'll also want to check out "SD Topics," a vast section that provides background information on over 50 topics, which are subdivided into the broad categories of "Business and Trade," "Communities and Society," "Danger Signs," "Environment," "Managing Sustainability," and "Regions."

For information on natural resources issues, try looking in the "Environment" section of the site index first. "Environment" is one of the numerous topics listed under the broad category of "SD Topics" in the index. You'll find resources on air, energy, forests, fresh water, grasslands, land, oceans and coasts, and rivers and wetlands. You can also search by region of the world, if you are interested in natural resources issues in a specific place. Scroll down the site index until you get to "Regions," which is also under "SD Topics." Choices include "Australia, New Zealand, Pacific Islands"; "Caribbean"; "Central America"; "Central and Eastern Europe"; "East Africa"; "East Asia"; and so on.

Sustainable Development Information Service
http://www.wri.org/sdis/
high school and up

This organization is concerned with guaranteeing people's access to information and decisions regarding natural resources and the environment. The menu at the left lets you search for resource information by region of the world for data tables, facts and figures, global trends, maps and indicators, multimedia resources, PowerPoint presentations, Internet resources, and more.

Go to the "Regional" section, pick your region, and you'll be given oodles of maps, data tables, articles, fact sheets, and more. "Global Trends" contains lots of interesting information on population statistics and human well-being, resources at risk, production and consumption, feeding the world, and other topics.

To access data in the "Data Tables" section of the site, click on the topic that best suits your interest. Options include "Agriculture and Food"; "Atmosphere and Climate"; "Basic Economic Indicators"; "Biodiversity and Protected Areas"; "Coastal, Marine, and Inland Waters"; "Energy and Resource Use"; "Forests and Grasslands"; "Freshwater"; "Population"; "Health and Human Development"; "Small Nations and Islands"; and "Urban Data."

NOMADISM

Best Search Engine: http://www.google.com/
Key Search Term: Nomadism

Nomadism
http://www.historytoday.com/index.cfm?articleid = 3695
high school and up

This *Historytoday.com* encyclopedia entry provides a thorough definition of nomadism to get you started in your research. It's a historical overview of nomadism with information on when and where nomadism has most often occurred in the world.

African Nomads
http://www.unesco.org/whc/exhibits/afr_rev/africa-c.htm
middle school and up

African Nomads provides a brief historical overview of seminomadic and nomadic cultures on the African continent. An exhibit of images illustrates daily life and artifacts in various nomadic groups.

NORTH ATLANTIC TREATY ORGANIZATION

Best Search Engine: http://www.google.com/
Key Search Term: NATO

North Atlantic Treaty Organization
http://www.nato.int/home.htm
high school and up

Naturally, if you're researching the North Atlantic Treaty Organization (NATO), you'll want to visit the organization's own Web site. The "Welcome" section offers an excellent overview of NATO itself and how it has evolved; you'll find background here on the original treaty, current member countries, and the fundamental role of NATO.

The section called "NATO Update" is an amazingly rich resource; it presents a complete chronology (1945 to the present) of all past and upcoming NATO-related events and activities, including links to information relevant to events in any given year. The "Issues" section is another gold mine, offering extensive background information, documents, multimedia, and fact sheets about issues on NATO's current agenda. Also, look in the site's "Document and Publications" section for basic texts, fact sheets, press archives, speeches, the *NATO Handbook*, and more.

CNN: NATO at 50
http://www9.cnn.com/SPECIALS/1999/nato/
high school and up

This *CNN In-Depth Special* looks into NATO's past and at how the organization's mission is evolving for the future. The site contains an interactive map, interactive time line (not as good as the one at NATO.int), and brief biographies of secretaries-general of NATO. You'll also find three meaty articles focusing on NATO's midlife crisis, its shifting role in the world, and on the reasons some countries are currently seeking NATO membership.

NUCLEAR ENERGY

Best Search Engine: http://www.google.com/
Key Search Terms: Nuclear energy + issues

Open Directory Project—Science: Technology: Energy: Nuclear
http://dmoz.org/Science/Technology/Energy/Nuclear/
high school and up

Created by the *Open Directory Project* (the largest, most comprehensive human-edited directory of the Web), this site offers hundreds of categorized and annotated links to information on nuclear energy.

The sites organized on this page are all relevant to research into the production of usable energy from fission of uranium, plutonium, and/or thorium. Categories include "Applications in Space," "Nuclear Fuel," "Nuclear Waste," "Chernobyl Accident," and "Power Plants." If you're looking for information relating to environmental concerns about nuclear energy, check the *Open Directory Project*'s "Society/Issues/Environment/Nuclear" (http://dmoz.org/Society/Issues/Environment/Nuclear/) page.

Nuclear Energy Institute
http://www.nei.org/
high school and up

Although the Nuclear Energy Institute (NEI) is clearly a cheerleader for nuclear energy, you will nonetheless find useful information here. Tap into the site's "Newsroom" and "Library" section for a primer on nuclear energy, fact sheets, other NEI publications, and a glossary of terms.

Click on "Nuclear Technologies" to learn about how nuclear energy is created and used. The section called "Nuclear Data" offers detailed current and historical nuclear industry statistics.

Under "Public Policy Issues," you'll find information about nuclear energy's economic benefits, environmental impact, nuclear waste disposal, transportation safety, and more.

OCEAN CURRENTS

Best Search Engine: http://www.yahoo.com/

Key Search Term: Ocean currents

Ocean Talk
http://oceanographer.navy.mil/oceantlk.html
middle school and up

This text-only site was originally written by a navy oceanographer for use in a booklet. Although a few photographs or graphics would surely spruce the site up, it does a decent job of giving you a basic understanding of ocean science.

To glean some history on oceanography, check out the section called "The Lure of the Sea." The next section, "Underwater World," does a nice job of describing parts of the ocean floor, including abyssal plains, midocean ridges, trenches, seamounts, and continental slopes, canyons and shelves. In "Oceans of the World," you'll find descriptions of the Pacific, Atlantic, Indian, and Arctic Oceans. "The Restless Sea" is a section that succinctly describes currents, swells, waves, breakers, upwellings, and tsunamis—and what factors cause them.

A Primer on Ocean Currents
http://www.whoi.edu/coastal-briefs/Coastal-Brief-94-05.html
high school and up

We're not convinced that "primer" is the right epithet for this site. Originally published by Woods Hole Oceanic Institution (WHOI), this primer on ocean currents is a good resource for researchers who are somewhat familiar with the subject. It offers scientific information on the following subjects: how current flow is recorded and measured, properties of seawater, water masses, and current velocity measurements.

OCEAN POLLUTION

Best Search Engine: http://www.google.com/

Key Search Term: Ocean pollution

Environmental Protection Agency Office of Water
http://www.epa.gov/ow/
middle school and up

This is water-central for resources related to water pollution in the United States, and you'll also find some links for international resources at various spots on this site. Start by browsing the home page, which has a menu on the left that includes the following sections: "Laws and Regulations," "Funding and Grants," "Publications," "What You Can Do," "Training," "Education Resources," "Databases and Software," and "For Kids."

You'll also see a little box of links for current information, which includes such things as "WaterNews," "Map Your Waters," "EPA News-room," and other current events resources.

The bulk of excellent research resources on the site are divided into the following sections, which are listed down the center of the home page: "Ground Water and Drinking Water"; "Water Science"; "Waste-water Management"; "Wetlands, Oceans, and Watersheds"; and "American Indian Environmental Office" which is the contact for all water issues on tribal lands. Go to "Wetlands, Oceans, and Watersheds" and you'll find subsections on all kinds of topics, including monitoring water quality; polluted runoff; oceans, coasts, and estuaries; wetlands; and wa-tersheds. Click on "Wetlands," for example, and you'll be able to explore "What Are Wetlands?", "Why Protect Wetlands?", and "How Are Wet-lands Protected?" Topics such as flood protection, fish and wildlife, shoreline erosion, economics, and recreation are discussed in detail.

Try "For Kids" back at the home page if you would like to find kid-friendly resources in the following areas: "Water for Kids," "What You Can Do," "Environmental Sites for Kids," "Education," and "Health."

Pollution at Sea
http://daac.gsfc.nasa.gov/CAMPAIGN_DOCS/OCDST/
    shuttle_oceanography_web/oss_122.html
middle school and up

This *Pollution at Sea* site gives you oceanography straight from the space shuttle. Photographs track pollution, particularly in the Persian Gulf and the Gulf of Oman, where long-term pollution has occurred. You'll see thumbnail images of oil slicks, oil dumps, surface debris, and routine dumps in the Red Sea, the Persian Gulf, and other bodies of water in the Middle East.

At the bottom of this page, you'll see a button for "Contents." Click here and you'll be taken to the home page for the whole site, which contains loads of useful information on the oceans and seas. There are sections called "The Coastal Science," "The Islands," "Local Winds," "Waves," "Ship Wakes," "Spiral Eddies," and "Suloys." Although these other sections do not necessarily show pollution at sea, they may be of interest.

Oceans in Peril
http://seawifs.gsfc.nasa.gov/OCEAN_PLANET/HTML/peril_buoys.html
high school and up

The menu made up of buoys at the top of this page offers you access to the following topics: "Pollution," "Habitats," "Fishing," and "Global." Click on the "Pollution" buoy to explore the issues surrounding oil pollution, toxic contaminants, marine debris, and ocean mining and dumping. Click on any one of these topics for a detailed page devoted to exploring the topic in depth. The "Oil Pollution" page, for example, is divided into three categories—sources, accidents, and cleanups. You'll find statistical information, photographs, legal information, links to further resources, and more.

Under the "Global" section of the site, you'll find some pollution-related resources, including "Swarming the Shores" and "Growing Pains" articles about the demands that growing populations place on coastal resources.

Another cool feature at this site is the link to the "Ocean Planet Exhibition" from the Smithsonian Institution's National Museum of Natural History. If you've got an extra minute, check it out. You'll see "Oceans in Peril," which is part of the exhibition, but you'll also see many other ocean-related resources that you may want to visit.

OCEANS

Best Search Engine: http://www.yahoo.com/
Key Search Term: Oceanography

National Oceanographic Data Center
http://www.nodc.noaa.gov/
high school and up

The National Oceanographic Data Center (NODC) Web site is *the* place to go for scientific global ocean data. The NODC collects physical, chemical, and biological oceanographic data from a variety of sources, including federal agencies, state and local government agencies, universities and research institutions, and private industry.

To access information on your chosen topic in oceanography, use the site's pull-down menu of data collections. You'll find info on buoys, coastal water temperatures, coral reefs, sea surface temperatures, plankton, salinity, waves, and far more. You can also use the site's search engine to find information using a specific keyword.

NODC's site offers a worthwhile FAQ section, as well as excellent links to research facilities and library and information services.

Bibliographies in Oceanography and Related Areas
http://scilib.ucsd.edu/sio/guide/bibliographies.html
high school and up

Maintained by the Scripps Institution of Oceanography Library, this site houses an enormous number of bibliographic links that will prove valuable for most ocean-related research projects.

The links are broken into the following broad areas: "Oceanography: Biological Features"; "Oceanography: Physical Aspects"; "Oceanography: General Topics"; "Regional Focus"; "Polar Focus"; and "Other Topics." Spend some time, however, just browsing this collection—you'll find links to such gems as the *Bibliographic Guide to the Study of Dolphin Intelligence*, a *Bibliography for AlgaeBase*, the *Bibliography of Biographies of Ocean Scientists*, and the *Cumulative Bibliography on the History of Oceanography*.

NOAA Ocean Explorer
http://oceanexplorer.noaa.gov/
high school and up

Although the *Ocean Explorer* site is only in its first year, it already houses an impressive collection of information on the National Oceanic and Atmospheric Administration's (NOAA) major ocean exploration efforts.

Here, you can follow ocean explorations in near real-time, learn about ocean exploration technologies, observe remote marine areas through multimedia technology, review NOAA's 200-year history of ocean exploration, and discover additional NOAA resources in a virtual library.

To learn about NOAA's recent ocean expeditions, go to the "Explorations" section. Here, you can read each expedition's mission plan, summaries and observations, daily updates, and more. Visit the site's "Gallery" for a collection of images, audio, and video. The "Technology" section offers photos and descriptions of the various technologies used in ocean exploration.

Earth's Water
http://ga.water.usgs.gov/edu/mearth.html
middle school and up

This page from the United States Geological Survey *Water Science for Schools* site is chock-full of things you might want to know about the earth's oceans and water in general. Click on the following sections to take you on a comprehensive tour: "Where Is Earth's Water?", "How Much Water Is There?", "The Water Cycle," "Water on the Earth's Surface," "Water in the Ground," "Rain," and "Glaciers and Icecaps." This site doesn't miss much.

Head back to the home page for information on "Water Basics," "Special Topics," a "Glossary of Water Terms," an "Activity Center," and more.

The Sea
http://www.the-sea.org/main.htm
high school and up

Although this is a personal page, written and maintained by a sea admirer, it contains reliable information that is presented in a pleasing format. One quirk, however, is that you will need to use the menu at the bottom of the page to access any pages once you leave the home page. It's a tiny little menu, but it's your ticket to lots of great info on the world's oceans.

Try "Oceans Map" where you can click on an ocean to read a detailed but accessible description of the ocean's geography. There's also a table that gives you all the seas connected to each ocean.

Other sections of this site include "Sea Creatures," "Hurricanes," "Currents and Waves," "Tides," and "Ocean Links" for other related Web sites.

ORGANIZATION OF AMERICAN STATES

Best Search Engine: http://www.google.com/
Key Search Term: Organization of American States

Organization of American States
http://www.oas.org/
high school and up

If you're initiating your research on the Organization of American States (OAS) with this site, we suggest you go directly to the "About OAS" section. Here, you can read about the role of OAS, its history, charter, and vision for the future. In the "Documents" section, you can access the OAS's annual report, press releases, treaties, and speeches. You can also use a pull-down menu to collect information from OAS's committees on democracy, drug control, human rights, trade, sustainable development, and other issues. Sadly, however, this site's overall content and structure struck us as bureaucratic and tough to navigate.

Background Notes: Organization of American States
http://www.state.gov/www/background_notes/oas_0398_bgn.html
college level

This textual U.S. State Department document provides an excellent primer on the Organization of American States (OAS). It offers extensive factual information on the organization, its history, purpose, member countries, permanent observer countries, official languages, principal organs, specialized organizations, other entities, and budget. The site also provides information on U.S. policy toward the OAS, as well as a description of the OAS's core concerns and objectives.

ORGANIZATION OF PETROLEUM EXPORTING COUNTRIES

Best Search Engine: http://www.google.com/
Key Search Term: OPEC

Organization of Petroleum Exporting Countries (OPEC) Online
http://www.opec.org/
high school and up

OPEC's Web site is well designed, with easy-to-find information resources. You'll see a handy navigation bar across the top of the home page with headings that include "News and Info," "About OPEC," "Member Countries," "Meetings," "Publications," and "FAQs." (The toolbar is present on every page of the Web site, making it a cinch to travel around the site.)

In the "News and Info" section, you'll find press releases, speeches, market indicators, and other general information. The "Member Countries" section opens with a map that you can click on to learn about OPEC's 11 oil-producing and exporting countries, including each country's oil and gas reserves and production. Look under "Publications" for OPEC's monthly oil market report; the annual report; a general information booklet that contains details about OPEC's founding, principal aims, and structure; and so forth.

OPEC Fact Sheet
http://www.eia.doe.gov/emeu/cabs/opec.html
high school and up

Created by the U.S. Department of Energy's Information Administration, this analysis brief provides factual and statistical information about the Organization of Petroleum Exporting Countries (OPEC). The subjects that are covered include background info, OPEC and the global oil market, limited non-OPEC support for OPEC, OPEC compliance, Iraq, and world oil pricing. The text is supported by excellent graphics and charts.

OZONE LAYER

Best Search Engine: http://www.directhit.com/

Key Search Terms: Ozone

                        Ozone layer

                        Ozone + education

U.S. Environmental Protection Agency: Ozone Depletion
http://www.epa.gov/ozone/
high school and up

The U.S. Environmental Protection Agency (EPA) has created an excellent resource for information on ozone depletion. Despite the labyrinth of extensive materials, this site is remarkably easy to navigate. You'll want to begin in the "Consumer and Business Resource Center," which is where you'll find the bulk of information. Click on "Information for the General Public," then go to "Science of Ozone Depletion." This page has extensive links to articles, fact sheets, and Web sites that provide scientific overviews, images, and animation of ozone levels. You'll find data covering the science of ozone depletion, as well as information on methyl bromide, the UV index, and the U.S. regulations designed to protect the ozone layer.

For more detailed information, such as full citations to original papers, you can access "NASA's Ozone Resource File" or use the search field. You may also want to look under "Information for Businesses," where you'll find news about specific substances that contribute to ozone depletion, as well as their alternatives. Finally, if you can't find what you want here, try the EPA hotline that's provided or check out the EPA's links to other ozone-related Web sites.

Beyond Discovery: The Ozone Depletion Phenomenon
http://www4.nas.edu/beyond/beyonddiscovery.nsf/web/
    ozone?OpenDocument
high school and up

This site was created by the National Academy of Sciences as part of the "Beyond Discovery" series, which traces the origins of important scientific advances. Here, you'll find a tutorial on the scientific history of the ozone problem and what scientists have done to mitigate it. You can read through the site's pages much like a book, or use the toolbar on the left side of the page to choose a particular topic.

Some of the topics covered here include earth's atmosphere, CFCs, chemical culprits, the first findings about the ozone hole, potential catastrophes, atmospheric science and policy decisions, and more. You'll also want to check out the links here, which include a multimedia tour and a teaching tool on graphing stratospheric ozone.

Corporate Watch: Push Back the Poison
http://www.corpwatch.org/trac/feature/bromide/index.html
high school and up

Providing news, analysis, research tools, and action resources, this site can help you investigate how corporate activity affects the ozone layer.

The "Push Back the Poison" section takes aim at corporations' continued use of methyl bromide. Click on "Barons of Bromide," to learn extensively about companies that produce the chemical. You can also read a lengthy article about its effects on human health, excerpted from the Methyl Bromide Alternatives Network Briefing Kit. In a section called "A First Class Ozone Destroyer," you'll find scientists' statements on the impact of delaying the phase-out of methyl bromide use. There's also a detailed fact sheet on alternatives to methyl bromide.

To uncover dirt on a particular industry or company, first run a keyword search on the site, and then go to the "Research Corporations" guide, which provides links to databases, publications, search engines, government resources, investigative news sources, and corporate sites.

PACIFIC RIM

Best Search Engine: http://www.google.com
Key Search Terms: Pacific Rim + geography

Countries of the Pacific Rim
http://geography.about.com/library/misc/blpacificrim.htm
middle school and up

This little *About.com* site lists all the Pacific Rim countries with links to numerous sites about each country. Check it out to get an overview of which countries are included in the Pacific Rim, and then follow the link to an individual country site to pursue your specific research interests.

Asia Pacific Network
http://www2.h-net.msu.edu/~asia/links/
high school and up

You'll find everything under the sun about the Asian Pacific countries at this great gateway Web site. Links are organized in the following categories: "Academic Sites," "Government Sites," "Teaching Resource Sites," "Media," and "Miscellaneous." You'll find each of these categories under "General," and then under each region—"Central Asia," "East Asia," "South Asia," "Southeast Asia," and "Aotearoa/New Zealand/ Australia."

PETROLEUM—PRODUCTION, CONSUMPTION, RESERVES (SEE ALSO ORGANIZATION OF PETROLEUM EXPORTING COUNTRIES)

Best Search Engine: http://home.rmi.net/~michaelg/
Key Search Term: Petroleum

American Petroleum Institute
http://www.api.org/
high school and up

Produced by the American Petroleum Institute (API), this is actually a three-sites-rolled-into-one Web site. From the home page, you can access the "Energy Consumer Site," the "Energy Professional Site," or API's "Media Center," each targeting a different share of the Web audience.

All three subsites offer the same basic information on petroleum policy issues, innovation in the field, classroom tools and curricula, industry statistics, environmental issues, and more. For press releases and the latest news, go to the "Media Center." The "Energy Professional Site" is your best bet for in-depth information on specific issues and policies, statistical reports and economic analysis, distinct industry segments, and industry publications.

Oil and Gas Exploration
http://www.mindspring.com/~michaelg2/HOTLINKS_24.html
high school and up

Created by the ever-reliable *Websurfers Biweekly Earth Science Review*, this list of links will probably provide enough fire power for all of your research on petroleum. The sites listed here all offer information on oil and gas exploration, with links sorted into the following categories: "Government Oil and Gas Web Sites"; "The Environment"; "Oil and Gas Exploration in Specific Countries"; "Professional Societies"; "Technology"; "Other Sources of Information"; and "Oil Companies."

PHYSICAL GEOGRAPHY

Best Search Engine: http://www.msn.com/

Key Search Term: Physical geography

Introduction to Physical Geography
http://www.free-ed.net/fr08/lfc/course%20080502_01/section01.htm
high school and up

This site is the one you'll find time and time again by plugging the phrase "physical geography" into a search engine. Created by a professor in the geography department at Okanogan University College in British Columbia, this site is truly a noteworthy resource.

It's organized into six major topics: the science of physical geography; the universe, Earth, natural spheres, and gaia; matter and energy; climatology; hydrology; and biogeography. Each topic further subdivides into an extensive information network from which you can easily pick and choose the areas you want to delve into.

Physical Geography Resources
http://www.geography.wisc.edu/resources/phys.html
high school and up

This site, created by the University of Wisconsin–Madison, provides a collection of links to Web resources in the field of physical geography. As such, it also gives you a broad sense of which topics are important to the subject of physical geography.

You'll find these links sorted and arranged by subject; the subject areas include current weather images, maps, and movies; current weather data; climate images; climate data; atmospheric composition; solar; earth topography; stream flow data; vegetation; soils; and frequently asked questions files. You'll also find a list of popular information libraries for the study of physical geography.

PLATE TECTONICS

Best Search Engine: http://www.directhit.com/

Key Search Term: Plate tectonics

You Try It: Plate Tectonics
http://www.pbs.org/wgbh/aso/tryit/tectonics/
middle school and up

This site, created by WGBH, a public television station in Boston, does a bang-up job of illustrating the theory of plate tectonics, using Shockwave software that lets you manipulate earth's plates yourself. (If you don't have or want Shockwave on your computer, there's also a very good text version of the activity.)

Next, you can move on to a section called "Slippin' and a Slidin' " to learn about convergent, divergent, collisional, and transform boundaries. Each of these subsections provides real-world examples of the type of boundary, along with clear graphics to illustrate the concept.

If you're looking for biographical or historical info, go back to the home page, where there's a link to sites within the WGBH "People and Discoveries" databank, such as pages about sea floor spreading, the mid-ocean rift, and scientists Harry Hess, Arthur Holmes, and Alfred Wegener.

Earthquakes and Plate Tectonics
http://neic.usgs.gov/neis/plate_tectonics/rift_man.html
high school and up

Here's a brief informative site from the U.S. Geological Survey's (USGS) National Earthquake Information Center. It explains how the relatively new theory of plate tectonics combined many of the ideas about continental drift and sea-floor spreading into one theory. You'll see a large world map depicting the major and minor crustal plates and read an explanation of the role magnetic fields play in plate tectonics.

The majority of the text here is devoted, not surprisingly given the source, to the connection between plate tectonics and earthquakes. You'll read about the four types of seismic zones that can be attributed to plate movement. The article also discusses how plate tectonics is used as a tool in predicting earthquake activity. For more information about earthquakes, you need only click on one of the links at the top of the page, which include "Current Earthquake Information," "General Earthquake Information," and "Earthquake Search."

Note: Since the text provided here was originally in a USGS bulletin in 1977, you'll want to compare it to more recent research material as well.

Geology: Plate Tectonics
http://www.ucmp.berkeley.edu/geology/tectonics.html
high school and up

This exhibit, created by the Museum of Paleontology at the University of California, Berkeley, is broken into three major sections. The first section consists of text explaining the history of plate tectonics, the second offers an overview of the mechanisms driving plate tectonics, and the third provides animation (in GIF, AVI, or QuickTime formats) of plate tectonics during the Cenozoic, Mesozoic, Paleozoic, and Precambrian eras. For each era, there's also a link for more information on that era in terms of stratigraphy, ancient life, tectonics, and localities.

The site uses images from maps created by the PALEOMAP Project at the University of Texas at Arlington, a well-respected endeavor that focuses on plate tectonic development of the ocean basins and continents, as well as the changing distribution of land and sea during the past 1,100 million years. For more in-depth research, you'll find links here to the PALEOMAP data.

This Dynamic Earth (U.S. Geological Survey)
http://pubs.usgs.gov/publications/text/dynamic.html
high school and up

You'd be hard pressed to find a better explanation of how plate tectonics impacts all geological processes. The contents are broken into sections, which include "Historical Perspective," "Developing the Theory," "Understanding Plate Motions," "Hotspots," "Some Unanswered Questions," and "Plate Tectonics and People."

Within each of these main sections, you'll find well-written articles, good graphics, and interesting sidebars. For instance, in "Historical Perspectives," there are links to "Inside the Earth," "What Is a Tectonic Plate?", "Alfred Lothar Wegener," and "Polar Dinosaurs in Australia."

Because of a booklike layout, the best way to use the site is to read (or at least browse) the sections sequentially. The site could be improved by a site index or search mechanism that would allow you to better locate specific facts.

POLITICAL GEOGRAPHY

Best Search Engine: http://www.google.com/
Key Search Term: Political geography

Gerrymandering
http://geography.about.com/library/weekly/aa030199.htm
high school and up

Political geography examines the geographical factors involved in politics as well as the political factors involved in geography, such as the creation and development of countries. This *About.com* site explores the former—how geographical factors affect politics, specifically how gerrymandering makes the reapportionment and redistricting of congressional districts unfair.

When the census is taken every decade, there are new population figures for states, which means that the number of representatives each state can send to the House of Representatives has the potential to change. States have the responsibility of redistricting themselves into the appropriate number of congressional districts. Gerrymandering occurs when the party in power uses its power to modify congressional districts for its own benefit.

While this may sound scandalous, it's actually quite common, and you'll find lots of interesting statistics and information about the process in this article. You can also link to sites on the census, the House of Representatives, the state of Massachusetts, which is where the term originated many years ago, and the Congressional Apportionment home page.

State Morphology: The Shape of a State
http://geography.about.com/library/weekly/aa102797.htm
middle school and up

This *About.com* article does a nice job of explaining how geography can directly affect politics. You'll get definitions of the various shapes of states, and by "state," the article means "state or nation." The five different shapes are compact, fragmented, elongated, perforated, and protruded.

A paragraph on each of these shapes explains what the shape is and gives examples of countries with the shape, including links to other *About.com* geography pages that discuss those countries in depth.

Enclaves of the World
http://www.vasa.abo.fi/users/rpalmber/enclaves.htm
high school and up

An enclave is a geographical territory located wholly within the boundaries of another territory. Places like the Vatican City, which is a country that lies completely within the boundaries of another country—Italy—are enclaves. You'll learn at this page that there are three main types of enclaves. The first type is like the Vatican City—an entire country surrounded by another country. The second type is when there is a portion of a country that is isolated from the main part of the country but not landlocked by foreign territory. The third type of enclave is when there is an isolated portion of a country that is surrounded by foreign territory.

At this page, you can explore enclaves from all over the world by scrolling down the alphabetical listing of countries and reading about the enclaves connected to each one. Countries you'll find here include Oman, Tajikistan, United Arab Emirates, Bangladesh, Belgium, and Cyprus. There are also several links to other enclave sites listed at the bottom of the page.

POLITICAL SYSTEMS

Best Search Engine: http://www.google.com/
Key Search Term: Political systems

Political Systems
http://dspace.dial.pipex.com/town/street/pl38/sect2.htm
middle school and up

Although not an academic site, this one appears to be fairly objective in its treatments of the various political systems of the world, and it's more comprehensive than other similar sites. You'll find a good list that is divided into two main categories—the collectivists and the individualists—and then subdivided by specific political system. Systems discussed include autocracy, communism, conservatism, democracy, fascism, imperialism, monarchy, pluralism, plutocracy, socialism, theocracy, anarchism/nihilism, liberalism, libertarianism, objectivism, capitalism, and republics.

Once you've read this overview of the systems, you'll probably want to locate further resources on a specific system. Some of the descriptions contain links to sites that discuss the political system in more depth. If you don't see any links to the system you want to explore, simply check out the other sites listed below or do a keyword search using Google.

History and Theories of Capitalism
http://hsb.baylor.edu/html/gardner/CESCH03.HTM
middle school and up

This gateway site from Professor Stephen Gardner at Baylor University was designed as a companion to his book *Comparative Economic Systems,* but you don't need the book to make good use of the site.

The list of links is divided into four sections: "Precapitalist Economic Systems," "Early Views of Capitalism," "Contemporary Views of Capitalism," and "Global Capitalism." If you're researching the history of capitalism, you'll probably be most interested in the links that fall under the "Early Views" section. "Classics of Economics," for example, will take you to a McMaster University archive site that has collected a large number of significant texts in the history of economic thought. It's an ongoing project, but already you can find a wide array of primary source material here, all organized by the names of historical economists.

The Labour Movement
http://www.spartacus.schoolnet.co.uk/socialism.htm
middle school and up

This encyclopedic site from Britain's *Spartacus Encyclopaedia* won't give you a historical overview in one brief article, but it will provide you with links to excellent resources on many of the people, organizations, movements, and events at the core of socialism's history. Scroll down the home page and you'll see sections on "Pre-Socialist Radicals," "Socialist Writers and Philosophers," "Political Organisations," "Labour Journals and Newspapers," the "Christian Socialist Movement," "Fabian Society," "Social Democratic Federation," "Independent Labour Party," "The Labour Party 1906–1950," and "The Zinoviev Letter."

The biographies of key socialists at this site are quite in-depth and contain links to related topics also found in the encyclopedia, so your explorations might proceed from Mary Wollstonecraft's biography to the hyperlink on the "Unitarian Society" to "factory reform."

FactMonster: History of Fascism
http://www.factmonster.com/ce6/history/A0858080.html
middle school and up

FactMonster has an excellent article that addresses the history of fascism. It's part of a larger fascism article, which has sections on "Characteristics of Fascist Philosophy" and "The Fascist State," as well as a "Bibliography," all of which might interest you, too, depending on your particular area of research. See the links at the bottom of the "History" page if you'd like to read more.

In any case, start with the "History" section, which contains the following: "Origins of Fascism," "Emergence after World War I," and "Fascism since World War II." This overview will go a long way toward helping you understand the rise of fascism in Europe, how it managed to win followers, and how its popularity was shaped by other events and movements of the time.

POLLUTION—AIR

Best Search Engine: http://www.google.com/
Key Search Term: Air pollution

Demographia: Air Pollution Ranked in U.S. Metropolitan Areas: 1997
http://www.demographia.com/db-usmetap97.htm
high school and up

For some basic stats on air pollution in U.S. cities, try this page from *Demographia.* You'll get a comparison of data between 1988 and 1997 for all 92 cities covered, their ranking in the list, organized by best to worst, and their change in rank over the decade covered.

Environmental Protection Agency Office of Air and Radiation
http://www.epa.gov/oar/urbanair/index.html
high school and up

This Environmental Protection Agency Office of Air and Radiation Web site lets you locate air quality information about your home state and town. Follow the link for the cool little page called "Where I Live" and then just click on your state on the colorful map to get today's forecast, tomorrow's forecast, an ozone map, and links to state and local air quality maps. Some states, like mine, which is Montana, lacked complete information, and the ozone maps are only available during ozone season, which is May through September, but this is still a useful site if you're trying to collect data on where you live.

There are also some good educational resources here. A menu at the bottom of the page gives you access to a list of health-related pamphlets and videos, all of them downloadable from this site. Just click on "Health" for resources like "Ozone and Your Health," "Smog—Who Does It Hurt?", and "Ozone Double Trouble." Click on "Kids" in this menu for a great resource page on general air pollution issues. There are sections to explore on "What Is AQI?", "Clean and Dirty Air," "What Can I Do?", and "Air Pollution Health." You'll probably find these resources most interesting if you're just beginning to explore the topic of air pollution.

If you're interested in international air quality information, look at the list of states, then go all the way to the end where you'll see a link for "International." Click it and you'll get links for Australia, Canada, Mexico, and the United Kingdom.

For other air-pollution topics, use the menu at the left side of the home page. There is "acid rain," "indoor air," "visibility," "toxic air pollutants," and more.

Aerias.org
http://www.aerias.org/
middle school and up

This organization is devoted to increasing awareness about indoor air quality issues. If you are interested in types of indoor air quality problems and how to recognize and address them, this is the site for you.

From the menu at the top of the home page, you can choose from the following sections on the site: "Home," "Office," "School," "Other Places," "Just the Facts," or "Testing." The site is searchable, too, so if you want to try a keyword search, just use the search feature at the top right of the page. You'll see a link there for a glossary, as well. Otherwise, just pick the type of locale you'd like to research—home, office, school, or other.

Under each of these sections, you can read the following sections: "Overview," "Indications of IAQ Problems," "Testing and Diagnosis," and "Prevention."

Special feature articles on this site include "Green Indoor Environments Are a Must" and "Poor Building Design Leads to Fungal Growth."

POLLUTION—WATER

Best Search Engine: http://www.google.com/

Key Search Term: Water pollution

Environmental Protection Agency Office of Water
http://www.epa.gov/ow/
middle school and up

This is water-central for resources related to water pollution in the United States, and you'll also find some links for international resources at various spots on this site. Start by browsing the home page, which has a menu on the left that includes the following sections: "Laws and Regulations," "Funding and Grants," "Publications," "What You Can Do," "Training," "Education Resources," "Databases and Software," and "For Kids."

You'll also see a little box of links for current information, which includes such things as "WaterNews," "Map Your Waters," "EPA News-room," and other current events resources.

The bulk of excellent research resources on the site are divided into the following sections, which are listed down the center of the home page: "Ground Water and Drinking Water," "Water Science," "Waste-water Management," "Wetlands, Oceans, and Watersheds," and "American Indian Environmental Office," which is the contact for all water issues on tribal lands. Subsections will inform you on all kinds of topics, including local drinking water information, source water protection, shellfish protection, beach watch, effluent guidelines, U.S./Mexico border, oceans, coasts, and estuaries, lakes, and many more.

Try "For Kids" if you would like to find kid-friendly resources in the following areas: "Water for Kids," "What You Can Do," "Environmental Sites for Kids," "Education," and "Health."

Exploring Estuaries
http://www.epa.gov/owow/estuaries/kids/
middle school

This pretty site from the Environmental Protection Agency will teach you all about estuaries, which are the places where freshwater streams and rivers flow into the ocean and mix with seawater. You can read about estuaries, take a virtual tour of two different estuaries, play games and activities, find other Web resources on estuaries, and look up estuary-related words in the glossary. The text of each of the tours is focused on exploring the pollution threats to these estuaries and what can be done to help protect and restore water quality in these areas.

You might want to start with "About Estuaries," which gives a good introduction, then click on "Take a Tour," which is located under one of the flying bird's wings, to explore some of our country's most fascinating estuaries. There are two estuary tours to choose from. You'll find out what makes these places so special and meet some of the plants and animals that live there. You'll also learn about some of the challenges the estuaries are facing along with how the local communities are working to protect them for the future.

The Barataria-Terrebonne estuary, located west and south of New Orleans, is a web of bays, lagoons, marshes, and swamps that covers a vast amount of land. On your tour of this special place, you'll encounter brown pelicans, alligators, and blue crab, read about how wetlands benefit the people of south Louisiana, and learn about what people are doing to preserve this endangered place.

The other estuary you can tour at this wonderful site is the Long Island Sound. After an introduction where you learn about the basic geography of the sound, you'll meet the winter flounder, bluefish, and oysters that the sound is famous for, learn about pollution issues in the sound, and discover a link to *Long Island Sound Study Online*, where you can find fact sheets, maps, posters, and more about this estuary.

Once you've taken the tours, you might want to search other resources or play some of the water games found here. Or maybe you're ready to find a way to get active and support the conservation of these estuaries or an estuary near you. If so, check out the following site for young activists.

Give Water a Hand
http://www.uwex.edu/erc/gwah/
middle school and up

Designed for kids who want to take an active approach to preserving water quality in their neighborhood, this site helps kids team up with educators, natural resource specialists, and concerned members of their community to work on water quality issues.

Give Water a Hand is a national watershed education program designed to involve young people in local environmental service projects. Just follow the steps in the *Give Water a Hand Action Guide*, which you can download for free at this site, and get your youth group or classmates involved in a community service project to protect and improve water resources.

There are links for finding other helpful water-related Web resources and for contacting Give Water a Hand partners, like the Conservation Technology Information Center and the Environmental Protection Agency.

This is a simple site with few graphics to slow down the loading time. It's available in Spanish as well as English.

POPULATION

Best Search Engine: http://www.google.com/
Key Search Terms: Population
                        Population + demographics
                        Population + geography

U.S. Census Bureau Population Division
http://www.census.gov/population/www/pop-help.html
high school and up

What better source of information on U.S. population issues than the Census Bureau's own population division? This page provides a road map to the material handled within the population division, such as population projections at the U.S. and state level; current population estimates; population survey results on social, economic, and demographic characteristics; and more.

At the bottom of the help page, click on "People" to go to a collection of data entitled "Population and Household Economic Topics." Here, you'll see U.S. and world population clocks ticking away, and you'll also be able to access specific population data that's grouped according to topics such as "Age," "School Enrollment," and "Fertility."

UNFPA Interactive Population Center
http://www.unfpa.org/modules/intercenter/index.htm
high school and up

If you're looking for information on issues related to world population, this is a great site. The United Nations Population Fund (UNFPA) helps developing countries find solutions to their population problems and is the largest international source of population assistance.

For starters, check out the site's "The Day of Six Billion" section, which houses media kits, population estimates and projections, issue summaries, and more. The "Publications" section of the site is another winner. You can read current and archived editions of *The State of World Population*, a remarkably comprehensive document, and the Population Issues Briefing Kit, which summarizes many of the major issues and challenges, such as gender equality, HIV/AIDS, and sustainable development.

Population Reference Bureau
http://www.prb.org/
high school and up

The Population Reference Bureau (PRB) has created a site that's hard to ignore. PRB is a nonprofit educational organization aiming to "increase the amount, accuracy, and usefulness of information about population trends and their implications."

A toolbar at the top of the page provides quick access to the site's most frequently used resources, such as lesson plans, quick facts, a glossary, data finder, and media tools. Use the pull-down menus to find information by region (Asia/Pacific, Europe, etc.), topic (family planning, migration, urbanization, marriage/family, etc.), or focus area (environment, HIV/AIDS, populations trends, reproductive health, etc.). The "Find an Expert" tool at this site provides a list of quotable U.S. and international analysts on world population, arranged by topic.

And if that's not enough, PRB also maintains *PopNet* (http://www.popnet.org/), an extensive directory of population information resources available on the Web. You can browse the *PopNet* directory by organization type, geographic region, or subject area. The directory is also searchable by keyword. But that's not all: PRB also maintains *AmeriStat* (http://www.prb.org/AmeristatTemplate.cfm), which truly delivers on its billing as a "one-stop source for U.S. population data."

POPULATION DENSITY (SEE ALSO POPULATION)

Best Search Engine: http://www.ixquick.com/

Key Search Terms: Population density

                      Population + demographics

U.S. Census Bureau
http://www.census.gov/population/www/censusdata/density.html
high school and up

This cranny of the U.S. Census Bureau's mammoth Web site provides you with data on population density within the United States. You can download PDF files detailing land area, population, and density for states and counties, for metropolitan areas, and for places. You'll also find a map showing population distribution within the country. (See full review of Web site under **POPULATION.**)

Population Reference Bureau (Data Sheet 5)
http://www.prb.org/Content/NavigationMenu/Other_reports/2000–2002/
    sheet5.html
high school and up

As part of the Population Reference Bureau's (PRB) extensive population data collection, this page can provide you with the population per square mile (i.e., population density) of many regions and countries around the globe. (See full review of Web site under **POPULATION.**)

POPULATION GROWTH

Best Search Engine: http://www.google.com/

Key Search Term: Population growth

Fundamentals of Population Growth (Population Reference Bureau)
http://www.prb.org/Content/NavigationMenu/PRB/Educators/
    Human_Population/Population_Growth/Population_Growth.htm
high school and up

Designed to provide an overview of population growth, this site by the Population Reference Bureau will make a good first stop in your research. You'll find a summary of population growth issues; excellent graphics illustrating world population growth (1750–2150) and world population distribution by region (1800–2050); definitions of relevant terminology; and a list of additional annotated Web resources on population growth from various credible sources. (See full review of Web site under **POPULATION.**)

Negative Population Growth (NPG)
http://www.npg.org/
high school and up

Negative Population Growth (NPG) is an organization advocating population control through voluntary incentives for smaller families and reduced immigration levels. On its home page, NPG states that the U.S. population has increased 85 percent in the past 50 years, growing from 151 million to 283 million. According to its estimates, if present trends continue, the U.S. population will reach 400 million by the year 2050.

If you're researching any issue related to population, this is an interesting perspective to consider. Since NPG is very much an advocacy group against population growth, there's a strong bias in the text found here. Be sure to weigh and perhaps address that bias if you use material found at this site. You'll find some good links to other Web sites about population sustainability.

Age-Sex Pyramids (AboutGeography)
http://geography.about.com/science/geography/library/weekly/aa071497.
   htm
middle school and up

If you're looking for a get-in, get-out explanation of population (age-sex) pyramids, this site delivers. As usual, *About.com's* geography specialist does a nice job of summing up this demographic tool. In language that's easy to understand, you'll read about how population pyramids are used. Graphs from the U.S. Census Bureau help illustrate the three key types of population pyramids: rapid growth, slow growth, and negative growth.

Population Projections
http://www.census.gov/population/www/projections/popproj.html
high school and up

The Census Bureau's Population Projections Program produces projections of resident population and the number of future households and families for the nation, each of the 50 states, and the District of Columbia.

Simply select the projection you want: national, state, households and families, or population of voting age. Under "National Population Projections," for instance, you'll find population projections by age, sex, race, Hispanic origin, and nativity. These projections are based on assumptions about future births, deaths, and international migration. Under "Households and Families Projections," you'll find data that's based on national population projections and assumptions about future household structure and family composition, such as age of householder, the number of persons in households, household type (both family and nonfamily), race and Hispanic origin, persons living alone, and families with children under age 18.

PRECIPITATION

Best Search Engine: http://www.google.com/
Key Search Term: Precipitation

Intellicast.com
http://www.intellicast.com/
middle school and up

For daily and weekly weather forecasts as well as historical weather data on the United States and the world, try this *Intellicast* site. It's well organized to give you easy access to precipitation forecasts and historical data on precipitation, as well as much other weather information, including reports and articles on topics such as "Why Tracking Global Climate Change Is Like Tracking the Stock Market" and "Compelling Evidence that the Sun and Oceans Play a Key Role in Our Warm Winter."

PRIME MERIDIAN

Best Search Engine: http://www.google.com/
Key Search Term: Prime meridian

Royal Greenwich Observatory
http://www.rog.nmm.ac.uk/
middle school and up

Home of the prime meridian of the world, the line of longitude adopted by international agreement (in 1884) to be the 0° meridian from which all longitudes worldwide would be calculated, the Royal Greenwich Observatory has a museum with original Royal Greenwich

Observatory artifacts, an astronomy information service, a national maritime museum, and more. At the Web site, you can search for astronomy information, visit the "Night Sky" page with information on the moon's phases, the planets, star charts, and more, or view one of the online exhibits.

We recommend visiting the "Online Exhibits" and the "Astronomy Leaflets" page to learn more about the prime meridian and the history of the Royal Greenwich Observatory.

RAIN FOREST

Best Search Engine: http://www.ixquick.com/
Key Search Terms: Rainforest
                    Rain forest

Rainforest Alliance
http://www.rainforest-alliance.org/index.html
middle school and up

As an organization dedicated to the conservation of tropical forests, the Rainforest Alliance offers numerous educational resources, as well as opportunities for direct involvement.

If you're searching for one-liner factoids for your research, click on "Resources/Facts." Here, you'll learn the rate at which tropical forests are being destroyed, and find information on the impact of deforestation on animals, plants, and indigenous people. There's also plenty of info here about conservation methods—in case your research involves creating an action plan. In another section for "Kids and Teachers," you'll find additional resources. However, most of it is directed at a K–8 audience.

Rainforest Action Network Information Center
http://www.ran.org/ran/info_center/index.html
middle school and up

The "Information Center" of the Rainforest Action Network (RAN) Web site is a great place to collect some facts about the rain forest and efforts to conserve it. Go to "Fact Sheets," where you'll find excellent data on rain forest destruction, economic alternatives, old growth forests, Amazon oil, rain forest animals, and specific RAN campaigns like the Protect-an-Acre program and the Campaign for a Sane Economy.

Under "Special Reports and Publications," you can read a handful of interesting online reports, such as *Drilling to the Ends of the Earth: The*

Ecological, Social, and Climate Imperative for Ending Petroleum Exploration and the *500 Year Plan*, which describes an approach to global forest protection, certified logging, sustainable economic development, and more. Other publications are offered for a fee.

Live from the Rainforest
http://passporttoknowledge.com/rainforest/intro.html
middle school and up

This site is aimed at providing student scientists with information about the rain forest. As part of the Passport to Knowledge series, which takes students on "electronic field trips to scientific frontiers," it is supported in part by the National Science Foundation and the National Aeronautics and Space Administration (NASA).

You'll find this site well organized and attentive to detail. Inside the "GEOsystem" section, you'll find in-depth descriptions of types of rain forests, their climate, structure, and characteristics. Here, you can also click to access maps and rain forest–specific data on South America, Brazil, Central America, North America, Africa, Southeast Asia, and Australia.

Want to know about the Gongora orchid, the capuchin monkey, or say, the cecropia cricket? Click on "ECOsystem" to get detailed information on the trees, plants, birds, animals, and insects of the rain forest. Additionally, there are sections about the scientists and students who collaborated on this site, an archive of their interactions, and a list of other books, articles, videos, CD-ROMs, and online resources.

REEFS (SEE CORAL REEFS)

REFUGEES

Best Search Engine:	http://www.google.com/
Key Search Term:	Refugees

U.S. Committee for Refugees
http://www.refugees.org/
high school and up

The U.S. Committee for Refugees (USCR) has created a stellar site for information on the global refugee situation. The section called "Worldwide Refugee Information" is loaded with information. Here, you can access reports and statistics on the refugee and asylum situation in countries throughout the world. You'll also have access to USCR's online publications on issues surrounding refugee conditions, such as detention, health/mental health, refugee/asylum law, religious persecution, repatriation, safe havens, and women and children.

In the "News and Resources" section, read current reports from various refugee hot spots around the world. You'll also find an excellent slide show entitled "Understanding Refugee Numbers: Where Do Refugees Come from and Where Do They Go?" that can be viewed online or downloaded as a PowerPoint presentation.

Human Rights Watch: Refugees
http://www.hrw.org/refugees/
high school and up

Human Rights Watch (HRW), a nonprofit organization committed to defending human rights, created this Web page as part of their Web series on critical global issues. You'll find HRW news releases, background reports, information kits, and commentary on the refugee issue. The full text of HRW's excellent and comprehensive "World Report 2002: Refugees, Asylum Seekers, Migrants, and Internally Displaced Persons" is also posted on the site. Finally, you'll find a number of useful links to related sites.

Center for Immigration Studies
http://www.cis.org/
high school and up

The Center for Immigration Studies (CIS) is an independent, non-partisan, nonprofit research organization devoted to research and policy analysis of the economic, social, demographic, fiscal, and other impacts of immigration on the United States. You'll find CIS's well-designed Web site easy to use for your research.

On the home page, headlines from current news and articles are compiled on a toolbar—just click on a headline to go directly to the full article. Another toolbar provides a list of common topics in immigration studies, and this is where you'll find lots of goodies on the subject of refugee resettlement and asylum, as well as other related topics such as terrorism and national security. Click on a topic to read about it, access relevant reports prepared by CIS, and find links to other useful Web sites.

REMOTE SENSING

Best Subject Guide: http://www.shell.rmi.net/~michaelg/
Key Search Term: Remote sensing

Online Remote Sensing Guide (University of Illinois)
http://ww2010.atmos.uiuc.edu/(Gh)/guides/rs/home.rxml
high school and up

The University of Illinois's *Online Remote Sensing Guide* is a two-module unit that nicely uses text, diagrams, and animation to introduce topics in the field of remote sensing.

The "Radar" module covers the basics of radars and target detection, interpretation of radar imagery, and the use of radars in forecasting and severe weather prediction. It's organized into the following four sections: "Radar Basics," which covers the sending and retrieving of signals, detecting a target, and different scanning modes; "Radar Imagery," which discusses WSR-88D and MDR radar imagery; "Velocity Patterns," which notes the wind patterns depicted through Doppler radar estimated winds; and "Applications," which describes how radar is used in tornado and hurricane detection, short-term forecasting, and other areas.

In the "Satellite" module, you'll explore Earth observing satellites and their capabilities in greater detail, focusing on two satellite orbital groups in particular: Geostationary Operational Environmental Satellites (GOES) and Polar Orbiting Environmental Satellites (POES). This module also demonstrates how to interpret visible, infrared, and water vapor channel satellite images.

Remote Sensing Tutorial
http://rst.gsfc.nasa.gov/
college level

This enormously useful tutorial on remote sensing, prepared by the National Aeronautics and Space Administration's (NASA) Goddard Space Flight Center, delivers just about everything you'd want to know about remote sensing . . . from thermal remote sensing to hyperspectral imaging spectroscopy to vegetation applications to planetary remote sensing and more.

The "Introduction" is a sensible place for you to begin. Here, you'll learn the basic concepts behind remote sensing, as well as technical and historical perspectives. Throughout the next 21 sections (wow—that's not even counting the four appendixes), you'll gain an understanding of the role remote sensing plays in the study of land, sea, air, and biotic communities and in exploring planets, stars, and galaxies. The tutorial also offers information that will help develop your skills in interpreting these visual displays and data sets.

The site's table of contents makes it easy to navigate the site's massive collection of information. Along with section headings, you'll find a brief annotation of what each section offers—so you won't waste time visiting sections that aren't relevant to your research.

RESOURCES—RENEWABLE

Best Search Engine: http://www.google.com/
Key Search Term: Renewable resources

Renewable Resources Data Center
http://rredc.nrel.gov/
high school and up

Where better to find resources on renewable energy than a data center dedicated to the subject? The *Renewable Resources Data Center* (RreDC) provides information (i.e., publications, data, maps) on types of renewable energy resources in the United States.

Scroll down the home page to "Information by Resource" to find material on the following renewable resources: "Solar Radiation," "Biomass," "Wind Energy," "Geothermal," and "Dynamic Maps and GIS Data." For each resource area, you're provided with links to publications, archived data, project summaries, and other relevant Web sites.

Be sure to look in the "Special Features" column for a glossary of terms, "EnergyTidbits" (factoids on sources of renewable energy), "KidzLinks" (a collection of links with renewable resource info geared toward students and teachers), and a unit conversions calculator.

Renewable Energy
http://solstice.crest.org/renewables/re-kiosk/index.shtml
middle school and up

This is the entryway into an excellent introductory education module on renewable energy, assembled by the Center for Renewable Energy and Sustainable Technology (CREST).

Just click to learn about five technology areas for renewable energy: small hydro, biomass, geothermal, solar, and wind power. Inside each of these sections, you'll find an overview, as well as information on theory, applications, case studies, environmental impact, and economic impact. For instance, under "Biomass," look in the "Theory" section to find the goods on the conversion processes of direct combustion, pyrolysis, anaerobic digestion, gasification, alcohol fermentation, landfill gas, and cogeneration.

The site's straightforward arrangement allows you to compare the various forms of renewable energy easily. Some sections, however, are woefully underdeveloped and disappointing. The "Case Studies," for instance, are sometimes little more than a captioned photograph.

RICHTER SCALE (SEE ALSO EARTHQUAKE)

Best Search Engine: http://www.askjeeves.com/
Key Search Term: Richter scale

USGS National Earthquake Information Center: Magnitude Scales
http://gldss7.cr.usgs.gov/neis/general/handouts/magnitude_intensity.html
high school and up

If you're looking for clear explanations of what earthquake magnitude and earthquake intensity are, this U.S. Geological Survey (USGS) site more than fits the bill. Click on "Richter Magnitude Scale" to learn when the scale was created, who created it, and how exactly it measures magnitude. (If you're interested in learning how intensity is measured, click on "Modified Mercalli Intensity Scale" as well.)

The section called "Measuring the Size of an Earthquake" goes into technical detail about body-wave magnitude formulas, fault geometry, seismic moment, and more. Other useful sections include "Why Are There So Many Magnitude Scales?", "Magnitude/Intensity Comparison," and "Magnitude Definitions Used by the National Earthquake Information Center."

Virtual Earthquake
http://vcourseware4.calstatela.edu/VirtualEarthquake/VQuakeIntro.html
high school and up

Here's a great site for those of you who learn about a subject by *doing*, rather than reading. Funded by the National Science Foundation, *Virtual Earthquake* offers an interactive program that teaches how an earthquake epicenter is located and how the Richter magnitude is determined.

Virtual Earthquake shows you the recordings of an earthquake's seismic waves detected by instruments far away from the earthquake. You get to locate the epicenter of an earthquake by making measurements on three seismograms that are provided for you. You can also determine the Richter magnitude of the quake from the same recordings.

RITES OF PASSAGE

Best Search Engine: http://www.dogpile.com/
Key Search Terms: Rites of passage + anthropology

Rites of Passage in America
http://www.balchinstitute.org/museum/rites/rites.html
high school and up

For a historical and multicultural view of rites of passage, try this site, which was created as an accompaniment to a traveling exhibition put on by the Balch Institute for Ethnic Studies.

The Web site consists of a preface and introduction to the exhibition, followed by three essays on the topic of American rites of passage. These are "The Life Cycle: Folk Customs of Passage," "Art and Rites of Passage," and "Reviving Rites of Passage in America." These are compelling, footnoted essays that combine research and storytelling to give an excellent and enjoyable introduction to their topics. Hyperlinks in the margins take you to photographs or other media that illustrate the ideas of each essay.

The section of articles is followed by a longer section of case studies. Some of these topics include " 'Doing the Month' and the 'Full Month' Party: Chinese Birth Traditions in America," "Day of the Dead: Mexican Memorial Traditions," and "Sunrise Ceremonial: An Apache Girl's Coming of Age" to name just a few of the offerings.

These are wonderful resources, and though the site is simply designed and does not offer much in the way of additional resources, other than a bibliography, you'll get plenty to ponder just by reading what's here.

Rites of Passage
http://axe.acadiau.ca/~047073m/ROPHomepage.htm
middle school and up

This site is basic but good as an introduction. It defines rites of passage, provides links to several sites that give examples of rites of passage—one deals with the Ndembu of Zambia and their rite of passage for boys making the transition from childhood to adulthood and another deals with American wedding rites of passage. There are some annoying broken links here, but just use this site for its definition and move on to the following sites for in-depth exploration.

LifeRites
http://www.liferites.org/
middle school and up

LifeRites is, in its own words "dedicated to serving the needs of those individuals who seek to affirm their life and death in a personal and individual manner by providing practical advice and guidance on Rites of Passage and Life Celebrations, empowering people to do things for themselves." At its comprehensive Web site you can learn about rites of passage related to birth, puberty, weddings, eldership, and death. There are sections for each of these topics at the site, as well as sections on community and celebrants.

Under "Birth," for example, you'll find information about rites of passage in general, pregnancy rites, naming rites, and more. Under "Death," there's information on rites connected to wills, do-it-yourself burials, woodland burials, funerals, and more. Each section has further information on books and Web links.

This site is geared toward contemporary folks who want to mark the important times in their life. You won't necessarily find a lot of historical information on rites of passage. Rather, you'll get a look at what rites of passage mean in contemporary American culture.

The Sacred Site
http://www.abc.net.au/compass/explore/rites.htm
middle school and up

For an index to religious rites of passage, try this comprehensive Web site from the Australian Broadcasting Company. *The Sacred Site* is divided into the following categories: "Rites of Passage," "African Rites of Passage," "Ancient America," "Ancient Roman Marriage Laws," "Catholic Sacraments," "Death and Dying," "Death Rites," "Druidic Rituals," "Hindu Rites of Passage," "Hindu Wedding Rituals," "Hospital Birth Rituals," "Jain Wedding Rituals," "Family and Society in Ancient Israel," "Feminist Jewish Rituals," "Korean Rites of Passage," "Lutheran Confirmation," "Mormon Confirmation," "Neanderthal Ritual," and many more. You get the idea. There's everything under the sun here. There's even a link at the very bottom of the page for "Secular Ceremonies and Rites of Passage."

RIVERS

Best Search Engine:	http://www.google.com/
Key Search Term:	Rivers geography

River Systems of the World
http://www.rev.net/~aloe/river/
middle school and up

There's nothing fancy about *River Systems of the World*, but you will find tons of excellent river information organized in a very accessible format. The page is constructed as a table with the name of the river system on the far left and columns for the following subjects: continent or island, length (defined in two different ways), drainage area (given

in miles and kilometers), discharge at mouth, distinction, notable trib-
utaries, and cities.

The data in the chart is organized from largest river system to smallest,
so the first river system listed is the Nile, followed by the Amazon, the
Yangtze, the Mississippi-Missouri, and so on. The last river system included in the table is the La Grande in North America.

Many of the river names, though not all, are actually hyperlinks to
sites that explore them in depth. Click on "Amazon" for example, and
you'll be taken to an *Exploratorium* site called *What's New in the World:
Discovering the Amazon: The World's Greatest River*, which is chock-full
of fun resources. Click on "Congo (Zaire)" and a site called *The Zaire
River* comes your way, which is part of the personal home page of a guy
named Arold who traveled around Africa on an old Yamaha XT 500
motorcycle. You'll see some really nice pictures taken by Arold along
the river.

Overall you'll find the external links diverse and fun, and the table
of river statistics comprehensive and extremely helpful if you're looking
for basic data and rankings of the world's great river systems.

All Along a River
http://library.thinkquest.org/28022/?tqskip1 = 1&tqtime = 0117
middle school and up

This *Thinkquest* site, created by students, uses animation to show the
physical properties of rivers. The design of the site leaves a little to be
desired—it's tough to read due to a chaotic layout—but the content is
useful, particularly in the section called "Student's Corner." Here you'll
find a section on physical aspects of rivers with detailed information on
river erosion, river velocity, river volume, and transportation along a
river. Click on "Transportation," for example, and you'll learn about
saltation, traction, solution, and suspension as they relate to the ways
rivers transport eroded material like mud, sand, and boulders. Click on
any one of these terms for an in-depth description of the particular
process.

Other sections of the site include "Case Studies," where you can learn
about the Singapore River and the River Rhine; a section that talks
about the trail of a river, from its source to its eventual meeting with
the sea; an online study area for rivers of the world; an interactive
section complete with games and a discussion forum; and an educator's
section with worksheets prepared by one of the teachers of the Chinese
students who developed this site.

"Rivers from Source to Sea" is an *About.com* article that discusses
how rivers interact with the land around them. It's an excellent intro-

duction to the basic physical properties of rivers and to their role in the larger environment to which they belong. You'll also find some links within the text to sites on the Nile River and on tributary streams.

SEX RATIO

Best Search Engine: http://www.google.com/
Key Search Terms: Sex ratio + geography

The Sex Ratio
http://www.ac.wwu.edu/~stephan/Animation/sexratios.html
high school and up

This cool little page is part of a Web site that contains dozens of animation projects on a wide variety of topics, everything from Galileo Galilei to moon phases to Charlie Chaplin. There's also one on sex ratios that demonstrates the number of males per 100 females between the years 1790 and 1990. You may have to reload the animation several times to catch all the changes covered, but it's a fun resource if you're interested in historical data and the changes in sex ratio over these two centuries.

The World Factbook: Sex Ratio
http://www.bartleby.com/151/a27.html
middle school and up

This page takes you directly to the *World Factbook* page that lists sex ratios for just about every country in the world—from Afghanistan and Albania to Zambia and Zimbabwe. And the listings are so easy to read. The only data on this page is sex ratio, so you don't have to muddle through lots of numbers and text. You'll get the male/female ratio at birth, for 15 years old and under, for ages 15–64, for 65 and over, and for the total population.

In case you want more information on the country, just click on its name and you'll go to the *World Factbook*'s home page for that country with all the basic stats, plus a table of contents for other information, including geography, people, government, economy, communications, transportation, military, and transnational issues.

SHINTOISM

Best Search Engine: http://www.google.com/
Key Search Term: Shintoism

The Geography of Shintoism
http://people.morehead-st.edu/fs/t.pitts/shinto.htm
high school and up

Courtesy of the useful *Geography of Religions* Web site (created by students in a university-level world religions course), this page focuses exclusively on Shintoism. Here, you'll learn the essentials of the faith— such as how and when Shintoism was founded, in which countries it is practiced, major teachings and significant texts, symbols, holy days, and major divisions within the religion.

Under the heading, "Details about Shintoism," you can read about the four affirmations, or basic beliefs, in Shinto. You'll also find a list of recommended print reference materials that might be of use in your research.

Shinto Religion
http://www.comedition.com/AAAA/Religion/ShintoReligion.htm
middle school and up

This comprehensive Shinto site is part of a larger site called *Religion at All American Family*, which is an excellent resource if you're looking into any religion and want to read a diverse collection of carefully selected resources. At the Shinto page alone, there's a wealth of useful information. Annotated links on the home page will take you to a variety of sites. Follow the link for "Shinto Documents," where you can read excerpts from key texts of the Shinto religion, including the creation story and the generation of key gods. There's a link to the "International Shinto Foundation" and to "The Way of the Gods," which is a photographic journal of Shinto shrines and festivals with a basic overview of the religion.

The best place to start your exploration of Shinto is by clicking on "Shinto: The Way of the Gods," which will take you to a nicely illustrated essay from the online magazine *Trincoll*. Or scroll down just a little on the home page and follow the link to "History, Beliefs, and Practices." This *Religious Tolerance* site goes into more detail about the various forms and practices of Shinto and gives more attention to current practice than to history, although you will find a brief historical overview at the top of this page.

New Religious Movements: Shintoism
http://etext.lib.virginia.edu/~jkh8x/soc257/nrms/shinto.html
college level

This site, with over 150 profiles of religions, was created in conjunction with a course at the University of Virginia called "New Religious

Movements." You'll find the comprehensive section on Shintoism to be incredibly useful in your own research. It is divided into the following areas: "Profile," "History," "Beliefs," "Links," and "Bibliography."

Under the "Profile" section, the author has collected information about Shintoism's founding, revered texts, world distribution of its followers, and more. The "History" section is lengthy, offering details dating back to A.D. 552, as well as modern-day information about the four current forms of Shinto (Koshitsu, Folk, Jinja, and Shuha). The "Beliefs" section is particularly thorough, providing you with a clear understanding of Shinto's fundamental beliefs and four affirmations.

Finally, if you haven't found the info you need here, chances are good that you will in one of the many annotated links and print references provided in the "Link" and "Bibliography" sections.

SLAVERY

Best Search Engine: http://www.google.com/
Key Search Term: Slavery

Anti-Slavery International
http://www.antislavery.org/
middle school and up

Anti-Slavery International is the world's oldest international human rights organization, founded in 1839. It is the only such organization in the United Kingdom that works at the local, national, and international levels exclusively against slavery and related abuses.

If your research involves contemporary slavery issues, this Web site can help you locate information about current slavery issues worldwide and campaigns to stop the modern slave trade that affects every continent in the world, news about slavery, and other resources to aid your research, including books, videos, films, and a long list of links to other Internet sites. This list is organized by category so that you can easily locate Internet resources on children, women, human rights, labor rights, and more.

In the "Links" section you can also connect to "Out of Sight, Out of Mind," *Anti-Slavery's* film on child domestic workers in the Philippines, which you can watch by logging on to http://www.communitychannel. org/.

If you want to do some background reading first, start by clicking on "About Us" and going to the "Issues" section, where you can read brief essays about modern slavery, child labor, trafficking of humans, and bonded labor. This will give you a good introduction and overview.

ECPATUK
http://www.ecpat.org.uk/
high school and up

ECPAT stands for End Child Prostitution, Child Pornography, and Trafficking of children for sexual purposes, and it's part of an international organization that campaigns to protect children from commercial sexual abuse.

At its Web site you can access "Background Info," "Press and Publications," and "Ways You Can Help," as well as information on contacting the organization. If you want to understand basic information about the trafficking of children for sexual exploitation, go to "Background." Look under "Press and Publications" for a November 2001 report called "What the Professionals Know: The Trafficking of Children into and through the U.K. for Sexual Purposes."

To get involved in antitrafficking campaigns, go to "Ways You Can Help."

The Global Alliance against Trafficking Women
http://www.ineet.co.th/org/gaatw/bodyframe.html
high school and up

This organization was formed at the International Workshop on Migration and Traffic in Women held in Chiang Mai, Thailand, in October 1994. It consists of both organizations and individuals worldwide who are working on issues related to human trafficking and women's labor migration. While its goal is to stop the trafficking of humans, it also works to insure that the human rights of trafficked persons are respected and protected.

The Web site contains a section on human rights standards for the treatment of trafficked persons and a resources center with a number of abstracts of books about trafficking in women around the world. The "Links" page is nicely organized with links to many important antislavery and human rights organizations.

Stop-Traffic
http://fpmail.friends-partners.org/mailman/listinfo.cgi/stop-traffic/
high school and up

Stop-Traffic is a facilitated, international electronic list dealing with human rights abuses associated with trafficking in persons, with an emphasis on public health and trafficking in persons for forced labor, including forced prostitution, sweatshop labor, domestic service, and some coercive mail-order bride arrangements.

If you would like to join such a mailing list or read the archives of past postings on these subjects, this is a good resource.

British History 1700–1930: The Slave Trade
http://www.spartacus.schoolnet.co.uk/slavery.htm
middle school and up

If you are looking for historical information on slavery with an emphasis on the British slave trade with Africa, this comprehensive site contains a wealth of compelling information that includes 30 "Slave Accounts"; a section on "The Slave System," with links to such topics as "African Slave Trade," "Cotton Plantations," "Slave "Markets," "Slave Breeding," and "Runaways"; and a section called "Slave Life," with links such as "House Slaves," "Marriage," "Whipping," and "Slave Music." There are also sections on "Events and Issues," "Women's Anti-Slavery Society," "Anti-Slavery Group," "Legislation," and "USA Campaigners Against Slavery," which boasts nearly 50 links to people such as Elizabeth Cady Stanton and Walt Whitman.

The organizers of this site have done a wonderful job of combining secondary and primary sources. Go to the section on the "African Slave Trade" under "The Slave System" and you'll first read a historical overview of Europeans trading slaves from Africa beginning in the fourteenth century. This account is followed by excerpts from two different slave narratives—a Scottish explorer's account of his travels in Africa, and another European man's book about the African slave trade.

The Slave Kingdoms
http://www.pbs.org/wonders/Episodes/Epi3/slave.htm
middle school and up

The Slave Kingdoms is again focused on the European and American slave trade with Africa, but this site blends contemporary resources with historical resources in a way that is both compelling and informative. It also presents information from the perspective of Africans, which makes it unique among other Web resources on the slave trade.

Not long after charting Africa's shores, Europeans began to trade with West African tribes—the Europeans traded guns and gold for human slaves. This Web site, which is part of the larger PBS site that is a companion to the television show *The Wonders of the African World* is one of the few top-notch sites that gives the history of the slave trade from the perspective of African history. *The Slave Kingdoms* focuses on the western African kingdoms that flourished because of their role in the slave trade.

The site combines essays, interviews, photographs, maps, and video clips to tell its story. For an excellent overview of the slave trade, select "Continue" at the end of the paragraph under "Confronting the Legacy of African Slave Trade." Return to the home page when you're ready for the site's in-depth features: "Wonders," "Retelling," "Gates' Diary," and "Cultural Close-Up." Select the topics that interest you from the menu at the bottom of the home page.

"Wonders" contains a history of two West African tribes that grew rich and powerful from the slave trade—the Ashanti and the Dahomey. "Retelling" has a wealth of fascinating material. You can watch an interview of a current Ashanti leader explaining the Ashanti role in the slave trade, as well as an interview of Martine de Souza, a descendant of one of the most infamous slave traders. There's also a written firsthand account of growing up in Ghana with the legacy of the slave trade, and the perspectives of African Americans who visit Africa and must confront the history of the slave trade. "Gates' Diary" is less helpful. It contains the written reflections of the show's narrator, Henry Louis Gates, on how the slave trade has affected African Americans. "Cultural Close-Up" has a short profile on the Gbeto warriors of western Africa.

SOCIAL GEOGRAPHY

Best Search Engine: http://www.google.com
Key Search Terms: Social geography + definition

Social Indicators
http://www.un.org/Depts/unsd/social/
high school and up

Here's a great place to hunt for statistics on all kinds of social issues. This recently updated site, compiled by the United Nations Statistics Division (UNSD), provides "social indicators covering a wide range of subject-matter fields." These indicators consist mainly of the list proposed for follow-up and monitoring at recent major United Nations conferences on children, population and development, social development, and women.

Here's a brief list of the categories you can use to search for social indicators at this site: population, human settlement, water supply and sanitation, housing, health, childbearing, education, literacy, income and economic activity, and unemployment.

Social Science Information Gateway
http://www.sosig.ac.uk/roads/subject-listing/World-cat/socgeog.html
high school and up

Social geography can be defined as the study of how societies and social norms arrange themselves around the globe. Consequently, a huge number of topics fall under this category. For an index to some of the possibilities in social geography, try the *Social Science Information Gateway*. It's a British index that does a wonderful job of annotating and categorizing its links. All the links found at this page relate to social geography—articles, papers, reports, databases, bibliographies, educational materials, government publications, and much more. Browse the list for the type of information you want first, then read the excellent and lengthy annotations to see if the particular resources fit your needs.

SOIL TYPES

Best Search Engine: http://www.google.com/

Key Search Terms: Soil type

Soil taxonomy

Keys to Soil Taxonomy
http://www.pedosphere.com/taxonomy/
high school and up

The U.S. Department of Agriculture and the Natural Resources Conservation Service pulled together to produce this site—a searchable version of the well-respected book *Keys to Soil Taxonomy*. You can peruse the book, chapter by chapter, or you can use the "Soil Taxonomy Key" to search for detailed information on each soil group. In the "Soil Taxonomy Key," you'll find descriptive information on gelisols, histosols, spodosols, andisols, oxisols, vertisols, aridisols, ultisols, mollisols, alfisols, inceptisols, and entisols. And, hey, if that's not enough, you can also get information on each soil group's subsoils.

The titles of the book's chapters give you a sense of what the text is about. They include "The Soils that We Classify," "Differentiae for Mineral Soils and Organic Soils," "Horizons and Characteristics Diagnostic for the Higher Categories," "Identification of the Taxonomic Class of a Soil," "Family and Series Differentiae and Names," and "Designations for Horizons and Layers."

The Twelve Soil Orders
http://soils.ag.uidaho.edu/soilorders/
high school and up

This site, prepared by the Soil Science Division at the University of Idaho, draws on the same general soil classification system as the site reviewed above. Focusing on the same 12 soil categories—or orders—this site also provides excellent images that illustrate each order's distribution, properties, and use.

Click on "Information" to find descriptions of each soil order and to view excellent images of example soils and landscapes. Use the "Global Distribution Map" to view a U.S. Department of Agriculture (USDA) map depicting global soil regions. For information on dominant soil orders closer to home, simply use the "United States Distribution Map."

SUBURBANIZATION

Best Search Engine: http://www.google.com/
Key Search Terms: Suburbanization
                                        Suburbs

Virtual World: The New Suburb
http://www.nationalgeographic.com/earthpulse/sprawl/index_flash.html
middle school and up

Urban planners everywhere are experimenting with new urbanist concepts—building suburbs using the traditional Main Street model, creating walkable communities that save more open space, and focusing on the creation of a connected community for residents and businesses alike.

To explore the new look of suburbs, try this new urbanism National Geographic site, which takes you on a virtual tour of a new urbanist neighborhood.

Just click on the "Explore" button on the home page to begin your tour. The tour takes a minute to load, but it's worth the wait. You'll see arrows at the bottom of the page that let you navigate left to right down the street. Just move your mouse over houses, businesses, cars, and streets, and click to get images and ideas related to those objects. Move your mouse over the trees, for example, and you'll read that many urban planners consider trees to be hazardous for cars. New urbanist planners, on the other hand, see them as buffers between pedestrians and cars. Click over the garage apartment located behind a corner house and read about the value of mixed housing. New urbanists prefer a mix in terms of types of housing and income levels because it brings people together from diverse backgrounds and enables families to move up without leaving their neighborhoods.

The tour is fun and informative. Once you're done, you can explore these ideas further by reading a National Geographic feature article on the subject, or by going to the "Resources and Links" page.

Demographia
http://www.demographia.com/db-cities.htm
high school and up

This fairly brief rant on the rise of suburbs and decline of inner cities in the United States will most likely provoke some questions.

Suburbanization and Highways
http://www.pbs.org/wnet/newyork/laic/episode7/topic3/e7_t3_s3-sh.html
middle school and up

This PBS kids' site explores the topic of urban renewal and the construction of expressways in postwar America. It's part of Episode 7 in a series called Learning Adventures in Citizenship. Episode 7 addresses the "The City and the World, 1945–Present." Among the topics explored in this episode are "V-J Day in New York," "Urban Renewal and Expressways," "Urban Despair," and "Economic Rebirth."

The *Suburbanization and Highways* site falls under the "Urban Renewal" episode and explores the forces at work in prewar and postwar America that brought about the flight of people from inner cities and the corresponding growth in expressway systems.

SUSTAINABLE DEVELOPMENT (SEE ALSO AGRICULTURE)

Best Search Engine: http://www.dogpile.com/
Key Search Term: Sustainable development

Center of Excellence for Sustainable Development
http://www.sustainable.doe.gov/index.shtml
high school and up

The Center of Excellence for Sustainable Development, a project of the U.S. Department of Energy, has created an impressive Web site for information on sustainable development within the United States. Look under the home page's "Topics in Sustainability" for wonderfully developed Web sites-within-a-site on topics that include an overview, green buildings, green development, land use planning, disaster planning, community energy, transportation, sustainable business, financing, rural issues, and resource efficiency. Within the "Overview" section alone, you'll find countless resources, including definitions and principles of sustainable development, success stories, codes and ordinances, articles and publications, educational materials, and other resources.

We also hunted around the land use planning page, which is oriented toward urbanization issues and grappling with land use considerations within the context of urban growth. The site contains sections on "Key Principles," "Strategies," "Civic Participation," "Success Stories," "Codes/Ordinances," "Articles/Publications," "Educational Materials," and other topics.

For a good introduction, go to "Key Principles" where you'll find a number of different links to sites that offer guidance on land use. There's *Principles for Better Land Use Policy* (put out by the National Governors' Association), *New Urbanism/Neo-Traditional Planning*, and *Land Use Agenda for the Twenty-First Century America*, among others.

The "Strategies" section contains land use planning strategies. Here you can read about transit-oriented design, mixed-use strategies, urban growth boundaries, infill development, greenways, Brownfield redevelopment, open space protection, urban forestry, and other topics that are hot among urban planners.

If you need to learn about the codes and ordinances that govern land use decisions in towns and cities, go to the page of the same name. You'll find links to sites all around the country—places like Burlington, Vermont, the state of Maryland, Scottsdale, Arizona, Napa, California, and other places that have literally shaped their communities through the thoughtful work they have done on land use codes and ordinances.

Elsewhere at the site, you'll find "Breaking News," "Coming Events," "Funding Opportunities," "Web Site of the Week," and "Success Story of the Week." Another useful section is "Ten Steps to Sustainability," which outlines a path for communities to follow in their efforts to promote local level sustainability. If your project requires specific keyword searches (i.e., solar + energy + Montana), simply use the site's "Resource Database." You'll enjoy the excellent planning that went into this great little site. It's packed with extremely useful information that's been organized in a logical and easy-to-access way.

Introduction to Sustainability: SD Gateway
http://sdgateway.net/introsd/
high school and up

This site, developed by the Sustainable Development Communications Network, provides a powerful overview of what sustainable development is and why it is important. The site contains a time line of sustainable development history, background material on important aspects of the concept, and suggestions for further exploration.

Inside the "Definition" section, you'll read how various groups and organizations describe sustainable development, and you'll find a searchable database, with access to the full text of many reports and articles on sustainable development. You'll also want to check out "SD Topics," a vast section that provides background information on over 50 topics, which are subdivided into the broad categories of "Business and Trade," "Communities and Society," "Danger Signs," "Environment," "Managing Sustainability," and "Regions."

Virtual World: The New Suburb
http://www.nationalgeographic.com/earthpulse/sprawl/index_flash.html
middle school and up

New urbanism is one of the hottest topics around in the field of sustainable development, and this National Geographic site takes you on a virtual tour of a new urbanist neighborhood. Urban planners everywhere are experimenting with new urbanist concepts—building suburbs using the traditional Main Street model, creating walkable communities that save more open space, and focusing on the creation of a connected community for residents and businesses alike.

Just click on the "Explore" button on the home page to begin your tour. The tour takes a minute to load, but it's worth the wait. You'll see arrows at the bottom of the page that let you navigate left to right down the street. Just move your mouse over houses, businesses, cars, and streets, and click to get images and ideas related to those objects. Move your mouse over the trees, for example, and you'll read that many urban planners consider trees to be hazardous for cars. New urbanist planners, on the other hand, see them as buffers between pedestrians and cars. Click over the garage apartment located behind a corner house and read about the value of mixed housing. New urbanists prefer a mix in terms of types of housing and income levels because it brings people together from diverse backgrounds and enables families to move up without leaving their neighborhoods.

The tour is fun and informative. Once you're done, you can explore these ideas further by reading a National Geographic feature article on the subject, or by going to the "Resources and Links" page.

TECTONIC PLATES (SEE PLATE TECTONICS)

TEMPERATURE

Best Search Engine: http://www.lii.org/
Key Search Terms: Temperature
                     Temperature scale

Project Skymath: About Temperature
http://www.unidata.ucar.edu/staff/blynds/tmp.html
high school and up

If you're looking for a comprehensive introduction to the subject of temperature, this is a fantastic site to visit. Although created to help middle-school teachers *teach* about temperature, the site does not dumb down the subject matter.

Its contents include "What Is Temperature?", "Development of Thermometers and Temperature Scales," "Heat and Thermodynamics," "The Kinetic Theory," "Thermal Radiation," "Temperature of the Universe," and more. You'll appreciate the good graphics, diagrams, and hyperlinked text, as well as the links to other reference materials.

Athena: Fahrenheit and Celsius Temperature Scales
http://www.athena.ivv.nasa.gov/curric/weather/fahrcels.html
middle school and up

The National Aeronautics and Space Administration's (NASA) educational sites typically hit the mark, and this one's no exception. As part of Athena, a NASA project for earth and science education targeted at grade levels K–12, this site covers the basics of the two major temperature scales.

You'll learn the difference between the Fahrenheit, Kelvin, and Celsius temperature scales, how to convert temperatures between scales, and an algebraic formula for conversion. For fast temperature conversions, simply use the graphic at the top of the page. There are also two links to conversion calculators at other Web sites.

TIME ZONES

Best Search Engine: http://www.google.com/
Key Search Term: Time zones

Time Zone Map
http://www.maps.com/explore/timeclock/
middle school and up

This time zone map gives you the current time in each of the world's 14 time zones. It won't interpret or analyze time zones, so go to one of the following sites for that.

The Time Zone Converter
http://www.timezoneconverter.com/
middle school and up

This site does more than tell you what time it is anywhere in the world. It offers historical information on the evolution of time measurement and on daylight savings time, in addition to numerous converters. You can convert time, meters, cooking measurements, and several other types of data here.

TOPOGRAPHY (SEE MAPS—TOPOGRAPHICAL)

TOXIC WASTE

Best Search Engine: http://www.google.com/

Key Search Terms: Toxic waste

Hazardous waste

Hazardous Waste: An Introduction
http://environment.about.com/library/weekly/aa061800.htm
middle school and up

This *About.com* introduction to hazardous waste will get you up to speed fast on the four types of hazardous wastes recognized by the Environmental Protection Agency—corrosive, ignitable, reactive, and toxic. You'll get a definition of each of these types of waste products with examples. From this introduction, you'll be able to navigate more effectively through the material at the following sites.

Greenpeace Toxics Campaign
http://www.greenpeace.org/~toxics/index.html
high school and up

The *Greenpeace Toxics Campaign* Web site will educate you on the issues involving toxic waste, give you the opportunity to get involved in reforming industry practices of waste disposal, and provide you with numerous resources for your research.

Read the material on the home page first. It explains POPs (persistent organic compounds) and PVC plastic, as well as toxic trade, which is the transfer of toxic waste from industrialized countries to newly industrializing countries. All of these are the focus of the toxics campaign.

Go to "POPs Producers" for more in-depth information on the specific POPs targeted by this campaign. There's a menu at the bottom of this page, where you can choose to read about pesticides, dioxins, PCBs, and Arctic POPs, among others. Click on "Producers" to get a detailed chart of which companies produce each of these toxic substances.

"Toxic Hotspots" (in the menu at the top of the page) is a stellar resource. It's a clickable atlas that highlights the places in the world where toxic waste problems are worst. Click on a country and you'll be given a map of that country with all the toxic hotspots within the country highlighted. Click on one of these hotspots for specific information about the contaminated area. Icons to the right of your map let you choose statistics, photos, or more information on the hotspot.

You'll also want to check out a part of the site called "Ban the Burn," which deals with the campaign to end the incineration of toxic waste. You'll learn about various types of incineration used around the world, alternatives to incineration, and reports on how it affects the environment.

Finally, this site offers reports, press releases, and a links page, all of which provide good info, too. In short, you can't go wrong at this Greenpeace site. Everywhere you click, there's excellent information that's easy to access and well organized.

Toxics Use Reduction Institute
http://www.turi.org/
high school and up

The Toxics Use Reduction (TUR) Institute of the University of Massachusetts is interested in developing strategies for pollution prevention. You can research specific kinds of toxic pollution, access government policy information, information on community projects and resources, and resources for education, as well as reference materials on toxics use and reduction and information about the institute's involvement with business and industry.

Go to the "Reference and Publications" page if you want to search for less toxic chemistries, alternative technologies, or innovative management methods related to stewardship and toxic use reduction programs. You can even send special requests for information to the institute reference staff.

If you want a basic introduction to toxics in the community—what they are, where they can be found, and what can be done about them, go to "Community Projects and Resources." You'll find answers to these basic questions and more.

If your research requires you to delve into the use of toxic substances in industry, you'll want to click on the "Business and Industry" page. At this useful part of the site, you'll get the details about the Toxics Use Reduction Act (TURA), the annual TURA data provided by companies, and some advice for developing a TUR plan. In addition, learn about TUR research, education, training, and information services available to companies in Massachusetts, where this institute is located.

The institute's Web site is easy to use. Just follow the menu at the left side of the page. One nice use of Web technologies is the shadow box that opens up when you place the mouse over one of the items on the menu. The box lists all the subtopics covered if you click and follow the link to that page.

TRANSNATIONAL CORPORATIONS

Best Search Engine: http://www.google.com/
Key Search Term: Transnational corporations

Transnational Corporate Research
http://www.trufax.org/menu/resource.html
high school and up

Be advised that this site represents a strong bias *against* transnational corporations. Nonetheless, you will find valuable research leads for this polemical topic.

The site is essentially a collection of links to other sites that contain information, articles, or reports about transnational corporations. Under the section "Research Treaties, Agreements, and Multinational Corporate Activity," for instance, you'll find links to the General Agreement on Tariffs and Trade (GATT) Treaty data, North American Free Trade Agreement (NAFTA) research, the journal *Multinational Corporation Monitor,* and more. The other sections of the site house "Research on Corporations, Corporate Havoc, and Planetary Disorder" and "Other Applicable Research Data."

Sierra Club: Conservation Policies: Transnational Corporations
http://www.sierraclub.org/policy/conservation/transcorp.asp
high school and up

If you want to know what heats activists up about transnational corporations, you'll appreciate the Sierra Club's clearly stated position. This site consists of a treatise that presents a statement of the problem, background information, and the Sierra Club's guidelines for responsible management, accountability, and trade.

World Investment Report 2001
http://www.industryweek.com/iwinprint/data/chart8.html
high school and up

Each year, the United Nations Conference on Trade and Development (UNCTAD) creates a top-notch document called the *World In-*

vestment Report. The 2001 report presents an overview of global business issues, with an entire chapter devoted to transnational corporations. The report also closely examines the issue of linkages between foreign affiliates of multinational enterprises and local companies in developing countries.

You can download the full report or individual chapters that are relevant to your research. Chapters 1 and 2 provide the global picture and a map of international production. In Chapter 3, "The Largest Transnational Corporations," you'll find information on the 100 largest transnational corporations worldwide, the 50 largest from developing countries, and the 25 largest from central and eastern Europe. The reports annexes provide additional statistics and figures.

TRANSPORTATION AND TRANSPORTATION NETWORKS

Best Search Engine: http://www.google.com/

Key Search Terms: Transportation + geography

Interstate Highways
http://www.geography.about.com/library/weekly/aa052499.htm
middle school and up

This *About.com* article provides a concise history of interstate highways, beginning with General Dwight D. Eisenhower's 62-day trip across the country in 1919, the memory of which played a large role in influencing him to push for the development of a national network of high-quality roads during his presidency. The article traces this development through the 1950s, revealing both the industrial/commercial and the military forces that drove the expansion.

See the *Lincoln Highway* Web site below for more about the history of highway systems in the United States.

Central Pacific Railroad Maps
http://www.cprr.org/Museum/Maps/
middle school and up

For historical maps of the Central Pacific Railroad, in particular, this comprehensive site is the ticket. There are nice images of a handful of maps—just click on a map for a larger image—and dozens of links to historic railroad maps on other sites. There are Nevada survey maps, maps showing railroad land grants in California, military maps from the Civil War, and lots more.

The images of maps are of very good quality, so you can actually follow the railroad lines as they crisscross the country.

Highway Route Markers
http://www.cprr.org/Museum/Maps/
middle school and up

Perhaps you're interested less in roads and rails than in the signs that direct people along their various routes. This excellent site on highway route markers around the world is organized into sections on the United States, Canada, Asia, Europe, Latin America, Oceania, and "Grab Bag," which is everything that doesn't fit into one of the previous categories.

In the United States section, you can view all kinds of signs, just state markers, or just state markers from the 1940s. Signs in other parts of the world are not divided into categories, so just click on the region of your choice.

Each image of a sign is accompanied by a link that gives you a larger image. There isn't any explanatory text here, just visual information, but you can check out "About this Site" for an overview of the site creator's mission.

The Lincoln Highway
http://www.ugcs.caltech.edu/~jlin/lincoln/
middle school and up

This Web site is devoted to resources on America's first transcontinental highway, the Lincoln Highway, which paved the way for the development of the interstate system. If you're exploring interstates and the changes wrought on the American landscape as a result of the automobile, you'll want to check out this collection of maps, history, articles, photos, and museum information.

Quite a few states have their own Lincoln Highway Association chapter, and you can link to their Web sites here as well. The "History" and "Articles" sections of the site are likely to contain the best resources for your research. You can read an article comparing the Lincoln Highway with Route 66, look at newspaper articles about the highway from 1910, as well as find current news articles on the road.

TROPICS

Best Search Engine:	http://www.google.com/
Key Search Terms:	Tropics + geography

Major Biomes of the World
http://www.runet.edu/~swoodwar/CLASSES/GEOG235/biomes/main.
   html
middle school and up

This site provides great information and pictures of the world's major biomes, including tropical forests and tropical savannah. Scroll down the table of contents to "Tropical Broadleaf Evergreen Forest" and "Tropical Savanna." Click on each of these to get an excellent introduction to the climate, vegetation, growth forms, tropical trees, soil, subclimaxes, fauna, and biome location.

Tropical forest is the rain forest, and it's considered earth's most complex biome. Rain forests can be found in the Amazon of South America, Central America, the Zaire Basin of Africa, the west coast of India, and several other places around the globe.

Tropical savannas or grasslands occur in many places, including the East African savannas of Kenya and Tanzania and the pine savannas of Belize and Honduras.

Journey into Amazonia
http://www.pbs.org/journeytoamazonia/
middle school and up

If the tropics you want to explore are those in the Amazon rain forest, this PBS site will take you there. Click on "Enter Amazonia" to begin your tour, which will take you through the following—"Waterworlds," "Life on Land," "The Big Top," "Powerful Plants," and "Sacred Ground." There are also pages devoted to an introduction to the site and "Teacher Resources."

"Enter Amazonia" is a good introduction to the region with some interesting historical facts and statistics thrown in. "Waterworlds" introduces you to rain, rain like you've never seen before, and creatures that like the rain—piranhas, a giant otter, turtles, and a manatee, just to name a few. "Life on Land" features jaguars, the anaconda snake, and vampire bats. Are you intimidated yet? You'll meet birds in "The Big Top" and plants of all shapes and sizes, including really, really huge ones. "Sacred Ground" will fill you in on conservation issues and activities in the Amazon Basin.

TROPOSPHERE (SEE ALSO ATMOSPHERE)

Best Search Engine:	http://www.infind.com/
Key Search Terms:	Troposphere
	Troposphere + geography

Discovery: Earth Journey: Peel the Planet
http://www.discovery.com/exp/earthjourneys/peel_atmos.html
middle school and up

This craftily named Discovery Channel Web site—*Peel the Planet* —
provides a look at the layers that make up our earth. By peeling through
"Atmosphere," "Crust," "Mantle," and "Core," you'll take a virtual trip
to the center of the earth. Although the section on "Troposphere" only
consists of two paragraphs, it will provide you with a concise base of
knowledge.

Troposphere (Encyclopedia of Atmospheric Environment)
http://www.doc.mmu.ac.uk/aric/eae/Atmosphere/Older/Troposphere.html
middle school and up

Produced by the U.K. Atmosphere, Climate and Environment Information Programme, this site is part of a handy resource for information
on atmospheric issues. The encyclopedic entry on troposphere is thorough and concise.

You'll also find a good introduction to other atmosphere topics, such
as aerosols, air, atmospheric gases, atmospheric layers, energy, exosphere,
ionosphere, magnetosphere, mesosphere, meteors, moisture, nitrogen,
oxygen, ozone hole, ozone layer, pollution, pressure, stratosphere, temperature, thermosphere, and trace gases. Many entries include a list of
Web links and recommended reading.

UNITED NATIONS

Best Search Engine:	http://www.google.com/
Key Search Term:	United Nations

The United Nations
http://www.un.org/
middle school and up

Here's the World Wide Web home of the world's foremost international organization. Click on the word "Welcome" in the language of
your choice, and the rest of the site will follow in that language. The
main menu includes links to the following: "UN News Centre," "About
the United Nations," "Main Bodies," "Conferences and Events," "Member States," "General Assembly President," "Secretary-General," "UN
Action against Terrorism," "Issues on the UN Agenda," "Civil Society/
Business," "The UN Works for Everybody," and "CyberSchoolBus."

Most of these pages within the site are self-explanatory from their name, but if you need a little help deciding where to go first, we'd recommend starting with the "CyberSchoolBus." It contains loads of wonderful information compiled and designed specifically with students like you in mind. There's a resources page, where you can read an introduction to the structure and activities of the UN, a curriculum page, a quizzes and games page, a community page, and lots of feature articles and reports.

If you're involved in Model UN activities through your school, you'll find a discussion group under the "Community" section of this page that's specifically for Model UN participants. It has a frequently asked questions page, a Starters' Kit, resources, and links that are probably just what you're looking for. Search the site for topics that relate to your area of research. Click at the very bottom of the "CyberSchoolBus" page to take a virtual tour of the United Nations.

Non-Members of the United Nations
http://geography.about.com/library/misc/blnun.htm
high school and up

This article about the three main nonmembers of the 189-member United Nations has a tiny bit of information on each country's status in regards to UN membership with links that take you to *About.com* maps and general information sites on Switzerland, Taiwan, and the Vatican City.

URBANIZATION

Best Search Engine: http://www.ixquick.com/
Key Search Term: Urbanization

For Schools: Tackling the Issues: Urbanization (The World Bank Group)
http://www.worldbank.org/html/schools/issues/urban.htm
high school and up

Part of the World Bank Group's educational collection on the Web, this site explores the increasingly important role cities play in the economic standing of nations and the challenges of rapid urbanization. You'll find some of the best resources around on global issues in urbanization. For instance, click on "Urban Development in World Regions" to access publications and data for numerous regions' urban indicators and urban development. (These regions include "Sub-Saharan Africa," "East Asia and Pacific," "Europe and Central Asia," "Latin America and Caribbean," "Middle East and North Africa," and "South Asia.")

Another standout is the section called "Urban Development Topics," where you can explore topics such as "City Development Strategies," "Local Economic Development," "Upgrading Urban Communities," and "Urban Waste Management." You can also tap into pages from *World Development Indicators, 2001*, to find more data on urbanization for over 140 of the world's countries.

Machine Space: A Case Study in Urbanization and Environment
http://www.colorado.edu/geography/virtdept/stylesheets//samples/
     machine_space/machine.html
high school and up

Created for the Virtual Geography Department Project, this learning module will provide you with both background information on urbanization issues and a hands-on exercise in which you consider the effects urbanization has on the environment. Best of all, the site gives you step-by-step instructions and tools for conducting an urbanization case study near your own home or school.

In the "Information" section, you'll gain an understanding of the concept of machine space and learn about urbanization's effects on environment and climate, the lithosphere and land resources, and the hydrosphere and water resources. The text material is nicely complemented by photographs, graphics, and a hyperlinked glossary of terms. You'll also find an excellent print bibliography to guide you in additional research.

VEGETATION

Best Search Engine: http://www.google.com

Key Search Terms: Vegetation + geography

Checklist of Online Vegetation and Plant Distribution Maps
http://www.lib.berkeley.edu/EART/vegmaps.html
high school and up

This comprehensive site from a couple of professors at the University of California, Berkeley is an index to vegetation and plant distribution maps for all parts of the world. The site is divided into "World," "Asia," "Africa," "Arctic," "Central America and West Indies," "Europe," "Indian Ocean," "North America," "Pacific," "South America," and "Other Sites." Each map is titled and is a hyperlink to its location on the Web.

If you're searching for a vegetation map for a certain locale, chances are that you'll find it here if it exists on the Web.

VITAL STATISTICS

Best Search Engine: http://www.ixquick.com/
Key Search Terms: Vital statistics + national
                      Vital statistics + international
                      Health + statistics
                      Mortality + statistics
                      Life expectancy + statistics

National Vital Statistics System (NVSS)
http://www.cdc.gov/nchs/nvss.htm
high school and up

The National Vital Statistics System is responsible for the United States' official vital statistics, which are provided through state-operated systems. This site offers access to the following categories of statistical data: "Birth," "Mortality," "Fetal Death," "Marriages and Divorces," "Linked Births/Infant Deaths," and "Family Growth" (i.e., infertility, sexual activity, birth control).

You can also access information via "FASTATS A to Z," which offers an alphabetical index that ranges from "Alabama" to "Birthweight and Gestation" to "Maine" to "Overweight Prevalence" to "Wyoming." In other words, "FASTATS" is an incredible resource for anyone seeking quick statistical info on a particular state or topic.

World Health Organization Statistical Information System
http://www.who.int/whosis/
high school and up

The World Health Organization (WHO) has created an international vital statistics resource comparable to the domestic site reviewed above. Here, you can search for statistics by disease or topic, or you can tap into the various sections of the site. These include "General Statistical Information," "Causes of Disease," "Statistical Annex of the World Health Report," "United Nations Population Division Data," "Healthy Life Expectancy," and others.

International Data Base (IDB)
http://www.census.gov/ipc/www/idbpyr.html
high school and up

The *International Data Base (IDB)* offers an extensive database with statistical tables of demographic and socioeconomic data for 227 countries and areas of the world.

The *IDB* combines data from country sources (especially censuses and surveys) with estimates and projections to provide information dating back as far as 1950 and as far ahead as 2050. The major types of data available in the *IDB* include: "Population by Age and Sex"; "Vital Rates, Infant Mortality, and Life Tables"; "Fertility and Child Survivorship"; "Migration"; "Marital Status"; "Family Planning"; "Ethnicity, Religion, and Language"; "Literacy"; "Labor Force, Employment, and Income"; and "Households."

VOLCANOES

Best Search Engines: http://www.yahoo.com/ and http://www.metacrawler. com/

Key Search Terms: Volcano + geography

Global Volcanism Program
http://www.volcano.si.edu/gvp/
high school and up

As part of the National Museum of Natural History at the Smithsonian Institution, the Global Volcanism Program (GVP) documents information on volcanic activity in order to understand and predict future volcanoes.

Start your general research at the site's "Volcanic Activity Reports." Here, you'll find *The Weekly Activity Report*, a cooperative project between the GVP and the U.S. Geological Survey that provides excellent summary material about recent volcanoes. More in-depth reports on volcanoes are published monthly in the *Bulletin of the Global Volcanism Network*. Within "Volcanic Activity Reports," you can also access a chronological archive of volcanic activity, dating back to 1968, which comes in handy for historical research. Use the excellent "Gazetteer" of volcano names, synonyms, and subfeatures to locate specific volcanic activity reports. If you're researching a particular region, simply click on the interactive map to find pages with detailed information about volcanic activity in that region.

Another excellent section is "Volcano NetLinks," where you'll find volcanology Web resources, annotated and organized by topic or region.

Types of Volcanoes
http://volcano.und.nodak.edu/vwdocs/vwlessons/volcano_types/index.
  html
middle school and up

This section of the colossal *Volcano World* site offers a classification system for volcanoes. The six types covered here are shield volcanoes, stratovolcanoes, rhyolite caldera complexes, monogenetic fields, flood basalts, and midocean ridges. For each type, simply click on the name to read a brief text description and view photos illustrating that type of volcano.

To view the rest of the *Volcano World* Web site, just click on the icon at the bottom of any page. From the home page, you can choose many excellent sections, including "Ask a Volcanologist" FAQs, "Interviews with Volcanologists," "Teaching and Learning Resources," "Today in Volcano History," and a powerful internal search engine.

How Volcanoes Work
http://www.geology.sdsu.edu/how_volcanoes_work/Home.html
high school and up

This educational site, sponsored by the National Aeronautics and Space Administration (NASA), describes the science behind volcanoes and volcanic processes. The site consists of six major units—"Eruption Dynamics," "Volcano Landforms," "Eruption Products," "Eruption Types," "Historical Eruptions," and "Planetary Volcanism"—and was designed for sequential use. In the "Volcanic Landforms" unit, you'll find specific info about volcano landforms' size, shape, composition, and eruptive history. Recent examples of each type of landform are provided, with excellent photographs and graphics.

You can also try your hand at a volcano crossword puzzle and check out a large selection of well-categorized, related Web sites. Each unit also offers a "Test Yourself" quiz on the material.

WEATHER

Best Search Engine: http://www.yahoo.com/

Key Search Terms: Weather + geography

                      Weather + education

Washington Post: Weather Calculators
http://www.washingtonpost.com/wp-srv/weather/longterm/calculator.htm
middle school and up

This page, courtesy of the *Washington Post*, features weather calculators that will do simple conversions or complex calculations based on your input. So if you need to know what the heat index is when the temperature is 80 degrees and the relative humidity is at 95 percent, you're at the right place.

There are five calculators featured here. Each one is easy to use—it's just a matter of pecking in a few numbers on your computer keyboard. If you've always wanted to spout out facts about the relative humidity or heat index like the local weather forecaster, here's your opportunity. Along with the "Fahrenheit/Celsius Converter," you'll find a "Wind Speed Converter," which converts between miles per hour, kilometers per hour, knots, and meters per second. The "Relative Humidity Calculator" calculates its data from temperature and dew point, and the "Wind Chill Calculator" uses temperature and wind speed. Finally, you can find out the heat index from temperature and relative humidity.

National Weather Service
http://www.nws.noaa.gov/
high school and up

With this site, you have access to the same info as your know-it-all local TV weather forecaster. The National Weather Service Web site is *the* place to go for official weather forecasts, weather maps, and historical and current weather data. There are several ways to access the information housed at the site. You can find it by geographic location (national or international) or by special topic (i.e., tropical prediction, marine prediction, storm prediction), or you can click on the projects highlighted at the center of the home page. These include 12-hour and 24-hour surface forecasts, daily temperature and precipitation outlooks, selected city bulletins, and more.

WEATHERING

Best Search Engine: http://www.google.com/
Key Search Term: Weathering

Weathering and Soils
http://www.tulane.edu/~sanelson/geol111/weathering.htm
high school and up

This site, designed for a college-level introductory geology course, provides in-depth information about weathering processes. The site breaks the topic into "Physical Weathering" and "Chemical Weathering."

In the text on "Physical Weathering," you'll find information about joints, crystal growth, the effect of heat, frost wedging, and plant and animal activities. In the "Chemical Weathering" section, the author describes the conditions and agents that cause chemical weathering. You'll find information here about hydrolysis, leaching, oxidation, dehydration, and complete dissolution. There's also an explanation of weathering rinds, exfoliation, and spheroidal weathering. You'll also learn about the key factors that influence weathering, such as rock type and structure, slope, climate, animals, and time.

If you discover that this site merely scratches the surface of your research needs, take a look-see at the remaining 19 chapters on geology.

Physical Geography: Weathering
http://uregina.ca/~sauchyn/geog221/wthrng.html
high school and up

Although this site is short and sweet, it provides a lucid explanation of weathering, the physical, chemical, and biological processes that alter the state of rocks and soil at or near the earth's surface.

The site's section on physical weathering examines frost shattering, pressure release, salt weathering, hydration, and thermal weathering. The section on chemical weathering explains carbonation, chelation, hydrolysis, and oxidation.

WINDS AND PRESSURE SYSTEMS

Best Search Engine: http://www.google.com/
Key Search Terms: Winds + pressure systems

Forces and Winds: Online Meteorology Guide
http://ww2010.atmos.uiuc.edu/(Gh)/guides/mtr/fw/home.rxml
high school and up

The University of Illinois's excellent series of online instructional modules strikes gold again. As a section within the *Meteorology Guide*, this "Forces and Winds" module is organized into the following topics: "Pressure," "Pressure Gradient Force," "Coriolis Force," "Geostrophic Wind," "Gradient Wind," "Friction," "Boundary Layer Wind," "Sea Breezes," and "Land Breezes."

You'll see that the first two topics provide a broad introduction to the subject of atmospheric pressure, while the remaining topics focus on specific aspects. The site is well designed, with good use of graphics and QuickTime movies. Highlighted text links to a glossary of terms and relevant case studies. On the "Pressure Gradient Force" page, for example, you'll be able to link to glossary entries, complete with graphic illustration, on "high pressure" and "low pressure." The "Boundary Layer Wind" page contains links to "convergence" and "counterclockwise," among other terms. Thanks to a toolbar on the left side of the home page, the site is also easy to navigate. And unlike other online courses that cater to students with lightening-fast computers, this one is available in both graphics and text-only versions.

Understanding Air Pressure
http://www.usatoday.com/weather/wbarocx.htm
middle school and up

Produced by *USA Today*, this site devotes itself to answering the questions of you weather hounds. The particular section found at the URL above sets out to explain how air pressure impacts the weather. You'll find explanations of how air pressure is measured, its relation to air density, how a barometer works, and how wind-barometer readings are used for forecasting. You'll also be supplied with the mathematical formulas used to describe air's decreasing pressure with altitude.

Simply click on highlighted words to link with related topics, such as atmosphere tables, a weather calculations index, the *Federal Meteorological Handbook*, a storms and fronts index, and how weather works. This last section, "How Weather Works," will give you numerous topics to explore, including "Winds, Jet Streams." Click on this link and discover how winds form, definitions of different kinds of winds, information on wind chill, jet stream formation, jet stream influence on weather, wind flow patterns, wind shear, the Beaufort wind scale, and wind calculations.

WOMEN—LIFE STYLES

Best Search Engine:	http://www.google.com/
Key Search Terms:	Women + geography
	Women's studies

United Nations Development for Women
http://www.unifem.undp.org/
high school and up

This organization within the United Nations is focused on working for women's empowerment and gender equality. Several sections provide resources of interest on women's lifestyles.

"Economic Capacity" explores the feminization of poverty and the United Nations' initiatives to expand the economic power of women.

"Governance and Leadership" also covers important ground. This page defines the need for women to gain access to political and economic power in order to attain gender equality in society. Subtopics include "Gender Responsive Budgeting," "Policy, Planning, and Programming," "Legislation and Constitutional Reform," "Leadership in Decision Making," and "Women, Peace, and Security."

"Women's Human Rights" is the section of the site that looks at all forms of discrimination against women and various initiatives within the United Nations to protect basic human rights for women.

To learn how the United Nations Development Fund for Women (UNIFEM) operates throughout the world, read the section called "About UNIFEM" at the top of the menu.

WomenWatch
http://www.un.org/womenwatch/world/index.html
high school and up

Here's an Internet gateway to women's empowerment and advancement issues. Following the international conference on women in Beijing in 1995, United Nations (UN) countries received a mandate to come up with strategies for improving the status of women in their countries. This Web site has been a catalyst for the United Nations in its efforts to direct attention to the status of women and to track the efforts of its member countries as they implement new plans.

The following sections of the site will take you to a wide variety of resources on women's lifestyles and other topics—"The UN Working for Women," "UN Conferences and Events," "Documents and Databases," "Women of the World," "News," and "Online Forums."

If you want to search for country- and region-specific information on women, go to "Women of the World." The page is divided into categories—"Africa," "Asia and the Pacific," "Eastern Europe," "Latin America and the Caribbean," and "Western Europe and Others." Click on the area of your choice, and you'll see a list of countries to choose from. Click on the country you're interested in, and you'll get links to resources of all types, including contact information for the UN committees working in the country on women's issues.

"Documents and Databases" is probably the most useful section of the site for researchers. It's divided into four sections—"Statistics and Indicators," "Good Practices Database," "Gender Training Materials," and "Selected UN Publications." There's also a "Women's Watch News Archive" link on this page if you're looking for older news on international women's issues.

For an introduction to United Nations programs, commissions, intergovernmental and treaty bodies, and international instruments related to women, go to "UN Working for Women."

WOMEN—STATISTICS ON

Best Search Engine: http://www.google.com/
Key Search Terms: Women + statistics

WomenWatch: Statistics and Indicators
http://www.un.org/womenwatch/resources/stats.htm
middle school and up

This is the page of the *WomenWatch* site (reviewed above) that deals specifically with statistics on women. It's an excellent source, with links to all kinds of statistical reports and databases. You'll find "World's Women 2000: Trends and Statistics" valuable for looking at a wide range of women's issues. This is the report from the United Nations of their main findings on women's situations as compared to men's worldwide in a broad range of fields that includes families, health, education, work, human rights, and politics.

Other reports include "Women in Government," a statistical database on women in the executive branch of governments, "Women in Parliament: World and Regional Averages," and "Who's Who at the UN: Women Ambassadors."

There are also loads of indicators you can use in your research. There are indicators on population, literacy, education, income and economic activity, and unemployment. These are all sorted by sex so that you can access the data for women.

WORLD TRADE FIGURES

Best Search Engine: http://www.google.com/
Key Search Terms: Foreign trade
                            World trade statistics

Foreign Trade Statistics
http://www.census.gov/foreign-trade/www/index.html
high school and up

This site's a winner for statistical information relating to the balance of trade. Look in the "Statistics" section to find current and historical information on imports, exports, and balance for just about every country in the world. You can also use this section to find out what categories of products were traded in any given year and month. In other words, if you need to know what the United States trade with Belgium was like during February of 1999, look no further.

Press releases, announcements, and papers relating to trade data are available in abundance here as well. And in case you're looking for information on a specific topic, the site contains an index as well as a search function.

Tracking Major Economic Indicators on the World Wide Web
http://www.methodist.edu/business/tracking.htm
high school and up

Created by the Reeves School of Business at Methodist College, this site provides excellent resources on the major economic indicators.

The section dedicated to "Balance of Trade" does a nice job of defining what balance of trade is and why it matters, as well as pointing you in the direction of other useful Web sites for researching world trade figures. Back at the home page, you'll also find sections with information on the consumer price index, Federal Reserve data, foreign exchange rates, gross domestic product, leading indicators, and more.

ZOOGEOGRAPHY

Best Search Engine: http://www.google.com/
Key Search Term: Zoogeography

Zoogeography and the Sea
http://publish.uwo.ca/~handford/zoogeog.html
high school and up

Part of zoologist Paul Hanford's home page, this site provides an excellent introduction, as well as some more advanced material if you read everything that's here. It's oriented toward understanding the role of the oceans in determining the geographic distribution of earth's animals.

Click on Part 1 for introductory material. This section begins with a good working definition and goes on to explore theories and other zoogeography terms and concepts in more depth. The page is sometimes difficult to read due to the lack of organization in the layout, but it contains an abundance of interesting material, including maps, inset boxes that highlight certain debates within the field, and links to other related resources.

If Part 1 leaves you wanting more, go on to Part 2, which explores three specific zoogeographic matters—"Wallace's Line, the Great American Faunal Interchange, and the entry of humans into the New World."

AnimalPlanet.com
http://animal.discovery.com/
middle school and up

Animal Planet is where you can find anything and everything about animals. To research animals from a zoogeographical perspective, your best bet is to go to "Explore by Subject." Click here and you'll be given a list of topics that includes "Pets," "Birds," "Bugs and Spiders," "Land Mammals," "Lizards and Reptiles," "Underwater Creatures," and "More Animals." Choose the one that best suits your interests.

Click on "Land Mammals," for example, and you'll encounter links to pages on pandas, rhinoceroses, elephants, dogs, grizzly bears, and more. There's also mammal cams, a video zoo, and other multimedia mammal resources here.

Nature: Triumph of Life
http://www.pbs.org/wnet/nature/triumphoflife/
middle school and up

If your interest in zoogeography relates to the evolution of life forms, you'll want to check out this PBS site, where six episodes take you on an exploration of evolution and the survival of the fittest. You'll start at the very beginning with "The Four Billion Year War" and work through "The Mating Game," "The Eternal Arms Race," "Winning Tams," "Brain Power," and "The Survivors."

An evolutionary time line will help you keep track as you skip through the millennia, and a filmmaker's diary may be of interest, too.

3

Materials and Resources for Geography Teachers

Each of the sites reviewed below reflects the unique needs of teachers of geography. Without a doubt, some of these sites will be ones you will want to bookmark on your computer. We've arranged the sites in this section into two broad categories: "Web Resources" and "Hands-On Opportunities." However, keep in mind that sites earmarked for teachers are by no means off-limits to other audiences. Parents who are home-schooling their kids, for instance, can use these sites to develop excellent at-home activities, lessons, and field trips. See also "The Basics" section in Volume I of this set for general sites.

WEB RESOURCES

Education Place: Outline Maps
http://www.eduplace.com/ss/ssmaps/

Looking for free outline maps? This site provides a wide selection of outline maps that you can freely print or download for use in the classroom or at home. (To open the maps marked PDF, you just need to have Adobe Acrobat, which can be downloaded from this site as well.)

Education World
http://www.education-world.com/soc_sci/geography/index.shtml

Geography teachers will find a "Timeline Teaching Tool," links to primary source material, lesson plans, thematic lessons, standards, and more. Use the toolbox in the center of the page to search for quick facts and statistics in the world country database. An assortment of other reference tools is organized at the bottom of the database.

The Gateway to Educational Materials
http://www.thegateway.org/

This is a must visit for busy teachers. Sponsored by the U.S. Department of Education, this site provides teachers, administrators, and parents with quick access to high-quality lesson plans, curriculum units, and other education resources on the Internet.

You can browse through lists organized by subject or keyword, or conduct a search by subject, keyword, title, or grade level. Under "Geography," you'll find 3,147 classroom resources, described in brief and rated for appropriate grade level.

The Geography Exchange
http://www.zephryus.demon.co.uk/geography/topics.html

The Geography Exchange, a British site, offers a worthwhile stop, particularly for educators or for parents who are homeschooling their kids. It offers excellent educational information via in-house topic sites written by geography teachers, along with a database of over 700 Web sites that have been reviewed and annotated by teachers.

The in-house sites cover the topics "Earthquakes," "Volcanoes," "Plate Tectonics," "Structure of the Earth," "Glaciers," "Rivers," "Fieldwork," and "The Environment." Click on "Online Lessons" to visit the "Virtual School" for high-school-age students. For each topic covered in the "Virtual School," you'll find instructional material, lesson plans, activities for students, information for teachers and parents, and recommended Web links.

NASA Education Programs
http://education.nasa.gov/

The National Aeronautics and Space Administration's (NASA) education program is an enormous enterprise, and the information you can access from this single Web site could keep you and your students engaged in learning activities from kindergarten through graduate school. From the home page, you'll see the site's major sections: "NASA Education Programs," "Education News," "Education Calendar," "Resources for Educators," "Resources for Students," and "Resources for the Informal Education Community."

The real heart and soul of the Web site—"A Guide to NASA's Education Programs"—can be accessed from any of the major sections. Here, you'll find a searchable database with brief descriptions of every NASA education project, which include such interactive standouts as the Jason Project and the GLOBE Project.

While your time would be well-spent exploring the entire site, teachers will also want to hone in on the "Resources for Educators" section. Here, you'll find descriptions of educator workshops and fellowship opportunities, curriculum support materials, educational television and video resources, and multimedia resources such as Webcams, 3-D models, satellite tracking, photographs, images, CD-ROMs, movie clips, and slide shows.

National Geographic Education Center
http://www.nationalgeographic.com/education/

National Geographic has pulled together an assortment of top-notch resources to help you teach your students about geography. You will want to check out the online thematic adventures, such as a trek through equatorial Africa or a tour of the Great Barrier Reef.

At the site, you can also find printable maps, well-designed lessons plans, quizzes to help students prepare for the National Geographic Bee, applications for teacher grants from National Geographic's Education Foundation, and a teacher store that's full of new educational products.

The New York Times Learning Network
http://www.nytimes.com/learning/

The "Teacher Connections" section provides daily lesson plans for grades 6 through 12. These comprehensive plans, written in partnership with the Bank Street College of Education in New York City, also provide reference articles that can be printed out for classroom use. You can find pertinent lessons by searching under a particular topic. Under the topic of "Geography," for example, you'll discover an impressive collection of lesson plans, covering timely issues such as "Making the Invisible Visible: A Lesson in Mapping the Mysteries of Cyberspace" and "Nepal in the Family: Exploring the History, Culture, Geography, and Politics of the Himalayan Monarchy."

World Bank Group: Development Education Program
http://www.worldbank.org/html/schools/depweb.htm

Sustainable development is a truly germane topic for many of the social sciences—from geography to history to economics. Teachers can utilize this site, which contains a wide range of curriculum materials, to explore sustainable development in their classrooms.

The "Learning Modules" section is divided into three areas: "Social," "Economic," and "Environmental." In each of these areas, you and your students can delve into learning modules on the specific issues of population growth, life expectancy, gross national product per capita, and access to safe water. You'll find texts, maps, charts and graphs, data tables, photographs, case studies, and research materials to help you examine these issues. The "For Teachers" area contains linear versions of all module activities (with and without answers) that you can print for offline classroom use. This section of the site also contains an introduction that addresses issues of particular concern to teachers, such as the goals and objectives of the learning modules and the point of view of the materials.

Odyssey World Trek: Teachers' Zone
http://www.worldtrek.org/odyssey/teachers/index.html

This is a fabulous site for high school geography teachers. At the *Odyssey* Web site, your students can follow a team of educators in their two-year trek around the world, learning about diverse cultures, critical global issues, and ways that they can help create positive change in the world.

The experiences of the traveling team are documented online in video, audio, photos, and text, posted twice a week. Students can also interact with the team, the people they meet, and each other. As a teacher, you have online access to excellent teacher's guides and lesson plans for the countries and regions the team has visited, including Mexico, Belize, Guatemala, Central and South America, southern Africa, West Africa, and Egypt. These lessons can be used in conjunction with the Web site or independently when they tie in with your own curriculum.

You can also use the message board to interact with other teachers—ask questions, schedule live chats with other classes, learn about what other teachers are doing, and share your own suggestions.

Parks as Classrooms
http://www.nps.gov/interp/parkclass.html

This is a great site for teachers who want to take their students out of the classroom and into the wild. Parks as Classrooms (PAC) programs and materials are the result of a partnership between national park sites and neighboring school districts. They provide on- and off-site learning opportunities via curriculum-based education programs, audiovisual materials, accredited teacher training, traveling trunks and kits, and teacher and student resource guides.

You'll find information on getting involved in PAC at this Web site, as well as information you can pass along to your students about Junior Ranger programs.

About.com: Geography Resources for the Social Studies Teacher
http://7–12educators.about.com/education/7–12educators/
    msub62historygeo.htm

You'll find plenty of material here specifically designed for secondary school educators. You'll find a section called "How to Teach Longitude and Latitude," a wealth of free blank outline maps of the countries and continents of the world that you can print out and use for class activities, links to other useful Web sites, and access to *About.com*'s extensive lesson plan library, organized by grade level and subject matter.

The National Center for Geographic Information and Analysis (NCGIA):
GIS Education Projects
http://www.ncgia.ucsb.edu/education/ed.html

The National Center for Geographic Information and Analysis (NCGIA) is an independent consortium dedicated to research and education in the field of geographic information science. This portion of NCGIA's Web site offers up the group's Geographic Information Systems (GIS) education projects.

You'll find information here about summer institutes for teachers, as well as a number of basic instructional resources for teachers. Click on "K–12 Level Materials" to tap into a series of learning modules that demonstrate the power of GIS software. You'll also find a "GIS in the Schools Resource Packet," with course outline notes and a plain language GIS glossary. If you are teaching more advanced students, look under "University Level Materials" for laboratory exercises and materials.

U.S. Census 2000: Census in Schools
http://www.census.gov/dmd/www/schindex.htm

The U.S. Census Bureau truly thought of everything when it designed its Web site. *Census in Schools* provides excellent teaching materials and tools to help your students understand data on the people and economy of the United States.

Be sure to check out the lesson plans, teaching suggestions, and worksheet, all designed to be used in studying Census 2000 results. These materials supply you and your students with an outstanding opportunity to learn about the demographic changes that took place in the United States during the 1990s.

You'll find an e-mail link to order free packets of additional teaching materials that are targeted to specific age groups. The packet includes a 24-page teaching guide and a 4' × 6' wall map.

Georgia Geographic Alliance
http://georgiageographicalliance.org/

The Georgia Geographic Alliance (GGA) is a nonprofit organization supported by the National Geographic Society and the Georgia Department of Education, whose goal is to improve the quality and quantity of geographic education in grades K–12 throughout the state of Georgia. You'll find useful information here, regardless of the state in which you teach.

Click on "Teacher Lesson Plans" to access a handful of lessons created by GGA's Teacher Consultants. These lessons, on topics such as pollution, urban geography, and the Aral Sea disaster, were designed to correlate with national standards for geography education. Click on "Notable Children's Books" for a list of fiction and nonfiction books recommended for classroom use by some of GGA's Teacher Consultants.

If you like what you find here, check out another regional site—the Geography Educators' Network of Indiana (GENI), found at http://www.iupui.edu/~geni/—which offers an even more extensive collection of interesting lesson plans. For both of these state organizations, you will also find information online about training seminars and summer institutes.

The K–12 Teacher Guide to Geography
http://tlc.ai.org/tgeogidx.htm

This Web site, part of the K–12 Teaching and Learning Center (K–12 TLC), is literally crammed with great resources for teachers. You might feel disoriented by the home page, which perhaps tries too hard to fit it all in one place.

Under "General Resources," you'll see a good selection of resources for teachers and students alike. In "Lesson Plans," you'll find excellent lesson plans organized by grade level and by country or geographic region. You can use the one-click links to access other relevant areas of K–12 TLC, such as the "Guide to Maps" or the "Guide to Travel Destinations."

National Wetlands Inventory Center: For Educators
http://www.nwi.fws.gov/educator.htm

At the *National Wetlands Inventory Center* Web site, you'll find a collection of resources compiled by the U.S. Fish and Wildlife Service that can be useful for teaching about wetlands.

Some of the highlights of the site include "The Young Scientists Introduction," a booklet designed to be downloaded and used as a teaching resource; "Educating Young People about Water," a searchable guide to help teachers develop community-based water education programs; and a link to *EcoScope*, a powerful and innovative approach to wetland education.

Geothermal Education Office: Educational and Classroom Material
http://geothermal.marin.org/edmatl.html

This site offers excellent information on geothermal energy, including an online slide show, an introductory lesson, an advanced lesson, and a glossary of terms—all of which you can incorporate into your own lesson plans. The Geothermal Education Office also assists in organizing workshops or community energy events and helping you locate expert guest speakers on geothermal energy.

The office also offers some freebies for teachers and students. The "Free Stuff" package includes an assortment of posters, brochures, fact sheets, booklets, and more. There's even more material available when you cough up some cash, including grade-specific curriculum, slide sets, videos, and CD-ROMs on topics related to geothermal energy and plate tectonics.

USGS Fact Sheets
http://water.usgs.gov/wid/indexlist.html

The U.S. Geological Survey (USGS) offers free fact sheets that summarize the organization's research and investigations. At this site, you'll find a list of available fact sheets, categorized by theme and/or scientific discipline. Within each of the themes—"Natural Resources," "Hazards," "Environment," "Information Management," and "States"—you'll find hundreds of online printable fact sheets.

Be sure to go to "Scientific Discipline" and click on "Mapping" to access an enormous collection of booklets, CD-ROMs, and grade-specific teaching packets on topics related to mapmaking and map reading. You'll also find links here to the many USGS education and outreach offices for specific divisions, such as Biological Resources, Water Resources, and Geology.

For more educational materials from the USGS, visit the "Learning Web" portion of its Web empire at http://www.usgs.gov/education/edulist.html, where you will find an exhaustive collection of teaching packets, posters, paper models, booklets, wall charts, activity sheets, and CD-ROMs.

Observatorium: Educator's Resources
http://observe.ivv.nasa.gov/nasa/education/edu_index.shtml.html

The Observatorium's Web site offers a number of information packets that can be useful for teaching about remote sensing, such as "Remote Sensing in History," "Remote Sensing Resources," "Remote Sensing Tools and Data," and extensive "Teachers' Guides."

The site also provides teachers with quick links to many of the National Aeronautics and Space Administration's (NASA) educational programs and materials. Click on "NASA's Education Projects" to browse material sorted by grade level (K–6, 7–9, 10–12, and post–grade 12) or topic ("Aeronautics," "Atmosphere," "Land," "Space," "Water").

Sustainable Seas Expeditions: Teacher Materials
http://sustainableseas.noaa.gov/aboutsse/education/teacher_materials.html

The Sustainable Seas Expeditions project provides high-quality marine science teaching materials that are linked to national standards on science and geography. From this site, you can download the "Sustainable Seas Expeditions Teacher Resource Book," which contains background information on the National Oceanic and Atmospheric Association's (NOAA) National Marine Sanctuaries, information about the submersible research missions, and suggestions for classroom activities (e.g., planning a submersible research mission, designing a submersible vehicle, and mapping a marine sanctuary). The book also lists many additional resources: books, Web sites, and CD-ROMs about the ocean and the sanctuaries.

There's also information about several training workshops for teachers—from single-day to multiweek to online—sponsored by NOAA. At these workshops, teachers acquire knowledge about national marine sanctuaries, learn strategies for integrating ocean studies into science and geography courses, participate in field investigations, interact with the research community, learn scientific monitoring techniques, develop lesson plans, and refine presentation skills. Adventurous sorts will want to look into NOAA's "Teacher at Sea Program" (described below in "Hands-On Opportunities").

HANDS-ON OPPORTUNITIES

AFS Global Educators Program
http://www.socialstudies.org/profdev/profdev1.html#opportunities

If you want to go abroad with one of the oldest and most established international organizations, AFS (American Field Service) is for you.

Open to teachers, librarians, and education administrators at any stage of their careers, these programs take you for one month or an entire semester to China, France, Argentina, Mexico, South Africa, or Spain.

AFS aims to provide educators with intercultural experiences that will affect the way they teach and learn throughout their careers. Your experience will combine class teaching with cultural immersion, allowing you to gain insight into a different way of life and educational system. There are also opportunities to meet with community leaders and local government officials to exchange ideas on education and culture.

If you'd like more information or an application, just contact AFS using the e-mail address or phone number provided at the bottom of the page.

Dar al Islam: Teacher's Institute
http://www.daralislam.org/programs/reach/ti.cfm

These are one- or two-week institutes, held in Abiquiu, New Mexico, for secondary school teachers who want to learn more about the faith, civilization, and worldview of Islam. There are morning and evening lectures, study groups, and research in the library and media room. Teachers learn from top-notch academic and traditional scholars about how to more effectively teach their students about Islam.

The application deadline is in the early spring of each year. See the complete application instructions online. You may also want to read some of the newsletters or other publications available from this organization's Web site.

Federal Reserve Bank of New York: Educator-Oriented Initiatives
http://www.ny.frb.org/pihome/educator/initeduc.html

The Federal Reserve Bank of New York offers several programs of interest to geography teachers. "The Global Economic Forum," for educators at all levels, is a three-day summer program in which educators gain an international perspective on a wide array of economic issues by assuming the roles of policy makers from various nations.

"In the Shoes of a Fed Policymaker" is very similar, except that the focus is on the making of monetary policy in particular. This is a four-day program. For more information on these programs, which are held in New York City, visit the Web site. If interested in enrolling, you will need to contact the Federal Reserve Bank of New York by phone or e-mail.

Global Volunteers
http://www.globalvolunteers.org/

If you'd like your hands-on experience to involve doing some good for people in another part of the world, Global Volunteers can help you make it happen. They coordinate service-learning programs that offer educators the opportunity to participate in short-term human and economic development projects in more than 15 countries worldwide, including Mexico, Poland, Spain, Vietnam, Greece, Ecuador, Ireland, Ghana, Tanzania, Romania, and Italy. Projects typically involve building community facilities, painting and repairing homes, teaching conversational English, providing health care services, and assisting in environmental projects.

Green World Center Study Retreat
http://www.greenworldcenter.org/content.html

Here's a more contemplative, low-key opportunity for those of you who might want some time to work on writing a book or article or developing a new curriculum. A residential program in the Appalachian mountains of Quebec, the Study Retreat brings together students, teachers, scholars, writers, artists, and others who need to take some time for themselves and their work. The center is especially interested in environmental civics; human ecology; literature and philosophy; cinema; photography; multimedia; peace studies; animals and society; anthropology; nature writing; and environmental education.

Click on "Study Retreat" on the home page to read more about the center's resources and the faculty, which includes such folks as Jane Goodall, Noam Chomsky, and Francis Moore Lappé.

Teacher at Sea Program
http://www.tas.noaa.gov/

If you are a teacher who is interested in oceanographic research, perhaps the idea of living aboard an oceangoing research vessel will intrigue you. The Teacher at Sea Program taps motivated K–12 and college teachers to work as crew members on one- to three-week cruises.

Teachers who participate in the program submit a report to the National Oceanic and Atmospheric Association Education Office detailing the cruise events and ideas for implementation in the classroom, including a mini-unit of lessons based on their experiences at sea. They are also expected to submit an article for publication or to conduct a presentation at an educators conference.

Check the site for upcoming cruise dates and mission descriptions. You can also read what past participants have written about their research activities and about life onboard a ship. You'll find downloadable application forms and health questionnaires right on hand.

Teachers Experiencing Antarctica and the Arctic (TEA)
http://tea.rice.edu/

If you're looking for a little adventure in the guise of continuing education, then look no further than this site. The centerpiece of the Teachers Experiencing Antarctica and the Arctic (TEA) Program is a research experience in which 12 to 16 K–12 teachers are selected to participate annually in a polar expedition. TEA teachers work closely with scientists and participate in cutting-edge research.

Click on "Meet the Teachers" to learn about the participants and to read portions of their journals. Be sure to visit the "Activities" section to glean excellent classroom material from teachers who were past TEA participants, covering topics such as polar chains and webs, Inuit culture, ice cores, global change in the Arctic, and much more. Look in "Polar Links" and "News" for links to other excellent sites on related subjects. And after you've done all that, why not cut to the punch—go ahead and download an application from the site.

Travel 2 Learn Rainforest Workshops for Educators and Naturalists
http://www.travel2learn.com/

Want a little adventure in the guise of continuing education? These workshops held in places like Belize and the Amazon give you the chance to work side by side with a spirited and engaging faculty in some of the most biologically diverse areas of the world. The faculty includes specialists in ornithology, botany, marine biology, archaeology, and entomology. Participants gain experience using hand lenses, binoculars, headlamps, maps, field guides, water testing equipment, and other simple field equipment. They may also be able to earn graduate credit or qualify for scholarship help. The program is open to anyone with an interest in the rain forest and a desire to explore.

Just scroll down the page to read comments from workshop alumni on every aspect of the workshops. Quotes are organized under the following categories: "Workshop Leaders," "Resources," "Inspiration," "Adventure," and "Group Dynamics." Links on the menu will take you to information about grants, slides from previous workshops, and detailed biographies of the faculty members.

4

———— ∞∞∞ ————

Museums and Summer Programs for Geography Students

In this chapter, we've scouted out the best Web sites for museums and summer programs for geography students. This part of the book is designed to help you learn about physical and human geography in a more hands-on style. We'll describe Web sites where you can manipulate earthquake fault lines, explore how the census was tabulated at the turn of the century, watch live video from a climb up Mount Everest, or hear an interview with a cultural anthropologist. We've also found amazing sites that'll convince you to log off your computer—to attend an ecology leadership workshop, spend the night in a paleontology museum, or even travel to a foreign country where Internet connections are far and few between. See also "The Basics" section in Volume 1 of this set for general sites.

MUSEUMS

American Museum of Natural History
http://www.amnh.org/

For geography students interested in topics such as biodiversity, paleontology, and world culture, the American Museum of Natural History (AMNH) Web site is a winner. Go to "Exhibitions" to explore current and past exhibits at the museum. While nothing compares to attending an actual exhibit, this site certainly rises to the challenge, offering movie clips, virtual tours, answers to FAQs, ideas for at-home activities, and excellent links to relevant Web resources. For example, when you enter the "Vikings: The North Atlantic Saga" online exhibit, you can see how your own name would appear in the runic alphabet, view a video about building a Viking ship, and hear an interview with the exhibit's curator.

For those of you living in or visiting New York City, click on "Kids and Families" to learn about the extensive offering of on-site workshops, lectures, and summer programs for children, young adults, and parents. The Precollege Science Collaborative for Urban Minority Youth (PSC) program, for example, is offered to high school juniors willing to commit to a two-year program of independent research under the guidance of a science mentor at the museum. There's also an Ecology Club for New York City teenagers interested in environmental issues. Club members participate in field explorations in a variety of habitats, from coastal dunes to Catskill highlands, conducting water quality investigations, biodiversity surveys, tree plantings, and a variety of other projects.

Franklin Institute Science Museum
http://sln.fi.edu/tfi/

It's no surprise that the U.S. Department of Education included *The Franklin Institute Online* on a list of family-friendly Web sites in a recent publication. The Franklin Institute Science Museum in Philadelphia, Pennsylvania, is clearly an innovative museum. Its educational exhibits and programs offer fresh interpretations of the social and historical impact of science and technology, along with forums for discussion of important scientific issues. Students who live in the Philadelphia area should click on "Programs" to learn about summer discovery camps, traveling science shows, science workshops, an excellent homeschool series of courses, and overnight camps at the museum.

Within the site's "Learning Resources" section, you'll discover an array of online learning options relevant to student geographers. Try "Inquiry Attic," for starters, to join in an online exploration of interesting scientific instruments (a new one is offered each month, along with an archive of previous inquires). You can explore, for instance, how the census was tabulated at the turn of the century. Another excellent learning resource is called "Spotlight." Here, topics such as Mount Everest, oceans, earthquakes, El Niño, and urban ecosystems are explored, incorporating outside Web resources into a package that would be useful in a geography classroom or at home. Be sure to also check out "Sciences Activities," where you'll find recommended science activities for home and school on specific topics in geography, oceanography, bioscience, and more.

The Exploratorium: The Museum of Science, Art, and Human Perception
http://www.exploratorium.edu/

Online since 1993, the Exploratorium was one of the first science museums to build a site on the Web. With a head start like that, it's no surprise that the site consists of more than 10,000 Web pages and hundreds of sound and video files, exploring hundreds of different topics. Some geography-related items here include an exhibition called "Life along the Faultline: Life and Science in Earthquake Country," a collection of artwork called "Turbulent Landscapes" that draws on the natural world, a "Sun-Earth Connection" tutorial, and Webcasts from the La Niña Summit.

While many of the online exhibits are patterned after real exhibits on the museum floor, the Exploratorium has, in some instances, created richer online versions than their physical counterparts by making the most of available technology. For instance, the museum was a forerunner in live audio and video broadcasts (Webcasts) that provide Web audiences the chance to hear or view interviews with scientists, meet interesting people, or tour unusual locations.

There's tons of content to explore here, so if you want to get right down to business, use the site's "Digital Library" for a quick guide to the online exhibitions, Webcasts, and more. Be sure to check out the section called "Science Explorer" to find scores of ideas for science activities you can do on your own, such as making a salt volcano, starting a mold terrarium, or building geodesic gumdrops.

"Science Snacks" is another must-visit section. The snacks are miniature exhibits that can be made in the classroom or at home, using common, inexpensive, easily available materials. Each snack is divided into easy-to-follow sections that include a photograph, a short introduction, a list of materials, assembly instructions, and an explanation of the science behind the snack.

Boston Museum of Science
http://www.mos.org/

The Boston Museum of Science has created a good Web site that allows you to quickly access its excellent online exhibits. Click on "Exhibits," then click on "Online" to find such gems as "Secrets of the Ice," which delves into the science behind an Antarctic expedition; "Mount Everest," which takes you on a tour of the path many climbers take to Mount Everest's peak; "Oceans Alive," which explores the global seas; and "Big Dig Archeology," a look at Boston's history and archeological artifacts.

Back at the home page, Bostonians (and Boston tourists) can click on "Learn More" to find out about museum courses and day trips, including extensive courses for adults age 16 and up on subjects such as planetary science, paleontology, mineralogy, New England weather, and forensic anthropology. There's also a great collection of educator resources here, such as video and CD-ROM loans from the museum library and a field trip guide. In addition, the museum sponsors a variety of excellent travel programs, which include a trip to the Amazon rain forest (specifically for teens), an African safari for the whole family, and a trip to the Galapagos Islands.

The Field Museum
http://www.fieldmuseum.org/

The Field Museum's Web site houses a collection of interesting online exhibits, which can be easily accessed from the "Quick Links" pull-down menu on the home page. These exhibits include "Sue on the Web," which centers on the largest, most complete, and best preserved *Tyrannosaurus rex;* "Man-Eaters of Tsavo," which focuses on the two lions that killed more than 140 workers building the Uganda Railway in 1898; "Underground Adventure," which examines the subject of soil from a unique perspective; and a virtual visit to the museum's "Anthropology Collections," nicely organized by world regions.

Back on the home page, click on "Education" to learn about the museum's extensive education programs for those in the Chicago area. These include free ongoing programs such as a fossil preparation laboratory, a replica of a Pawnee Earth Lodge, and other cultural learning stations. The museum recently launched Project E.R. (Environmental Rescue), an e-field trip for students that examines the connections between the environment and culture. Project E.R. features a broadcast and online curriculum that takes students behind the scenes at the museum and out to field sites. The museum also sponsors numerous courses on geography-related topics such as field ecology and paleontology; special family workshops; and behind-the-scenes evenings with museum scientists. You can also learn about the Harris Loan Program, which brings artifacts, specimens, audiovisual materials, and activity kits to Chicago area classrooms.

University of California Museum of Paleontology: History of Life Online Exhibits
http://www.ucmp.berkeley.edu/historyoflife/histoflife.html

This Web site, created by the University of California Museum of Paleontology, provides an excellent overview of paleontology, the history of life, and the diversity of Earth's biota.

The site's three exhibit wings—"Phylogeny," "Geology," and "Evolution"—are each packed with information. The "Geology" wing (a must-visit section for geographers interested in plate tectonics and geologic time scales) explores the history of Earth, looking at Earth and its life at particular points in time. The "Phylogeny" wing examines the diversity and relationships between the major groups of living things on Earth. The "Evolution" wing focuses on the people who have developed and contributed to current theories on phylogeny and geologic history. Each wing has an "Entrance Hall," allowing you to begin exploring from a fixed point. As you wander from hallway to hallway, you will be presented with options on which direction to go. You'll also run across some self-contained special exhibits on related topics.

Back at the site's home page, you'll also find "K–12 Resources," which is full of good classroom lessons, teacher resources, and student activities.

Yahoo! Directory of Natural History Museums
http://dir.yahoo.com/Society_and_Culture/Environment_and_Nature/
    Natural_History_Museums/

Yahoo! offers an excellent directory of museums and exhibits that are dedicated to the natural sciences. If you're searching for a good museum in your area or in a region you plan to visit, this site can help you find it. The list includes biggies such as the Smithsonian Institute's National Museum of Natural History and the American Museum of Natural History, along with smaller regional museums like the Alabama Museum of Natural History, the High Desert Museum, and the Natural History Museum of the Adirondacks. Brief annotations for most of the museums can help you decide if it's a site worthy of your next click.

Smithsonian National Museum of Natural History
http://www.mnh.si.edu/

If you are planning a visit to the Smithsonian National Museum of Natural History in Washington, D.C., you should definitely spend some time at this Web site first. It'll help you decide how to best use your time at the museum. Click on "Exhibits" to see what current exhibits are at the museum and, in some instances, get an online preview. For the "African Voices" exhibit, for instance, you'll find a special online introduction to the history, dynamism, and influence on global culture of Africa's people and cultures.

The section called "Educational Resources" is worthy of your click as well. Here, you can view past electronic field trips, such as "Exploring Ecosystems," "Messages from Outer Space," and "Stories Written in Stone." Each of these field trip sections offers educational activities, virtual museum displays, and relevant links for students in grades 7 through 12.

National Geographic
http://www.nationalgeographic.com/

The National Geographic Society's Web site offers online exhibits that rival what the best online museums have to offer. For example, in an "Expedition Online" entitled "Dispatches from Extreme Antarctica," you'll follow the dispatches (video, audio, and photographs) of a National Geographic correspondent aboard an icebreaker off west Antarctica.

Another interactive feature called "Go West with Lewis and Clark" lets you play a game in which you help map the rivers and try to find a water route from coast to coast. In the site's "Xpeditions" section, you'll find the official home of all 18 U.S. geography standards, extensive lesson plans and activities, an atlas chock-full of black-and-white maps designed for printing and copying, and "Xpeditions Hall," an interactive learning museum. The section called "MapMachine" contains great resources, including dynamic maps, atlas maps, flags and facts, and additional features like "Round Earth, Flat Maps," which explores every mapmaker's fundamental dilemma.

Be sure to check out the events calendar for a roster of lectures and public programs, most of which take place in Washington, D.C., Seattle, Chicago, and Cincinnati.

SUMMER PROGRAMS

Green World Center Study Retreat
http://www.greenworldcenter.org/content.html

Here's a more contemplative, low-key opportunity for those of you over 18 who might want some time to work on a self-directed project. A residential program in the Appalachian mountains of Quebec, the Study Retreat brings together students, teachers, scholars, writers, artists, and others who need to take some time for themselves and their work. The center is especially interested in environmental civics; human ecology; literature and philosophy; cinema; photography; multimedia; peace studies; animals and society; anthropology; nature writing; and environmental education.

Click on "Study Retreat" on the home page to read more about the center's resources and the faculty, which includes such folks as Jane Goodall, Noam Chomsky, and Francis Moore Lappé.

Rainforest and Reef
http://www.rainforestandreef.org/

The Rainforest and Reef Conservation Fund is a nonprofit organization based in Grand Rapids, Michigan, committed to conservation and education. The group's Web site describes a number of educational rain forest and marine ecology field courses, well suited to geography students with a special interest in ecology and conservation. Undergraduate and graduate credits are offered for the field courses, which take place in Belize, Costa Rica, Honduras, Panama, Ecuador, Peru, British Columbia, Hawaii, and Australia, typically over the summer months.

If you're looking for a more expansive program, there are also semester-long and yearlong college-level field courses, as well as specialized field courses with Spanish immersion for middle school, high school, and college students. For each field course listed on the Web site, you can click to read a general description, get a detailed daily itinerary, and pull up a printable registration form.

Conservation Leadership Schools
http://www.cas.psu.edu/docs/casconf/CLS/CLS.html

If the topics in geography that interest you include forestry, wetlands, and conservation, you'll definitely want to visit this Web site. Pennsylvania State University's Conservation Leadership Schools are two-week outdoor workshops for high school students interested in natural resource management, conservation, and exploring solutions to environmental problems.

The instruction and fieldwork involves groups of 8 to 10 students supervised by a faculty member. Subjects include forestry, water quality management, soil analysis and use, conservation legislation and regulation, public speaking, environmental issues, low-impact recreation, general natural history, speleology (study of caves), and more. To be admitted to the program, you'll need to be 15 to 18 years old, finished with ninth grade (with at least one ninth-grade science course), and have a genuine interest in conservation. You'll find all the information you need to apply right at the Web site.

You can also learn more about the Advanced Conservation Leadership School, which emphasizes leadership and problem solving. It's designed for students (ages 16 to 18) interested in leading environmental education activities and in becoming involved with local, state, or national resource management and conservation issues. The Advanced School is for students who have attended the two-week Conservation Leadership School or an equivalent program.

Living Routes—Student Programs
http://www.siriuscommunity.org/LR/programs.html

The study of sustainable development is an increasing part of the advanced geography curriculum. Living Routes is an organization offering educational programs—in connection with a consortium of colleges and universities—in which students gain hands-on experience in sustainable development by living and working in eco-villages around the world.

At Living Routes' Web site, you'll find thorough descriptions of the array of student programs offered. The Summer Institute in Sustainable Living, for instance, is a six-week program for students. The first five weeks of the institute take place at an educational center and eco-village in western Massachusetts, with the final week at Ecovillage at Ithaca, an ecological co-housing community in upstate New York. During the institute, students focus on topics such as green building, ecological design, appropriate technology, organic gardening, sustainable food systems, eco-village network outreach, conference center management, and personal and community health.

Other Living Routes programs include the Appalachian Ecovillages Semester and the Geo Communities Semester (in India and southern France). These longer programs provide students the opportunity to immerse themselves in sustainable living practices and to learn firsthand about issues like world population, globalization, habitat destruction, and biological restoration.

Teton Science School
http://www.tetonscience.org/

The Teton Science School in Grand Teton National Park offers hands-on programs in ecology, geology, botany, zoology, astronomy, and the unique natural history of the Yellowstone ecosystem. Whether you're a high school student, college student, graduate student, or teacher, there's a program to suit you.

At the Web site, you can read descriptions of five-week summer courses for high school students in field ecology and natural history, one-day and multi-day seminars for adults, teacher workshops, and three- to five-day customized programs for school groups. You can also use the Web site to learn about how you can participate in the Journeys project, which explores the idea of a sense of place through the physical and natural environment, cultural history, and present-day community.

Recent college graduates might be interested in applying for the Teton Science School Professional Residency in Environmental Education and Natural Science (PREE), a one-year training program in environmental education. Eighteen college graduates are selected each year; these candidates typically have training or experience in some combination of science, environmental studies, education (classroom or nonformal), and outdoor pursuits, as well as a strong interest in working for nonprofits, natural resource agencies, or public/private schools.

School for Field Studies
http://www.fieldstudies.org/pages/programs/programs.html

If you would like to take your geography studies out of the classroom and into the rain forest or savanna, check out this Web site. The School for Field Studies offers semester-long and summer courses at its field study centers in Australia, British Columbia, the British West Indies, Costa Rica, Mexico, and Kenya.

Semester programs allow students to enroll in four courses of four credits each, with a curriculum of lectures, research presentations, field trips, and lab work. Summer courses are intense 30-day experiences, comprised of lectures, field exercises, research, and expeditions. Whether your interest is in physical geography or human geography, these programs will move you beyond textbook analysis of issues and allow you to learn firsthand about conservation, sustainable development, and other relevant topics.

From the Web site, you can order a catalog of programs and download the admissions application form.

There's even a special section just for parents, in case you need help convincing Mom and Dad to let you live in Kenya for four months.

Youth for Environmental Sanity (YES) Action Camps
http://www.yesworld.org/summer_camps.html

Youth for Environment Sanity (YES) is a nonprofit organization that educates young people and encourages them to work together for social justice and environmental issues. At the YES Web site, you learn about Summer Action Camps, which focus on topics such as ecology, social justice, solutions to environmental problems, and globalization.

The camps are designed for students ages 15 to 25, with some exceptions made "for mature younger folks and youthful older folks." You can even earn three college credits for the camps held through the New College of California Program in Culture, Ecology, and Sustainable Community. A sliding scale of fees helps make the camps affordable for students who are watching their dollars.

StudyAbroad.com
http://www.studyabroad.com/

If you're looking for a study abroad program that matches your specific educational needs, *StudyAbroad.com*'s search engine will prove to be a huge timesaver. Those of you who have a certain country in mind can simply use the country portals to find student programs, travel information, maps, and more. You can also easily search by subject area, using a pull-down menu to select from such choices as agricultural economics, cultural/regional studies, ecology, environmental science, geology, geography, international relations, marine science, urban planning, and more.

In addition to full academic year and semester programs, you can find information here about summer programs abroad, internship and volunteer opportunities, high school programs, and intersession programs.

5

---ↁ⊶---

Careers

Whether you're simply gathering information to help you turn your passion for geography into a livelihood or you're actively searching for your first job in the field, the World Wide Web can play an integral role in the development of your career.

Your idea of a perfect job in geography may involve cartography or GIS technology or urban planning or conservation or perhaps you're interested in demographic and statistical applications of geography—the choices are remarkably varied.

We've selected what we consider to be the best career-building geography Web sites, with the needs of upper-level high school and college students firmly in mind. These sites, which include professional organizations and societies, federal and state agencies, private companies, and nonprofit groups, should give you a good jumpstart on your career. See also "The Basics" section in Volume I of this set for general sites.

PROFESSIONAL ORGANIZATIONS AND SOCIETIES

American Association of Geography: Careers in Geography
http://www.aag.org/Careers/Intro.html

The American Association of Geography (AAG) has created a Web site that should be a requisite stop for students exploring career options in geography. The site offers a basic primer on geography careers and is broken into meaningful sections that can help you evaluate job prospects, educational requirements, and your personal aptitudes.

Start with the section called "What Can You Do as a Geographer?" to learn about specific private sector and government jobs that utilize geography skills and training. In the next section, "Geographic Fields," the AAG divides geography into eight academic fields: regional geography, environmental studies, cartography and geographic information systems, urban and regional planning, economic geography, geographic education, physical geography and earth science, and cultural and human geography. Each of these areas is briefly described and accompanied by a short list of related job descriptions.

"How Do You Know If You Want to be a Geographer?" offers a 10-question checklist to help you determine your aptitude and interest level. Several other sections ("Job Search and Internship Guide" and "Geographers at Work") provide good tips on how to present your skills during the job hunt and what to expect on the job. Finally, for those of you in the throes of deciding where to go to college, there's a nice interactive map of geography departments in the United States and Canada.

American Society of Limnology and Oceanography
http://aslo.org/

If you're drawn to the study of underwater geography, it's likely you've already discovered the American Society of Limnology and Oceanography (ASLO) for yourself. ASLO—a group devoted to promoting the interests of limnology, oceanography, and related aquatic sciences—has created a Web site with excellent educational and career resources.

From the home page, click on "Student Information," which is broken into categories such as "Aquatic Science Careers," "Career Links," "Education Resources," "Student Awards," and "Student Opportunities." Within "Student Opportunities," there's a list of summer courses and research opportunities for students interested in freshwater and marine science, such as a field course in lake ecology in Pennsylvania, a summer field course in limnology in Michigan, nationwide sea grant research programs, graduate opportunities in remote sensing, and a coastal studies program for undergraduates. Be sure to check out "Career Links" as well—it's ASLO's free service helping to connect students with potential mentors and employers.

Geospatial Information and Technology Association (GITA)
http://www.gita.org/hq/scholar.html

You techie breeds of geographer should check out the Geospatial Information and Technology Association's (GITA) Web site. GITA has taken a role in connecting qualified students with spatial information technology companies for excellent internship opportunities.

Click on "Resources" to read about GITA's Internship Stipend Program, which provides financial assistance to college juniors who are pursuing degrees in GIS-related areas. The program, designed for students who are college juniors or above, places students in terrific summer paid internship positions with GITA's extensive corporate member companies or other organizations. If you're lucky, you'll receive one of the nine $2,000 stipends offered each year to help offset travel and living expenses for students.

American Meteorological Society
http://www.ametsoc.org/AMS/

The Web site for the American Meteorological Society (AMS) offers several excellent resources for geography students with a meteorological bend. Start by clicking on "Student Information and Resources," to access the "Career Guide for Atmospheric Sciences." The career guide provides a thorough explanation of job opportunities, job market and salary outlook, and tips on getting a job. There's also a lengthy list of scholarships and fellowships offered by AMS and affiliated organizations each year to future meteorologists, oceanographers, hydrologists, and climatologists.

The site also offers access to a list of summer opportunities for students in atmospheric and related sciences, which includes federal jobs, corporate internships, and unpaid spots at television and radio stations.

National Council for the Social Studies
http://www.ncss.org/

Defined as an information service for educators, this organization's Web site contains sections on conferences, standards, teaching resources, awards and grants, meetings, membership, and more. If you're considering a career as a teacher, you'll find lots to think about here, and if you're already headed down that career path, you'll be able to take advantage of all the resources offered. Click on "Professional Development" to learn more about educational and work opportunities as a geography teacher.

Student Conservation Association
http://www.sca-inc.org/

If environmental studies is your area of interest within geography, check out the Student Conservation Association (SCA). Dedicated to "changing lives through service to nature," this group's Web site is bursting at the seams with listings of volunteer and internship spots across the country.

Click on "Volunteer and Internship Opportunities" to learn how you can lend a hand in month-long team projects for the National Park Service, the U.S. Forest Service, the Bureau of Land Management, and other agencies. This site makes finding an unpaid internship or volunteer position almost too easy: you can access a list of current positions, get information, and request an application all online.

Paid internships in areas such as endangered species protection, archaeology, environmental education, wilderness patrol, and marine biology are also available by tapping SCA's online searchable database. You may also be eligible for SCA's Diversity Internship Program, which offers paid seasonal internships to college students who traditionally do not work within the conservation field (ethnic populations, women, and others).

FEDERAL AND STATE GOVERNMENT ORGANIZATIONS

Peace Corps Master's Program
http://www.peacecorps.gov/volunteer/masters/index.html

Trying to decide between graduate school and the Peace Corps? The Peace Corps has come up with a way that you don't have to choose. Thanks to partnerships with more than 40 campuses across the United States, the Peace Corps Master's International (MI) program allows you to incorporate Peace Corps service into a master's degree program.

Students apply to both the Peace Corps and the participating graduate school, and must be accepted by both. You would typically complete one year of graduate studies before starting a Peace Corps assignment. Your Peace Corps assignment then serves as the foundation for a thesis or other culminating project.

You can use the Web site to learn more about the participating graduate schools and the specific areas of study, which include geography-friendly subjects such as agribusiness, forestry, environmental education, environmental engineering, and urban planning.

U.S. Geological Survey: Student Educational Employment Program
http://interactive.usgs.gov/Student/Benefit/seep.asp

The U.S. Geological Survey (USGS) offers two programs for students interested in gaining meaningful career experience in geology, biology, mapping, water, and administration. They're called the Student Temporary Employment Program (STEP) and the Student Career Experience Program (SCEP)—and this Web site explains all about them. Both programs offer flexible work schedules to accommodate your academic schedule and needs.

In STEP, you'll find temporary positions with the USGS, ranging from summer-long programs to one-year positions. While these jobs are not necessarily in your academic field, they often provide a stepping stone to the more prestigious SCEP program. In SCEP, you gain work experience directly related to your academic field of study. This program combines academic classroom learning with practical, on-the-job experience and may lead to permanent employment after graduation.

Within both STEP and SCEP, you'll find positions geared toward a range of academic levels, including high school, vocational and technical, associate degree, baccalaureate degree, graduate degree, and professional degree students.

U.S. Geological Survey: Earth Science Corps
http://interactive.usgs.gov/Volunteer/EarthScienceCorps/index.asp

Here's another way to get your foot in the door at the U.S. Geological Survey (USGS). The Earth Science Corps offers volunteer opportunities that let you test your interests in earth sciences and to buff up your resume at the same time.

You'll be surprised at the broad range of volunteer gigs listed at the site. Using the search engine, you can locate positions according to site location or career interests. For example, we quickly found volunteer positions in cartography in Colorado, in seismic imaging in California, and in volcano hazards in Hawaii. While the positions are unpaid, some of them offer good perks such as free lodging (a cottage in Hawaii, no less!), free transportation to the job site, and/or meals while you're working.

U.S. Census Bureau Jobs
http://www.census.gov/hrd/www/

If you have an interest in demographics, it's easy to use this Web site to investigate career possibilities with the U.S. Census Bureau.

From this Web site, click on "Professional Jobs: Student, Entry, and Mid Career" to see areas of interest, such as "Geography/Cartography/ Urban Studies/Planning" and "Sociology/Demography/Psychology." Each area offers a description of the type of work and job responsibilities involved.

After you've ascertained your own interests and aptitudes, click on "Nationwide Positions" to view a list of jobs available with the Census

Bureau. There's even a special section for "Student Employment," where you'll find information on summer internships and cooperative work programs for geography students. If you're further along in your education, and drawn to statistics and demography, you'll also find info here about the Census Bureau's postdoctoral research program.

Youth in Natural Resources (YNR)
http://www.dnr.state.co.us/edo/ynr/ynr.html

The Youth in Natural Resources (YNR) environmental education program is a great way for high school and college students in Colorado to get a handle on various careers in natural resources. The nine-week program, sponsored by the Colorado Department of Natural Resources, requires you to attend college preparation workshops, complete environmental education assignments, and participate in field trips. You'll earn minimum wage, a $100 savings bond, and possible high school or college credit. The program targets students who are typically underrepresented in natural resource fields.

In the YNR program, you'll be given an incredible amount of responsibility for such projects as teaching angler education clinics, conducting wildlife inventories, building interpretive trails, mapping abandoned mines, identifying geologic hazards, performing water sample analyses, relocating geese, documenting and removing noxious weeds, and participating in hunter education.

U.S. Department of State: Student Programs Index
http://www.state.gov/www/careers/rstudprogindex.html

If you're interested in a career in foreign affairs, you'll want to visit the U.S. Department of State's comprehensive Web site.

The department manages several student employment programs that can provide you with invaluable on-the-job experience in a foreign affairs environment. If selected for one of the programs, you could work in Washington, D.C., or at an embassy overseas. Positions are both paid and unpaid and are available during spring, summer, and fall.

Use the comprehensive Web site to learn details about the various programs, which include a cooperative education program; a graduate fellowship program; the presidential management intern program; domestic and overseas student internships for university juniors, seniors, and graduate students; and student-worker trainee opportunities for high school, vocational school, and undergraduate students.

The Jack Kleinman Internship and Research Grants for Volcano Research
http://vulcan.wr.usgs.gov/News/Announcements/Kleinman_intern2000.
   html

Yep, it's another U.S. Geological Survey (USGS) site, this one targeted at you burgeoning volcanologists. The U.S. Geological Survey, through its Cascades Volcano Observatory in Vancouver, Washington, selects stipend recipients for volcano research. Grants of up to $2,000 are available to undergraduate, graduate, or postgraduate students conducting research in volcanology, preferably in the Cascade Range, the Aleutian volcanic arc, Hawaii, or the Long Valley region.

Typical grant recipients work on field projects involving geologic, geochemical, or geophysical investigation of a volcanic region. Cooperation with a staff member at the Cascades Volcano Observatory, Alaskan Volcano Observatory, Hawaiian Volcano Observatory, Long Valley Observatory, or a university earth science department is strongly recommended.

Bureau of Land Management: Student Career Experience Program
http://www.nc.blm.gov/jobs/SCEP/SCEP.htm#About the Student Career
Experience Program

In case you think BLM stands for some kind of sandwich, it's time for a proper introduction. The Bureau of Land Management (BLM) is an agency within the Department of the Interior that administers 264 million acres of America's public lands, located primarily in 12 western states. If you happen to live in one of those 12 states—or wish you did—read on. Like many other government agencies, the BLM offers two employment programs to help students build their careers while still enrolled in school.

The Student Temporary Employment Program (STEP) places students in temporary (up to one year) jobs that are not necessarily related to their academic fields. The Student Career Experience Program (SCEP) hires students—often those with STEP experience—to work in their academic field. SCEP students generally attend college on a regular semester or academic quarter schedule, and work for the BLM during summer vacation and holiday periods. You'll find specific and current info about both programs' openings at BLM's Web site.

U.S. Department of State: Student Programs Index
http://www.state.gov/www/careers/rstudprogindex.html

If you're interested in a career that involves you in foreign cultures, you'll want to visit the U.S. Department of State's comprehensive Web site.

The department manages several student employment programs that can provide you with invaluable on-the-job experience in a foreign affairs environment. If selected for one of the programs, you could work in Washington, D.C., or at an embassy overseas. Positions are both paid and unpaid and are available during spring, summer, and fall.

Use the comprehensive Web site to learn details about the various programs, which include a cooperative education program; a graduate fellowship program; the presidential management intern program; domestic and overseas student internships for university juniors, seniors, and graduate students; and student-worker trainee opportunities for high school, vocational school, and undergraduate students.

PRIVATE COMPANIES, NONPROFIT ORGANIZATIONS, AND SPECIALIZED WEB SITES

Jobs in GIS
http://gis.about.com/science/gis/cs/jobs/index.htm

This site, created by the ubiquitous *About.com*, provides valuable information on cultivating your career in Geographic Information Systems (GIS). Start by clicking on "Building a Career in GIS" for tips on appropriate education paths and on how to build your job skills and experience.

To get a handle on what kind of jobs are available in the field, look under "GIS Job Descriptions." Here, you'll find a collection of job descriptions submitted by individuals working in the field, conveniently grouped by job type and industry.

"How to Survive a GIS Job Interview" will strike a nerve among those of you making your first foray into the workforce. The "GIS Salary Survey" section provides helpful information to help you gauge the market value of your skill set. The site also provides links to several good GIS career sites—such as *Dice.com, Earthworks,* and *GeoJob Source*—where you can post your resume and browse job listings.

ESRI
http://gis.esri.com/jobs/jobs.cfm

ESRI, a leading firm in geographic information systems (GIS), offers several career goodies for geography students. For starters, there's ESRI's Summer Internship Program, a well-respected program that provides on-the-job experience for students. Interns work on GIS software team projects in the areas of software and development, implementation and programming services, and Internet development. If you're savvy enough to be selected for one of these paid 12-week internships, you'll work at ESRI headquarters in Redlands, California, or in one of the regional sales offices.

In addition, ESRI sponsors up to 60 students in the ESRI International User Conference, an annual GIS technology conference with over 9,000 participants. If you are a graduate student or fourth-year undergraduate student who uses GIS software, you can apply for this assistantship program. Selected students receive a full registration package for the conference, hotel accommodations, and a small stipend for meals, but pay for their own travel and personal expenses.

Cyber-Sierra's Natural Resources Job Search
http://www.cyber-sierra.com/nrjobs/index.html

This site is loaded with well-described links to great sites for job seekers in the fields of GIS, forestry, water resources, and natural resources. You'll enjoy the friendly and conversational tone of this site: It's like the world's best school counselor, giving you ideas and tips on how to find a job in your field. You'll find information on locating and getting hired for those competitive government, private sector, and nonprofit positions. For geography students simply deciding on what to do this summer, the "Summer Jobs" section offers extensive links to seasonal jobs and internships.

Environmental Careers Organization
http://www.eco.org/

The Environmental Careers Organization (ECO) provides environmental career information and services to over 50,000 people each year through its paid internships database, career conferences, and publications.

If it's an internship you're hankering after, click on "Career Services," then "Paid Internships." From here, you can search the ECO internship database, which is conveniently divided into regions of the country (eastern, northwest, central, and southwest). Each internship is described comprehensively, with details about necessary qualifications, pay scale, job responsibilities, and time frame required.

In the "Career Services" section of the Web site, you'll also want to check out ECO's annual National Environmental Career Conference, which provides a great opportunity for you to learn where the jobs are, what you can do in a particular field, necessary skills and degrees to get ahead, salaries, and resources for job hunting particular to the field.

Bigelow Laboratory for Ocean Sciences
http://www.bigelow.org/

Given that oceans cover more than 70 percent of the earth's surface, it's no surprise that marine sciences are an integral part of the geography curriculum. Bigelow Laboratory's Web site offers excellent educational resources for geography students interested in ocean sciences, including information on opportunities at the laboratory itself.

Located in Maine, the Bigelow Laboratory sponsors the Keller-BLOOM Program, a hands-on research experience in which 16 high school juniors are selected to spend a week working with oceanographers at the lab. This program's research activities and field studies, which focus on the Gulf of Maine, allow students to learn about diverse careers within the marine sciences. Other opportunities at the Bigelow Laboratory include a summer course series (worth two to four credits) for upper-level undergraduate and graduate students and a number of summer internships.

Brookhaven National Laboratory: Minority High School Summer Apprenticeship Program
http://www.scied.bnl.gov/mhsap.html

Here's a great career builder for minority students interested in environmental and energy research, a topic of importance to many geographers. The Brookhaven National Laboratory, in Upton, New York, developed the Minority High School Summer Apprenticeship Program to offer research apprenticeships to ninth and tenth grade underrepresented minority (African American/Black, Hispanic, Native American, or Pacific Islander) students who have shown ability and potential in science-oriented studies and activities. Each Suffolk County and Inner City Outreach high school is invited to submit nominees, with approximately 45 students selected for the program.

If selected, you'll participate in two four-week sessions during the months of July and August, in which you'll receive instruction and get a chance to do your own experiments in physics, biology and hydroponics, chemistry, and environmental science.

Index

Page numbers in bold indicate main discussion of a topic.

About the Authors

ELIZABETH H. OAKES is the author of more than 15 books, including *Career Exploration on the Internet* and *International Encyclopedia of Women Scientists*.

JEFFREY A. GRITZNER is Professor of Geography at the University of Montana. His areas of specialty include cultural ecology, public policy, Africa, the Middle East, and environmental geography.